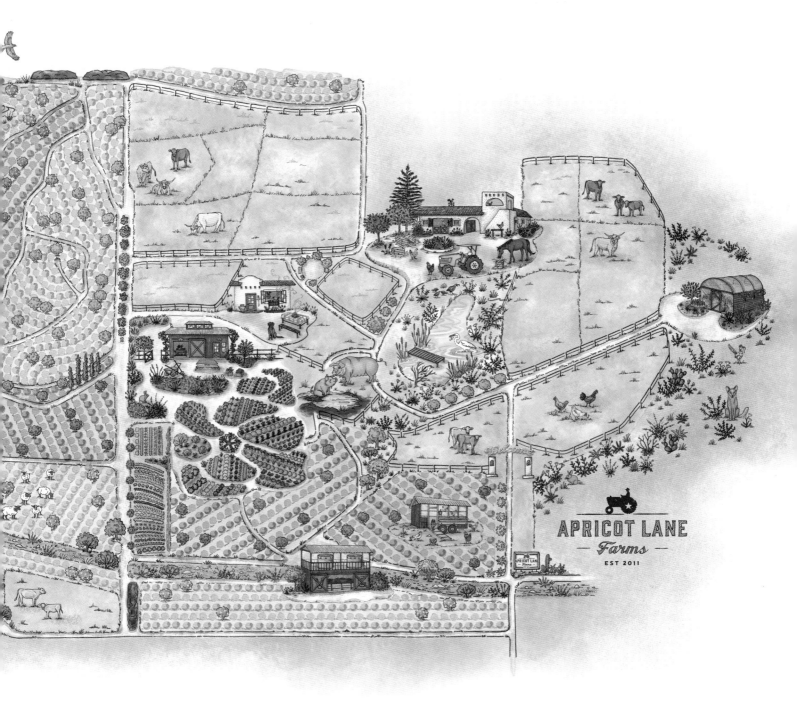

APRICOT LANE
— Farms —
EST 2011

THE
APRICOT LANE
FARMS
COOKBOOK

AVERY
an imprint of Penguin Random House
New York

THE

APRICOT LANE FARMS

COOKBOOK

Recipes and Stories from
the Biggest Little Farm

MOLLY CHESTER

WITH SARAH OWENS
PHOTOGRAPHS BY ED ANDERSON
ILLUSTRATIONS BY ANDY RAVILLE

Photographs on pp. 14, 15, 30–31, 72–73, 75,
96–97, 98, 103, 132–133, 158, 164–165,
200–201, 204, 230, 245, 252–253, 255,
280–281, 283, 299 (right), 304, 342–343,
and 345 courtesy of Apricot Lane Farms.
Photograph on pp. 206–207 by Keri Oberly.
Photograph on p. 299 (left) by Yvette Roman
Photography. All other photographs by
Ed Anderson.
Illustrations by Andreana Marie Raville

Most Avery books are available at special
quantity discounts for bulk purchase for sales
promotions, premiums, fund-raising, and
educational needs. Special books or book
excerpts also can be created to fit specific needs.
For details, write SpecialMarkets
@penguinrandomhouse.com.

ISBN 9780593330333
Ebook ISBN 9780593330340

Printed in China
10 9 8 7 6 5 4 3 2 1

Book design by Ashley Tucker

To my dad

CONTENTS

Foreword

I first visited Apricot Lane Farms in 2020, and it stopped me in my tracks—not just because of its beauty and abundance, but because of the journey it took to create it. I had seen *The Biggest Little Farm* several years earlier, and knew that, in less than a decade, Molly and John had turned a barren landscape stripped of its nutrients into a thriving, thoughtfully interwoven ecosystem. But of all the beauty and abundance on the farm, what I remember most from that visit was the soil. We were walking through a field of mixed grasses when John dug his fingers into the dirt and came up with a handful. He held it out to me: It was soft, dark as chocolate cake, and teeming with worms and bugs. I was delighted. It is this radical transformation of the soil that has given me hope in our fight against climate change—and hope for the health of our food.

Molly and the chefs of Apricot Lane Farms have an intimate, firsthand understanding of the universal truth that health *and* taste begin in the soil. Even more important, Molly is able to welcome readers into this understanding with warmth and approachability. The seasonal recipes you'll find here are easy to love: Delicious, surprising, and frugal, they are also a celebration of biodiversity, which is essential when we talk about food and cooking. This endless world of possibilities is what made me fall in love with food; Molly too—you can tell from the way she describes the farm's heritage breeds of chickens and their multicolor eggs (page 246), or the many surprising varieties of avocados (page 374). This biodiversity can inspire us all year long, even through the seasons we don't traditionally think of as plentiful. When I look at the beauty of radicchios and chicories in wintertime, they take my breath away: blush-pink Rosalba, chartreuse Castelfranco shot through with magenta, the twisting shoots of puntarelle. I could eat them every single day until the season is over—and when it's over it's over, and then we're onto the next vegetable.

Cooking in rhythm with the season changes your life—it has irrevocably changed mine, and the philosophy and mission of Chez Panisse—and, crucially, it changes our food system. You can't find ripeness and true taste in ingredients that have been industrially grown and shipped unripe from the other side of the world; you can only find them when you are eating seasonally and locally. Molly demonstrates how pleasurable it can be to eat this way: You can feel her excitement about the creaminess of summer eggplant or the myriad flavors of edible spring flowers. Preserving foods is also represented here in these pages, which is critical too—you can help to extend the seasons and stock your pantry through the skillful use of canning and fermentation. Above all, Molly shows us the profound rewards that can come from growing and harvesting your own food. Even if you have only a tiny garden plot or a fire-escape planter box, it can connect you to nature.

Molly, John, and the team at Apricot Lane Farms have succeeded in living, farming, and cooking completely in harmony with the land, and the farm has become an important place

of education and teaching. With every year that the farm evolved, Molly and John increasingly understood the interconnectedness of everything on their farm: The vegetables, cover crops, orchards, cows, ducks, and even slugs are all linked with one another in a delicate balance. Vitally, Molly and John didn't force conformity onto the land, as practitioners of industrial agriculture do. Instead, they allowed nature to be all that it could be. And that is the most remarkable achievement of all.

In order to find a way forward, we all need to have successful models like Apricot Lane Farms; when I first saw the film, I remember thinking, "Oh my goodness. We can really *do* this." The exhilarating fact is, *it can be done*. The farm is the proof of it, this book is the proof of it, and this is our work for the future. All the values we need to teach the next generation are imbedded here: equity, community, stewardship, nourishment, a love of nature. It's all at Apricot Lane Farms. This beautiful book is an extension of all that they have learned. And what a delicious way to learn.

Alice Waters

Introduction:

WELCOME TO
APRICOT LANE FARMS

In 2011, when my filmmaker husband, John, and I packed our bags to move from Santa Monica to a neglected farm an hour north of Los Angeles, everyone thought we were crazy. I had been working as a chef and food blogger, and the few tomato plants I had wedged onto my tiny patio just weren't cutting it anymore. Besides that, our beloved rescue dog, Todd, had been annoying our neighbors for months with his incessant barking! As we considered our options, we pined for a ten-acre parcel where we could create a traditional farm that worked in harmony with nature while Todd roamed freely. We were motivated by a desire to live with purpose, create a closer connection with our food, and cook with the most delicious and nutritious ingredients possible. Word of our ambitions circulated through friends and family, and with the backing of a like-minded investor, we found ourselves contemplating hundreds of acres instead! Visions of every conceivable food I wanted to cook danced in my head as we drove down dusty roads lined with monoculture crops typical of California's farming belt. We arrived at a dilapidated farm, nervous but giddy with excitement to embark on a journey of regenerating the land. Spurred on by eager optimism and undaunted by inexperience, we set to work.

Learning the Hard Way

Many of you reading this have already become familiar with our tale as chronicled in John's heartwarming documentary *The Biggest Little Farm*. The movie reveals our early days settling into the farm, and the challenges we faced, including the friction between our first animals and their eager predators. Each triumphant piglet that Emma the Pig reared under Greasy the Rooster's protective gaze has brought us a strong relationship with our food that has only deepened over time. And as I stand on the hill overlooking our orchard at Apricot Lane Farms, which we affectionately call the Fruit Basket, it is difficult not to be inspired by the sheer abundance of life teeming forth from the blossom-laden branches of our trees. In the spring, insects drink the flowers' nectar and bounce from understory to canopy, pollinating this year's harvest, while birds chase them to keep their population balanced. Plump earthworms convert organic matter like fallen leaves into nutrients for the tree roots. In this sacred part of the farm, the great circle of life unfolds before me.

But, the first year was a comedy of errors with a steep learning curve. Honestly, we spent a lot of time being jealous of our dog. Most days, Todd was living his best life lying in the sun or chasing after squirrels while John and I grappled with epic drought, wildfires, all-night lambing sessions, and rampant pests. The area that we marked for our vegetable garden was a compacted and dry old horse arena. We tried to make the ground more fertile by reusing the waste in our neighbor's horse barn, but little did we know that planting tomatoes in forty tons of raw manure is risky business! Those tomatoes didn't make it to market, but we still reminisce about how insanely delicious they were.

We made do while learning hard lessons, and I cooked with what little was available besides those tomatoes. We inherited one gigantic rosemary plant from the prior owners, and it became my constant companion in the kitchen, even after we were utterly tired of eating from it. At the time, the farm's soil couldn't support growing much of anything else, and I was simply too busy with planning to wrap my head around creative meals, let alone drive to the grocery store.

But our path to Apricot Lane Farms had been years in the making, and we knew that quitting wasn't an option.

A Delicious Journey to Health

There is a rhythm of life described in the film that I've long been drawn to involving cooking, tending the soil, and coexisting with plants and animals in a healthy ecosystem. As a young adult, I experienced various health conditions, including polycystic ovary syndrome and gut and joint inflammation, that challenged my ability to enjoy life to its fullest. It was a confusing time as I navigated conflicting health advice and fad diets. What's worse, I wasn't able to enjoy the simple pleasure of eating. And I loved food—I became a chef, after all! While I'd followed a vegetarian diet my whole life, I began to embrace the idea of incorporating meat and animal products to help ground my blood sugar and give my system the vitamins and minerals it needed to thrive. But I didn't have the tools or the knowledge to truly embrace the shift.

This began to change during my culinary education at the Natural Gourmet Institute of Health & Culinary Arts in New York City when I discovered Sally Fallon's *Nourishing Traditions*, a book based upon the research of Dr. Weston A. Price that is devoted to the healing wisdom of ancestral cultures and culinary techniques that enhance the nutrient values of foods. It became obvious to me that the choices farmers make about the soil (essentially the earth's gut) are just as important to our bodies as what happens in the kitchen. Integrating pastured animals and their composted manure is important to the microbial health of the soil. This "living soil" encourages the roots of plants to take up nutrients and helps them thrive. In turn, the plant produces more flavorful and nutritious fruits and vegetables. The overall farm ecosystem flourishes, including the health of the animals. You can not only taste but *feel* the difference in the meat and eggs from these happy pastured livestock!

I began seeking healthy animal fats and grass-fed meats, full-fat raw dairy, and pastured eggs more than ever before. It was a drastic leap for me, but I had a better understanding of my body's needs and how this way of eating fit into traditional cultures. I knew this approach was indeed the right way forward for me. For the very first time, I felt strong in body and infinitely more grounded in spirit. But to make a fully committed transition away from vegetarianism, I needed to figure out how to honor the animals that would be feeding me. I tried to buy meat and dairy from farms that encouraged their animals to live as they were meant to—foraging for food and moving freely—and helped them have a long, happy existence. I began to connect the dots between grass-fed pasturing and holistic approaches to caring for the land. As I immersed myself in this new knowledge and way of eating, I continued to feel better.

Oh—and how tasty that healing proved to be! Fat is not only an essential part of a healthy diet but a remarkable carrier of flavor. Raw dairy has a silky mouthfeel that, when cultured, provides a creamy and tangy addition to any meal. The rich orange yolk of a pastured egg carries amazing flavor—as do grass-fed pork and beef, with their earthy, nutty undertones. They have inspired my cooking in a whole new way. Likewise, I've learned techniques to coax both flavor and nutrition from ingredients. Studying the science as to why soaked nuts and seeds are more nutritious is one thing; biting into the satisfying, natural sweetness of a soaked and dehydrated walnut is all the argument one needs to take this easy step. Nurturing health through flavor is at the heart of this book. Healthy, delicious fats combined with organic, farm-fresh fruits and vegetables can provide a lifetime of nourishing, seasonal meals.

After culinary school, John helped me build my first big, beautiful garden in Maryland during what happened to be the hatch of the seventeen-year cicada. Those loud alien-looking things were everywhere and tried to run me out of town, but I persisted! If I was going to grow my food, I had to become comfortable with the roly-polies, ants, spiders, and other insects that make up an ecosystem. Soon after, we relocated to Los Angeles and I intended to become an organic personal chef. Since I had restored my health through food, I wanted to find pathways to help others do the same. All I had was my porch, but that didn't stop me from creating an organic potted garden, complete with mediocre tomatoes. Although our move to Los Angeles was an exciting step forward in my professional career, I felt as though I was just getting started. Motivated by my own health improvements, I wanted to be a bigger part of the solution.

Restoring the Soil

When we arrived at Apricot Lane Farms, the land was tired and depleted. Though part of a once fertile valley created by the Arroyo Simi River, the soil had suffered through drought and the conventional practice of using synthetic pesticides and fertilizers, which had stripped it of the microbes that are the building blocks of a productive, sustainable farm. We found the dry clods of soil stubborn as rocks, impenetrable to even the toughest of our tools, let alone a tiny germinating vegetable seed! While we had quit city life for the fantasy of nurturing plants and animals, we soon realized that our job was to grow a "living soil," which was the initial step toward that dream. To do this, we needed to disrupt a problematic system of farming that had been in place for decades. It was a mindset shift that would prove to be more challenging than anything we had previously undertaken.

Realizing that we needed guidance, we called upon Alan York, a pioneer in biodynamic farming who had a reputation for honoring natural resources. Biodynamic practices extend beyond an organic approach to treat the farm as a unique, individual ecosystem by participating with the natural cycles of the land and incorporating the lunar cycles of the cosmos. Based upon the lectures given by Austrian philosopher and social reformer Rudolf Steiner in 1924, biodynamics aspires for a farm to generate its own soil fertility through composting, animal integration, cover cropping, and crop rotation. Alan was one of the most respected leaders in progressive farming practices at the time and had the most experience with our specific challenges and climate. Until his premature death in 2014, we relied on Alan to lead us through the rough switch from conventional, chemical stewardship of the existing orchards to an organic, soil-building methodology. For years before our arrival, the avocado and citrus trees had been treated with synthetic liquid fertigation. When we stopped that practice, the trees had to adjust to using their roots again and develop the symbiotic relationship with the soil microbes that is necessary for natural nutrient uptake. As the trees went through withdrawal, we rebuilt the soil microbiology, and Alan was there to guide us through this slow and steady transition. He became a friend and confidant, and someone who helped us begin to navigate our long-term vision.

Working with Alan was a test in learning to trust and develop patience, two important keys to success that we still work to master every day. He taught us to use our own observations

and our intrinsic connection to the land to handle any challenge. He was unusually gifted in being able to combine abstract thinking and practical strategy. For example, one day he called me into a meeting in an empty field with a box of crayons and a huge sheet of paper so that we could map out our plans for our orchard. Alan was out of the box, in this case a crayon box, which pleased me entirely. As silly as it seemed at the time, the scribbled drawing we made of swooping and swirling rows of diversely colored fruit trees turned our playful imaginations into a practical strategy. Alan's encouragement to follow our intuition with a childlike spirit and curiosity has influenced our evolving methods of both farming and cooking since.

We are an organic- and biodynamic-certified farm, but beyond this, Alan taught us to stay open to creative solutions, rather than to dogmatically adhere to any one set of farming strategies. We have become more efficient and effective because of this philosophy of gentle stewardship; for example, instead of trying to eliminate pests (and, trust me, I really wanted to eradicate those coyotes and snails!), we learned to let them control one another, naturally, as they should, rather than using more immediate, harsh solutions that are not in alignment with balancing the farm's ecosystem.

The path to incorporating natural solutions is less linear than conventional farming, and often what solves one problem can create the right conditions for another. For example, cover cropping in the orchards is key to aerating the soil and building soil microbial life. Yet, pesky gophers love the cover crop's roots and can severely damage the fruit trees with their gnawing. Watering with above-ground sprinklers to grow the cover crop can also create prime environmental conditions for fungal diseases on the trees. Working our way through these layers of the onion created a consciousness and a connection to the land that has enhanced and honed our instincts with each new challenge.

The Biggest Little Regenerative Farm

From the smallest compost microbe to our magnificently fluffy-headed hens, everything on our farm now serves a purpose. Animal husbandry is key to our practices, including pasture rotation to increase soil fertility and maximize moisture retention in our arid climate. Cows are grass-eating herbivores, and we allow them ample space to roam and forage. Rotating animals on pasture is not only better for the land but also healthier for the animals themselves, since they are moving to fresh new ground daily, instead of being confined to a pen or small space with their own waste. The "cleanup crew" are our naturally foraging, happy chickens, which rotate into the pasture once the cows have grazed the paddocks. These industrious (and hilariously animated) flocks of egg-layers peck through and spread the cow's manure, manage pests, and leave behind their own . . . nitrogen-rich gifts. You will get to know them later in the book, each breed contributing its own character to the farm (page 246).

Heirloom livestock breeds, combined with the gradual progress of time, allow us to complete the circles of life in a more natural way and cycle fertility and nutrients. In addition to Akaushi and Highland cattle and various heritage-breed chickens, our pastured heritage pigs happily root for grubs and acorns, and our Dorper sheep keep the cover crops in check underneath our healthy lemon orchards. This way of farming is eco-restorative, as it conserves natural resources such as water and replenishes topsoil and increases biodiversity. The result of this approach is not only happy animals and resilience against climate change but also deliciously flavorful meat and eggs! I strive to honor every edible gift from our cows, chickens, pigs, and sheep, and I do all I can to help them live their best lives while roaming our pastures.

Our unconventional approach has created unique, thriving microenvironments: We have our diverse orchards woven with cover crops, a native plant wetland initiative, a prolific vegetable garden with rotating beds of more than one hundred roots, shoots, fruiting vegetables, and herbs, and intensively grazed animal pastures that collectively act like a sponge for sequestering water. In addition to our animals, we have a forty-foot vermicomposter squirming with red wigglers to help us create and maintain soil health on the farm. Our Farm Fertility & Vermicompost Center, which is the home of that worm bin, is focused on building the farm's immunity against epidemics of pests and disease by enhancing our microbial quality and diversity. Our worms recycle about ten thousand pounds a year of juice scraps and coffee grounds from local businesses, instead of leaving that waste for a landfill.

I will admit that John and I were naive in understanding that using a gentler approach to restore the soil's health would involve time and labor-intensive strategies like these, but our dedication to organic and biodynamic methods has finally paid off. Now after more than a decade (and plenty of worm, cow, pig, and poultry poop!), we and our growing team have turned Apricot Lane Farms into a lush and edible oasis. A farmer's work is never done, but we are finally living the dream, fueled by one tasty bite at a time!

Growing for the Future

In the beginning, it was just me and John and a few patient team members. Through the years we've grown to add other departments vital to our mission and our goal to continually improve our practices. These include an Avocado Conservation Project (you can read more about this on page 374) and a Native Pond Restoration Project inspired by Paul Gurinas, our partner and conservationist. We are lucky to have investors who believe in our approach and who support partnerships with scientific research teams that aid us in developing natural solutions with long-term goals.

Under the stress of balancing our passion and the opportunity at hand, we reached a point where the human component of our ecosystem needed further fortification. An often-overlooked truth is that a farm reflects the health of its stewards. Farming can prove such hard work that this practice can understandably get lost in the maze and weight of relating to biology, but the land will ultimately suffer that oversight. From the onset, we treated our farm team with respect and appreciation, paid them a fair wage, and nurtured a safe and chemical-free working environment. We welcomed our volunteers to our home for dinners on Wednesday nights, enjoyed potluck gatherings to celebrate collective and individual milestones, and regularly met as a group. But as the farm matured and our team grew, connection and proper care became infinitely more challenging. We had to evolve as leaders to rise to the challenge through personal work, business coaching, and, for John and me, couples counseling! We sharpened our focus on cross-training, educational exchanges, leadership training, and conferences that further developed our team's interests and skills. The farm has taken on a life of its own in return, and the ancient knowledge of traditional farming has been revived as a common language among this new generation of farmers.

Immersed in the many responsibilities that accompany any given day, I often have to stop and remind myself how far we've come since embarking on this wild ride. Now that I'm at the helm of an incredibly complex farming operation, I have less time to be hands-on in the garden, or out working with our animal herds. The trade-off is the honor of being a visionary for the farm and both steering and empowering such a remarkable and diverse group of people unified in growing delicious and vibrant foods with respect for our plants, animals, and the environment. There is never a dull moment, from the windstorms and terrifying fires that push us to our limits to the abundance of summer, which feels as though nature is literally throwing fruit at us, all while a new calf is born or a guinea fowl finds itself wedged in a tree! Each day is a new discovery in the fields and a chance to create something comforting on the stove, colorful in the salad bowl, or primal and smoky in the wood-fired oven. There is not a finish line to the business of growing food. The learning and work is never done, but I sure am grateful in the process of it all.

Now as a mother, I am so happy to pass this wisdom on to our young son, Beaudie. At seven years old, he is maturing in strength and intuitive character the more connected with the natural world he becomes. As soon as he was old enough to sit upright, into a sling he went, and I wore him everywhere those first few years! He now hops on to the back of the cart to head each morning to our newest endeavor, the Farm School. Led by educator Jenny Seeds, it is a one-room school we founded, with nine current students. The farm is the classroom and a deep reverence for Mother Nature as our greatest teacher is both fostered and felt. We hope that nurturing a close relationship with the diverse ecosystem of the land will give Beaudie, and his peers, a rich education and help them become changemakers in the world.

Bringing the Farm into the Kitchen

In 2013, we installed a barn kitchen to fine-tune the quality and flavor of the food we grow and to indulge my fantasies as a chef. Especially in the early years, our team needed loads of patience and creativity to make use of some wonky produce! The garlic cloves were tiny and a bear to peel until we perfected their growing cycle and they became the creamy and aromatic heads we sell today. One year we grew gargantuan jicamas that lovingly became known as Buddha's Belly by the farmers market team. They were certainly novel, but a jicama the size of a soccer ball is difficult to work with! But then the tides turned. Our eggplants and cucumbers became sweet, our lettuce lost its bitterness, and I'll let Beaudie tell you about our irresistible blueberries. With each successfully grown crop, our inspiration has multiplied exponentially, and I'm excited to share this tasty culinary journey with you in these pages.

That first kitchen has since expanded into two fully equipped kitchens, including an updated test kitchen. We use these to provide meals for our team and to develop farm market products like our orange blossom honey lemonade and bourbon lemon marmalade. Our cooking program is steered by my cooking philosophy and preferences, and our kitchens are run by an assortment of talent from various cultural backgrounds who have all embraced the foundations of a plant- and animal-rich diet. On any given day, our culinary team is busy at work, slicing and dicing ingredients for meals that burst with seasonal identity. We love bouncing ideas off one another, and I eagerly anticipate the aromas that will emerge after a collective brainstorming session. Head Chef Kayla Roche might serve up Perfectly Brined Pastured Pork Chops with PB&J Sauce (page 292), highlighting our rich and nutty meat, a reflection of our healthy heritage pigs and their foraging life. Other days, Maria, who is on our kitchen team, will be flipping Corn Tortillas (page 44) for Smoky Potato and Greens Tacos (page 150). And I dutifully carve out time each week to perfect A Simple Sourdough Sandwich Loaf (page 54), which we use to make our unforgettable BLT Sandwich with Egg, Avocado, and Basil Mayonnaise (page 384). And if it's fall, we've definitely made some Autumn Kuri Squash Bars (page 130). In this book, you'll find these and other recipes that our chefs and I have created together, as well as some classic recipes from my blogging days.

When the produce starts rolling into the kitchens, it sets our to-do lists for the season. With farming, we get only one chance a year to grow (and cook with) the perfect peach. If it doesn't work out, we wait a whole year to try again! Prepping fresh produce can be time consuming, and we like challenging ourselves in the kitchen to try something a little different every year. The day I learned to freeze elderberries before destemming them, I even had enough time left over for a nap! Learning new techniques to work with plants gives me confidence and makes me feel safe, knowing when and how to utilize our seasonal abundance to lead a healthier life. If you don't live in California or on a farm, we have made helpful suggestions in this book about how to bring similar ingredients into your kitchen. That is where the fun really begins!

The culinary techniques that have inspired me for nearly fifteen years to follow this path initially came from the profound wisdom of traditional cultures. As I gained more experience, I was led back to the place where the instincts for these techniques and ingredients originated: Mother Earth herself. When we cook in harmony with the rhythms of our surroundings, we understand their natural cadence, including seasonality and the cycle of life. We notice each subtlety and offering of the land in its infinite abundance. Our cooking gains not only wisdom but an unbelievable depth of flavor—this insight is the secret ingredient in the recipes in this book! I hope to pass my fervor for farm-fresh flavor on to you, with recipes that will bring you an equal sense of delight in your own kitchen.

May this book inspire a meal, maybe a trip to a farmers market, or even a new backyard garden. And when you create a dish that was inspired by your own ecosystem, I want you to tell me all about it. Happy cooking!

Part I

THE
LARDER

Cooking is simpler, faster, and more delicious when your pantry is flush with the essentials. Because this book focuses on wholesome, unrefined foods, the following chapters will help you stock the freshest and most basic ingredients while also expanding your larder with wide-ranging, high-quality flavors.

....

Ingredients

Cooking in rhythm with the seasons celebrates abundance and nurtures cravings that honor precious resources. Using farm-fresh fruits, herbs, and vegetables as well as pastured, grass-fed meats and eggs is a uniquely nourishing experience that benefits from a few considerations. Supporting quality, organic, and local produce and meat whenever possible is the core of our approach, but I do make a few exceptions for ingredients that provide flexibility and freedom from food intolerances. Food choices are ultimately very personal, however, and I hope the recipes in this book will inspire you to explore the many flavors and feelings that result from eating whole, unprocessed foods. The following are some tips on sourcing to get you started in stocking your pantry for delicious, wholesome meals!

Organic and Biodynamic Produce

Produce that has been grown in bioactive soil without the use of chemical fertilizers, pesticides, or herbicides will naturally elevate your cooking, and it will give you a resilient mind and body. Source either organic or biodynamic produce that has been harvested shortly before it is cooked, frozen, or preserved, to ensure that the ingredient's vibrancy is maintained and harnessed. Because farmers market produce can vary in size depending upon the grower, we have included a number count or weight in addition to volume measurements so you may get a better idea of how the dish should be seasoned. Fresh produce grown naturally also creates the most active fermentation for pantry staples such as Jalapeño Kraut (page 68) or medicinal tonics like Beet Kvass (page 149).

Purchasing from farmers you know and trust builds community-driven relationships and strengthens a connection to your food beyond its enjoyment. Choose the best of what your budget will allow and be mindful to store it properly once it has journeyed to your kitchen.

Grass-Fed Meat and Eggs

Cooking with meat and eggs that have been farmed in this way, however, requires a different approach than when using conventional, store-bought counterparts. The recipes in this book account for the difference in both muscle development and improved flavor that truly pastured animals embody. Utilizing low-and-slow cooking methods not only tenderizes but also heightens the complex taste and aroma of these nourishing foods. Although the cooking method for pastured eggs is similar to conventional, the mouthfeel and richness of the pastured eggs elevate an everyday food to an experience of luxurious delight!

Sourcing grass-fed and finished products can be challenging, depending upon your location and budget. Pastured meat or eggs are generally more expensive than those produced in industrial concentrated animal feeding operations (CAFOs). This is because the farmer needs to dedicate increased acreage, as well as time, for each animal to reach maturity at a natural pace. With the rising costs of organic feed and the labor associated with smaller, family-owned farms, this mindful approach also inevitably leads to smaller profit margins. We feel the investment is worth it, though, particularly when the environmental and ethical costs of the alternative are considered. Although our limited supply prevents us from offering whole or half animals, if farms near you do, this option can decrease processing costs and be economically resourceful, particularly if you have the freezer space for long-term storage. Sharing the butchering of a whole or half animal with another household can also help, and potentially diversify your freezer stash!

Raw Dairy

Whole-fat, grass-fed milk that comes straight from the cow without pasteurization or homogenization is used throughout the recipes in this book for several reasons. It contains helpful digestive enzymes and is often more nutritionally beneficial, especially once cultured (see Crème Fraîche, page 71). Fermented dairy such as milk kefir also gives a delicious tang to desserts such as Honey Panna Cotta with Milk Kefir and Fresh Passion Fruit (page 318). The fat within dairy specifically aids digestion and your body's absorption of vitamins and minerals, and so it is best to choose whole-fat milk whenever possible.

When choosing raw dairy, it is important to purchase from a farmer you know and trust, as the health of the animal that is grass pastured and the careful practices of milking are paramount to the safety of the milk. Give it a good shake before using to break up the cream, and enjoy the rich flavor in our recipes. If you are not able to source raw milk, choose a brand that is not ultrapasteurized for best performance, flavor, and nourishment.

Unrefined Fats and Oils

These important pantry ingredients are an opportunity to improve both the flavor and nutritive value of food, but perhaps more importantly, to make us feel full and satisfied!

When considering a cooking fat or oil for a recipe, it's important to note the smoke point. This is the conventional gauge for measuring the absolute highest temperature to which an oil or fat should be heated before it literally smokes, becomes oxidized, and begins to turn rancid. When fats and oils are heated beyond the smoking point, the bonds between their glycerol and fatty acids are broken and release toxic fumes and free radicals. When free radicals build up in excessive amounts, they can overwhelm the body. This oxidative stress is harmful and can trigger inflammation or lead to diseases such as cancer when free radicals are consumed in high amounts.

Smoke point, however, is not the only consideration for how an oil or fat will perform in a home kitchen. Rather, the factors that predict an oil's safety and stability at high heat are the percentage of polyunsaturated fatty acids (the lower the better when heated) and the extent to which the oil has been refined (the less the better). Many manufacturers use industrial-level refinement processes like bleaching, filtering, and high-temperature heating to extract and eliminate extraneous compounds to create a neutral-flavored oil with a longer shelf life and a higher smoke point.

An unrefined oil's characteristics will vary by season, plant or animal type, growing conditions, and the sample taken and tested. Additionally, fat from one part of the animal may have a makeup that performs very differently than from another part of the same animal.

We use unrefined plant fats that are tested each season to determine the smoke point and delicious and nourishing animal fats within a generally accepted range of temperatures for home cooking. Standard domestic cooking temperatures average around 250°F for sautéing, 320°F to 360°F for deep-frying, 350°F for indirect and up to 450°F for most direct grilling, and 390°F to 500°F for most baking.

Luckily there is a wide range of healthy and delicious plant and animal fats to choose from! The following unrefined fats and oils are used frequently throughout this book. It's worth investing in quality products from farms, producers, or health food stores that you trust (see Resources, page 392).

Centrifuge-Extracted (Unrefined) Avocado Oil

This luscious oil is a versatile and delicious healthy fat, rich in oleic acid, which has been known to reduce inflammation. We make an avocado oil at Apricot Lane Farms from our biodynamic Hass avocados that are picked at peak season and ripened to perfection before we use a centrifuge process to capture their opulent oil. This process keeps the avocado flesh and some skin cool during pressing to avoid rancidity caused by higher temperatures. Centrifugal forces extract a greater amount of oil with lower energy and water inputs than a refined avocado oil, resulting in a high-quality product with greater health benefits. Our oils made in this way have a bright green color and robust, buttery flavor. The smoke point of our oil registers 400°F, making it suitable for high-heat applications and a wide range of cooking methods, such as sautéing, indirect grilling, roasting, broiling, or frying. Its characteristic flavor is delicious in vinaigrettes, marinades, and sauces, such as Avocado Oil Mayonnaise (page 90). When sourcing other avocado oils, choose a label with clear information about processing and avoid the bleaching and deodorizing of a more refined product with a higher smoke point. Most unrefined avocado oils typically range in smoke point from 375°F to 480°F.

Cold-Pressed or Centrifuge-Extracted Extra-Virgin Olive Oil

This common pantry staple can range in flavors and has a smoke point of between 325°F and 425°F, so be sure to read the label before purchasing. For low-temperature frying, such as the Potato and Butternut Squash Rösti Cakes with Chive Crème Fraîche (page 116), you'll want a buttery and mild olive oil instead of a bold and peppery oil, which is better for making vinaigrettes or sauces, or for finishing a recipe. For our farm olive oil, we handpick a diverse assortment of our own organic olives, including Mission, Manzanillo, Arbequina, and Lucca.

The result is a complex and richly flavored blend, with an impressive smoke point of 425°F, which can be used as a cooking or finishing oil. An important note: the term "extra-virgin" doesn't necessarily mean that the oil has not become rancid due to poorly milled olives or inappropriate storage. Purchase from producers you trust.

Cold-Pressed or Centrifuge-Extracted Virgin Coconut Oil

This oil, which is solid at room temperature, is made from the fresh meat of mature coconuts. It contains beneficial antioxidants and both antifungal and antimicrobial properties. Virgin coconut oil has not been subjected to the chemical refinement, bleaching, or deodorizing that is typical of standard coconut oil. It also has a distinctive, slightly sweet coconut flavor that can add character to sweet and savory dishes. It has a smoke point of around 350°F and is best used for sautéing meats and vegetables, low-heat frying, or baking. Purchase brands that use ethically sourced, sustainably harvested coconuts grown with organic methods. The high saturated fat in virgin coconut oil remains stable for long periods at room temperature, but it is best to store it in a cool, dark place.

Ghee

Originating in ancient India, where the domestication of cattle began, ghee has been used in culinary and medicinal traditions throughout the Indian subcontinent, Middle East, and Southeast Asia for millennia. It is similar to clarified butter but is heated for a longer time to remove all the water before straining the milk solids. The result is a rich, nutty, and slightly caramelized flavor. It can be suitable for those who are lactose intolerant, though some may still not tolerate it. It is also magically shelf stable, even in the most sweltering temperatures. It is held in high regard in Ayurvedic medicine and benefits the digestive tract with its anti-inflammatory properties. You can easily make ghee at home, or you can find jars of grass-fed ghee at health food stores (see Resources, page 392). Unlike butter, which has a smoke point of around 300°F, ghee can generally be heated up to 480°F without burning and is excellent for frying.

Lard

This semisolid saturated fat comes from the rendered fatty tissues of the pig. It is easy to make (page 37) and has a distinctive, savory flavor. Its smoke point lies between 360°F and 370°F, making it best for sautéing meat and vegetables or for frying.

Pastured Bacon Fat

This precious rendered fat maximizes both the value and flavor from tasty bacon. Cook the bacon low and slow to crispy perfection to release the most fat before straining and transferring to a lidded glass jar. It adds a wonderful, slightly salty flavor to fried eggs or sautéed meats and vegetables, especially when rendered from our Simple Salt and Pepper Bacon (page 38). It has a smoke point of between 325°F and 360°F and will remain thick and somewhat solid at room temperature for several weeks or close to forever in the refrigerator or freezer—if it lasts that long!

Unrefined Sweeteners

One of the most important ways I've improved my personal well-being has been by limiting my sugar intake. Although this has helped tremendously in alleviating inflammation and encouraging proper digestion, it doesn't mean I don't enjoy something sweet on occasion! In California, we are lucky to have plentiful sources of honey but also locally grown dates that can be purchased whole, as syrup, or as flavorful granules. I have also embraced making and using Powdered Green Stevia (page 160) to bring balance to dishes such as tomato sauce, granola, soups, or smoothies. This powerful green powder is worlds away from the saccharine, synthetic flavor of refined stevia you buy at the store. Although there are few desserts in this book, the ones we have shared provide nutritious, nourishing calories and are a light way to end a satisfying meal.

Honey is a natural sweetener that we use often in our recipes, particularly in its raw form that is extracted straight from the honeycomb without further processing. It often contains trace amounts of bee pollen and propolis, which carry extra benefits such as health-enhancing phytochemicals, flavonoids, and ascorbic acid, which act as antioxidants. These compounds protect us against oxidative stress from free radicals that can contribute to chronic illness such as heart disease and cancer. Raw honey also carries anti-inflammatory benefits, can soothe a sore throat or upset tummy, and is naturally antibacterial and antimicrobial. These valuable advantages are thought to be compromised by the heating that is done to pasteurize and stabilize honey. To preserve honey's benefits, it is best to use raw honey that has not been heated above 110°F.

Although our farm contains plenty of year-round forage material for honeybees, it is a small oasis in a manicured landscape of conventional agriculture typical of Southern California. When monoculture farms aren't flowering, honeybees have limited resources due to the lack of biodiversity. With this in mind, we don't harvest the honey produced by our hives so that our bees have access to the essential micronutrients they need to thrive. Additionally,

honey acts as an important insulator for the hives, providing protection from cold in the winter and allowing the hives to remain cool in the summer. Our hives are vital to the pollination of our fruit trees, and we respectfully purchase raw honey instead from producers we know and trust who can harvest a sustainable surplus.

The nutritional benefits and composition of raw honey will vary depending upon the flowers the bees gather their nectar from as well as the overall health of their environment. Purchase honey from reputable sources with a label that clearly identifies the honey as raw and pure. It will often describe the kind of flowers the bees have pollinated. For our recipes, mild-tasting varieties are best, but you can experiment with stronger honeys to create exciting flavor combinations. Creamed honey is natural liquid honey that has been whipped to encourage crystallization, producing a smooth, spreadable consistency. Keep in mind that creamed honey will have a much sweeter flavor profile. Taste as you go when adding honey to a recipe, adjusting the amount according to your preference.

Whole Grains, Flours, Seeds, and Nuts

These common pantry staples are the workhorses of many of our recipes. Grains, flours, seeds, and nuts can be difficult for some people to digest because they contain enzyme inhibitors that bind to the healthy digestive and metabolic enzymes in our body. They also contain phytic acid, which binds to essential micronutrients in foods such as zinc, iron, magnesium, and calcium, making them impossible to absorb into our system. Exposure to these foods without proper preparation can lead to irritation and intolerance over time.

In our baking recipes, we often ferment flour before it's baked, as in A Simple Sourdough Sandwich Loaf (page 54), A Crusty Hearth-Style Sourdough Boule (page 59), or Sourdough Pizza and Flatbread Dough (page 62). When sourcing flour, choose freshly milled, stone-ground flour, ideally from a local and reputable source (see Resources, page 392). I prefer the nutritional profile and flavor of heirloom wheats like Red Fife, but there are other modern, non-GMO hybrids, such as Glenn, that have been developed to more closely cooperate with sustainable farming practices, especially in hot and dry regions. To extend the shelf life of this specialty flour, store it, protected from moisture, in either the refrigerator or freezer. When making bread, bring it to room temperature before mixing the dough and note the deliciously nutty aroma when it is combined with water. The nutritional integrity of stone-ground flour will also help with creating and maintaining an active Whole-Grain Rye Sourdough Starter (page 52). When using flour for other recipes, such as Zucchini Fritters with Lemon-Cucumber Yogurt Sauce (page 180), look for sprouted wheat flour (see Resources, page 392), which has more available nutrients and is easier to digest.

When cooking with edible seeds, give them a pretreatment by first soaking and dehydrating (page 41), sprouting, alkalizing (page 46), or fermenting with sourdough. Similarly, nixtamal (page 46) is a method that has been used for thousands of years to make maize (corn) more nutritious and delicious before adding it to soups or using it to make Corn Tortillas (page 44). Choose heirloom varieties of maize that are not only rich in color and aroma but preserve and honor Mesoamerican foodways.

Sustainably grown organic nuts provide excellent nutrition and healthy fats, but again, we are careful to soak them first to assist in digestion and absorption of their vitamins and minerals. We grow macadamia nuts and source biodynamic or wild-grown nuts when possible (see Resources, page 392). Store them in a cool, dark place until ready to soak and dehydrate (page 41). All nuts in the recipes of this book should be soaked and dehydrated first; it is worth dedicating time to prepare them in large batches, as they store for long periods of time in the freezer. They are delicious as is, but some recipes call for toasting the nuts after soaking and dehydrating them (bake in a preheated 350°F oven for 5 to 10 minutes before using).

Raw Vinegar

Incorporating live, probiotic ingredients such as vinegar into recipes is a wonderful way to improve the healing power of food. Brands that offer small-batch raw vinegars (see Resources, page 392) often work with sustainably minded farmers to procure the best ingredients. Look for labels that indicate the vinegar includes the "mother" or has not been pasteurized. When making a brine with raw vinegar, keep the heat below 110°F to preserve the probiotic benefits.

Miso

This ancient Japanese seasoning paste is traditionally made by fermenting soybeans with salt, kōji, and sometimes rice, barley, sweet potatoes, seaweed, or other ingredients. Kōji is a filamentous culinary fungus (mold) that, when intentionally grown under the right conditions, transforms the ingredients it's used with into a complex, concentrated flavor profile packed with umami. The hormonal properties of soy have a negative effect on my body and have caused me to experience breakouts and delayed menstrual cycles. Because I do not tolerate it, the recipes here have been developed with miso that uses chickpeas instead. I've suggested substitutions if you can't find this alternative, but use your best judgment and choose a miso according to your taste and dietary preferences. "White" miso is typically milder and more floral, whereas "red" misos tend to be more robust and carry their flavor forward in sauces, marinades, or vinaigrettes. You'll find misos with the best microbial and probiotic benefits in the refrigerated section of Japanese groceries or health food stores. Or, purchase them online from artisan, small-batch brands that have not been pasteurized (see Resources, page 392).

Filtered Water

Tap water varies widely by location, and I encourage you to review your local quality report to help you make informed choices about drinking water based upon mineral content and possible contamination. But beyond basic safety, water quality can affect both the nutritive value and performance of ingredients (particularly in fermented recipes) and influence their flavor. I recommend filtered water—removing chlorine, chemicals, pesticides, heavy metals, and bacterial contaminants provides better-smelling and better-tasting water.

Sea Salt

There are many different sources of salt, including evaporations from both land and sea. Although the natural moisture present in sea salts means they can easily clump, we prefer using these mineral-rich salts (see Resources, page 392) for both cooking and fermenting.

Chapter One

PRESERVED, CURED, and ACTIVATED INGREDIENTS

YOU CAN CAPTURE AND STORE THE ABUNDANCE OF THE SEASONS easily by using a few key techniques and recipes. The following are some of our favorite ways to preserve farm-fresh foods to add bright and savory flavors to any meal. Properly preparing nuts and seeds will ensure you are able to digest these powerhouse ingredients and benefit from the full spectrum of their nutrients. This chapter introduces the concept of soaking and dehydrating to eliminate phytic acid and digestive enzyme inhibitors and, just as importantly, to enhance flavor!

Recipes

PICKLED PERSIMMONS

The Coffee Cake persimmon is my very favorite fruit on the farm, and I eagerly await the first bite each season. It is a nonastringent variety, meaning it can be eaten sweet off the tree like an apple. Late in the season, however, a handful of fruits turn astringent for an unknown reason and must be fully ripened to a pudding-like softness before eating. Before I solved the mystery, this tricked me into thinking we had planted a rogue variety in our Coffee Cake tree row, but alas, it is just nature's sense of humor telling us the end of the season is near! Coffee Cake has a rich flavor and distinct speckled brown flesh that hints of nutmeg and spice. If you cannot source them, the more common Fuyu persimmons will work equally well. Choose firm but ripe fruits for best pickling results, avoiding soft flesh that will disintegrate in the jar. Use in the White Bean Tartine with Bacon, Arugula, and Pickled Persimmons (page 334), as a topping for pizza, or to dress a cheese and charcuterie board.

MAKES
1 QUART

3 large Coffee Cake persimmons

½ cup champagne or rice wine vinegar

3 tablespoons mild raw honey

1 cinnamon stick (about 4 inches)

5 whole cloves

5 whole allspice berries

½ teaspoon ground coriander

1 teaspoon whole black peppercorns

1½ teaspoons fine sea salt

1 tablespoon peeled and thinly sliced ginger (1 × 1½-inch knob)

2 tablespoons thinly sliced garlic (3 to 4 large cloves)

1. Remove the stems and sepals of the persimmons, and using a vegetable peeler, remove the skin. Slice the peeled persimmons into ¼-inch-thick wedges and transfer to a 1-quart glass jar.

2. In a small saucepan, warm 1 cup of water, the vinegar, and honey over medium heat. Stir until the honey is fully dissolved. Off the heat, add the cinnamon, cloves, allspice, coriander, peppercorns, salt, ginger, and garlic and stir. Cool for 10 minutes.

3. Pour the mixture over the persimmons and let the jar cool without a lid for 1 hour at room temperature. Fasten the lid and store in the refrigerator for at least 4 hours before eating. The pickled persimmons will keep in the refrigerator for at least 3 weeks and up to 2 months before softening.

PRESERVED LEMONS

Although common lemons can be picked year-round in California, the winter season is one of the most joyful and abundant times for this cheerful citrus. This recipe allows you to preserve the fresh flavor of lemon well into the summer months. Use a 1-quart mason jar with an accompanying airlock lid (see page 67). Lisbon lemons are a common juicy, medium-size fruit with a smooth, medium-thick, and bright yellow rind that is slightly bitter but excellent for preserving. You may substitute similar Eureka lemons or fleeting Meyer lemons, whose floral fragrance, thinner skin, and mild bitterness are delightful! Chop the rind into Potato Salad with Preserved Lemon and Mint (page 115) or Sugar Snap Pea Salad with Shaved Radish, Carrot, and Preserved Lemon Vinaigrette (page 139), stir into strained yogurt, or use to marinate or roast meats and fish (try the Braised Pastured Chicken Thighs with Lemon, Spring Onion, and Honey, page 221).

MAKES
1 QUART

8 medium lemons (2¾ pounds)

6 tablespoons fine sea salt

1. Using a knife, remove the stem end of the lemons. Cut each lemon lengthwise into 4 to 6 equal wedges. Remove all the seeds and the white central core using the knife's tip, and transfer the wedges to a medium bowl.

2. Sprinkle the lemon wedges with the salt and toss to combine. Rest at room temperature for 15 minutes to initiate maceration and brine formation.

3. Using a muddler or the end of a rolling pin, firmly crush each lemon wedge as you place it in the jar, pushing down to compact the wedges and extract the juice. If there is salt or liquid left over in the bowl, transfer it to the jar. It may not seem like they will fit, but they will continue to relax as you work. The juice will combine with the salt to create a brine that will cover the lemons. Insert a fermentation weight to submerge the lemons under the brine. If there is not enough brine to cover the lemon wedges, squeeze 2 to 3 additional lemons and add the juice to the jars to cover.

4. Clean the rim of the jar and firmly secure the airlock lid. Ferment at room temperature until the peel has slightly softened and the lemons taste pleasantly tangy, 7 to 12 days. Check the lemons every other day and skim off any suspicious surface film. The brine will become thick and the salt may settle. Shake the jar once a day to mix up the salt. Once fully fermented, the lemons will turn pale yellow and smell fresh and lemony with some musky undertones. Discard the lemons if they develop an acetone scent or if they have discoloration.

5. When the lemons are fermented to your liking, replace the airlock with a noncorrosive lid and transfer to the refrigerator for up to 6 months.

TOMATO RAISINS

Tomatoes are one of summer's most delightful gifts from the garden, but for the first few years on the farm, we struggled with soil fertility and pesky diseases that prevented us from growing the delicious, sweet tomatoes we do today. This technique not only preserves any cherry tomatoes in bite-size form but elevates ho-hum fruits that may be lacking in sweetness or flavor complexity. The results are plump, slightly tart, tomato "raisins" that are naturally sweet and perfect for preparing Spaghetti Squash Coins with Mascarpone and Tomato Raisins (page 113) or Summer Corn Salad with Tomato Raisins, Basil, and Chèvre (page 176). They are also delicious eaten as a snack, chopped into vinaigrettes, tossed into pasta sauces, stirred into stews, or as a substitute to sun-dried tomatoes preserved in oil.

MAKES
30 OR
ABOUT 1 CUP

2 cups medium cherry tomatoes (30 tomatoes)

2 tablespoons cold-pressed extra-virgin olive oil

¼ teaspoon fine sea salt

¼ teaspoon freshly ground black peppercorns

1. With a toothpick, evenly prick the skin of each tomato four times to allow air and moisture to escape the tomato while it dries.

2. On a large baking sheet, spread the tomatoes in a single layer. Transfer to the oven's middle rack and adjust the temperature to the lowest setting, ideally 175°F to 200°F or lower. The lower the temperature, the more time is necessary, but the sweeter the tomato raisins will be. Crack the door to ventilate until the tomatoes resemble large raisins and do not exude juice when squeezed, at least 10 hours. When they are finished, they will shrink to almost half their original size, but their skins will remain pliable. If using a dehydrator instead, spread the tomatoes over a 15 × 15-inch tray and set to 140°F for 36 hours.

3. Remove the tomatoes from the oven or dehydrator and set aside to cool. Place the tomatoes in a small bowl and toss with the oil, salt, and pepper.

4. Store the seasoned tomato raisins in a sealed container in the refrigerator for up to 1 month.

DRIED SUMMER STONE-FRUIT MEDLEY

During peak stone-fruit season, our surplus fruit seconds are used as puree for fruit butters; enhancements to our kombucha; or are pickled, fermented, or dried. In the dormant season, when we long for the essence of summer, recipes such as Summer Orchard Shredded Chicken Salad with Dried Stone Fruit, Fresh Lemon, and Pistachios (page 217) spoil us with the memories of sunny days in the orchard picking ripe fruit. We do not use synthetic preservatives and instead store the dried fruit in the freezer to prolong its life and avoid discoloration from unwanted oxidation. Some of our preferred dried fruits are tart apricots, sweet peaches, and mellow nectarines. Preserving your own medley at home is simple and takes only a little prep work, a dehydrator, and some time. Although this syrup method is not necessary, it can greatly enhance fruit that lacks in natural sweetness. It also benefits the texture, and the color will be preserved if stored for short periods at room temperature. We use 15 × 15-inch dehydrator trays for this recipe (see Resources, page 392).

PRESERVES
ABOUT
5 POUNDS
FRESH FRUIT
(Yields about
1 quart dried fruit)

3 tablespoons mild raw honey

3 tablespoons fresh lemon juice
(about 1 large lemon)

5 pounds ripe stone fruits (apricots, cherries, plums, or peaches work well)

1. In a small bowl, whisk together the honey and lemon juice until the honey is dissolved into a thin, golden syrup.

2. Line dehydrator trays with perforated mats. Using a small paring knife, slice the fruit in half lengthwise and remove the pit. Cut the fruit into ½-inch-thick slices. Dip the slices in the syrup, shaking off any excess before placing on the dehydrator trays. The fruit can be spaced close together on the trays but should not be touching. Continue this process until all the fruit has been dipped or you have filled the trays.

3. Slide the trays into the dehydrator and secure the door. Set the temperature to 135°F and the timer for 6 hours before checking the fruit. Drying times may vary slightly depending upon the moisture content of the fruit. To determine doneness, place a piece of fruit in a plastic bag while it is still warm from the dehydrator. If condensation forms on the inside of the bag after 2 to 3 minutes, too much moisture is still present in the fruit. Continue drying for an additional 1 to 2 hours if needed before testing again. Some of the syrup may drip to the bottom of the dehydrator—be sure to clean it up when the fruit is done to avoid the unwanted appearance of ants.

4. Store in sealed plastic bags or lidded glass jars at room temperature for 1 to 2 weeks or in the freezer for up to 1 year.

LARD

Pastured pork is well known for the mouthwatering and nutty flavor of its fat. Although we are equal-opportunity fat lovers, we prefer to source the fat from the soft and visceral areas around the loin and kidneys to produce what is known as leaf lard. It has a clean, delicate flavor and spreadable consistency useful for some applications. If you have a trusted local butcher, let them know your intended use and that you're happy to relieve them of trimmings!

In contrast to shelf-stable, store-brought brands, home-rendered lard is fresher and lacks preservatives and bleaching and deodorizing agents, but it will easily turn rancid at room temperature. Keep it stored in the refrigerator or freezer and use it to make Cinnamon and Orange-Infused Crispy Carnitas (page 285), Chorizo (page 297), Bacon-Wrapped Pastured Pork Meatloaf with Yellow Pepper Sauce (page 295), or Shepherd's Pie with Sweet Potato and Chimichurri Sauce (page 259). Dicing the pork fat into small bits is very important to efficiently render the fat—try portioning large chunks into more manageable pieces and freezing them first to avoid a slippery and sometimes challenging task! Use water as both a buffer and a gentle start to rendering—without it, you run the risk of scorching or, worse, catching the fat on fire! Trust us from experience; we render lard often and safely but do not recommend doing so unattended. This recipe makes not only a beautiful, smooth white fat but also some crispy leftover bits affectionately called cracklings in the southern cuisine of the United States or chicharrones in Mexico. Add these precious morsels to Masa (page 46), fold into sourdough bread dough (pages 54 or 59), or mix into cornbread for a savory, textural treat!

MAKES
2 QUARTS

6 pounds pork fat, chopped into ½-inch cubes (about 4 quarts)

1. In a 6-quart pot, add 3 cups of water and the pork fat. Cover and bring to a boil over medium-high heat. Boil for about 10 minutes, and then reduce the heat to medium. Slowly render the fat until the cubes are less than half their original size, about 2 hours. Remove the lid and continue cooking over medium heat until the fat is fully liquid and translucent and the residual solid bits have turned a distinctive golden color, about another hour. Remove the pot from the heat and set aside to cool for 20 minutes.

2. Line a sieve with cheesecloth and set over a 2- to 3-quart heatproof container. When the fat is still liquid but not scalding hot, carefully ladle it into the sieve. The leftover solid bits can be returned to the pot and cooked over medium-low heat until crispy, 30 to 60 minutes. Be careful to avoid being splattered with fat as these continue to render and "crackle."

3. Keep the lard and cracklings stored separately in covered containers in the refrigerator or freezer. Use the lard in 2 to 4 weeks if stored in the refrigerator and the cracklings within 5 days of rendering, or place both in the freezer for up to 1 year.

SIMPLE SALT AND PEPPER BACON

The day we made our own bacon on the farm was the day I felt like we had finally arrived! It has since become a mainstay of our meal program and is used to create everything from Bacon-Wrapped Pastured Pork Meatloaf with Yellow Pepper Sauce (page 295) to Arugula and Pickled Morello Cherry Salad with Bacon, Chèvre, and Borage Flowers (page 314) to White Bean Tartine with Bacon, Arugula, and Pickled Persimmons (page 334) and Winter Frittata with Butternut Squash, Leeks, Collard Greens, and Bacon (page 236). This recipe uses a manageable 1 pound of pork belly to make bacon, which will encourage success if you are a beginner. But you can scale the recipe up to multiple or larger pieces once you are comfortable with the process, up to 5 or 6 pounds at once, depending on the size of your smoker. We make a salt and pepper rub in large batches and use it as a percentage of the weight of the meat for proper curing. We prefer the handling and timing of using a 1.5 percent application of the meat's weight in this rub; it highlights the subtle flavors of our pastured pork. You can also experiment with flavors using dried herbs such as rosemary, thyme, summer savory, or sage.

If you are using store-bought conventional pork belly, it will naturally carry more water weight than pastured meat, leading to more brine accumulation in the curing process. Using pastured pork and a low percentage of salt, however, will allow the natural, woodsy flavors to emerge from the finished bacon. We use an electric smoker with a calibrated temperature range (see Resources, page 392) in combination with applewood chips presoaked in water for the best flavor. To source applewood for splitting into chips, check with local farmers, as they may be keen to offload their scraps from pruning! If you are in a more urban area, you can purchase applewood chips at hardware stores in the outdoor cooking section.

MAKES
ABOUT
¾ POUND

50 grams fine sea salt

10 grams freshly ground black peppercorns

1 pound pastured pork belly, skin removed and trimmed of excess fat to 1 inch

1. Place the salt and pepper in a small container with a lid. Fasten the lid and shake the container to combine. Set aside.

2. Wearing gloves, wash any blood from the pork belly and use a clean cloth or paper towel to pat it dry. Place the pork belly on a clean scale and record its weight in grams. Calculate 1.5 percent of the weight of the piece and record. This will be the amount of the salt and pepper rub you will use to season the meat. For a 1-pound piece (454 grams), this would be rounded to 7 grams of salt and pepper rub.

3. On a clean work surface, season the pork belly with the calculated amount of salt and pepper rub, ensuring all sides are evenly covered. Transfer to a stainless steel or food-safe plastic container and cover tightly with a lid or plastic wrap. Label the container, indicating the date, and transfer to the refrigerator. Cure the belly for at least 7 days and up to 14 days, turning once a day. After 2 to 3 days, the salt will have pulled moisture from the pork belly and a natural brine will begin collecting in the container. Rub this brine into the belly daily, ensuring that the salt and pepper remain evenly distributed. The bacon will be ready for rinsing when the color has slightly oxidized, and it smells sweet and fragrant. If it becomes slimy or smells sour, this is an indication the meat has turned and must be discarded.

4. Nestle a wire rack into a large baking sheet. Remove the pork belly from the container and rinse under cool water, brushing off the salt with your fingers in soft, quick motions, as if you were dusting a piece of furniture. With paper towels, blot the cured bacon until completely dry. Place the bacon on the wire rack and transfer to the refrigerator. Air-dry, uncovered, in the refrigerator for 24 hours, or until a noticeable dry skin forms.

5. Submerge 2 ounces of applewood chips in warm water and soak for at least 1 hour. Meanwhile, remove the pork belly from the refrigerator and let it rest at room temperature for 1 hour.

6. Assemble and preheat the smoker: Cover the bottom floor and the top of the wood-chip holder with foil for easy cleanup and to prevent a grease fire. Set the smoker to 225°F and the timer to 5 hours.

7. Using tongs, carefully place the soaked wood chips in the chip holder. Position the rack and place the pork belly on top, making sure the meat does not touch the walls of the smoker or other belly pieces, if smoking multiple pieces. Using clean tongs, turn the meat every 45 minutes to ensure even smoking.

8. Take the temperature of the meat after the first hour and every 45 minutes thereafter. When the internal temperature reads 130°F or above, check the temperature more frequently until the thermometer reads 155°F. The bacon will have shrunk to about three-quarters its original size with fat dripping off the sides. It will be a deep caramel color with slightly crispy corners. Using a sharp knife, slice into the thickest part of the meat—it should appear brownish-pink but

RECIPE CONTINUES

thoroughly cooked. Remove and rest, uncovered, on wire racks, about 30 minutes. Once cooled to room temperature, transfer to a covered container and place in the refrigerator overnight.

9. The next day, slice the bacon to the desired thickness, about ⅛ inch thick for average use. Shingle the pieces on a 24-inch-long piece of parchment paper and create a folded pouch. Wrap tightly with plastic film, or vacuum pack if possible. Store in the refrigerator for up to 2 weeks or freeze for up to 6 months.

COOKING TIP: *Crispy Bacon*

We prefer to cook bacon in a preheated 350°F to 400°F oven for a crispy texture and high amounts of rendered fat. Nestle a wire rack in a rimmed baking sheet and lay the bacon flat in a single layer across the rack. Place on the middle oven rack and cook for 15 to 20 minutes for even results. Alternatively, cook on the stovetop in a covered cast-iron skillet over medium heat until crispy, 8 to 12 minutes, depending upon thickness. Don't forget to strain and save the bacon fat for later use!

SOAKING AND DEHYDRATING NUTS

Nuts are a densely nutritious, conveniently snackable food that adds crunchy texture to meals or can be blended into creamy butters (page 42) for spreading. Like other seeds, it is helpful to soak nuts before consuming them to remove both phytic acid and digestive enzyme inhibitors (see page 28) and to enhance their flavor. Soaking nuts will remove bitterness (especially present in walnuts) and allow a subtle sweetness to step forward. Anytime I introduce this idea to someone new, I use walnuts to win them over with flavor alone! Please note, this method does not act as a remedy for those with an *allergy* to nuts, seeds, or grains.

MAKES
1 QUART

4 cups raw nuts (pecans, walnuts, almonds, cashews, pistachios, or pine nuts work well)

1 tablespoon plus a few generous pinches fine sea salt

1. Combine the nuts and salt in a nonreactive container three times their volume. Fill the container with water, leaving at least 2 inches of space below the rim, and stir to dissolve the salt. Soak for 4 to 24 hours, depending upon the nut (chart follows).

2. Drain and rinse the nuts in a fine-mesh sieve. Spread in a single layer on a 15 × 15-inch dehydrator tray. Sprinkle lightly with sea salt, if desired, and place in the dehydrator. Set the temperature to between 155°F and 165°F and check the nuts periodically until they are dry and crispy (see suggested times below).

3. When the nuts are fully dehydrated, transfer them to a clean and dry container and secure the lid. Store at room temperature for 2 months or in the freezer for up to 6 months.

Raw Nut	Soaking Time	Dehydrating Time
Almond	12 to 24 hours	12 to 24 hours
Pecan	12 to 24 hours	12 to 24 hours
Walnut	12 to 24 hours	12 to 24 hours
Macadamia	4 to 6 hours	24 to 36 hours
Cashew	2 to 4 hours	12 to 36 hours
Pistachio	4 to 6 hours	12 to 16 hours
Pine Nut	4 to 6 hours	8 to 12 hours

HOMEMADE TOASTED NUT BUTTERS

Homemade nut butters are economical to make and yield the freshest, most digestible results without additional refined oils or sugar. Presoaked cashews, pecans, and almonds (page 41)— no need to dehydrate!—are our favorite and blend to a mostly smooth finish with some rustic texture remaining. Add salt if desired, but remember that the soaked nuts may have already been slightly salted at the time of drying. To blend the nuts properly, use a 5-cup food processor if possible. For a thinner consistency, add 1 to 2 tablespoons of coconut oil after blending while the nut butter is still warm.

MAKES
ABOUT 1 CUP

2 cups soaked and dehydrated pecans, almonds, or cashews (page 41)

1. Preheat the oven to 350°F and position a rack in the middle.

2. Spread the nuts over a large baking sheet and place in the oven. Toast until a nutty fragrance fills the kitchen and the nuts are a light brown color, 5 to 7 minutes. Remove from the oven and set aside for 10 minutes, or until cool.

3. Transfer the nuts to a 5-cup food processor. Process the pecans for about 4 minutes, the almonds for about 8 minutes, or the cashews for about 9 minutes, scraping down the sides as needed. The food processor will produce a thick, slightly grainy paste rather than a completely smooth nut butter.

4. Transfer to an airtight glass or stainless steel container and store at room temperature for up to 2 weeks or in the refrigerator for up to 2 months.

CASSAVA AND COCONUT FLOUR TORTILLAS

When the farm first began, our culinary program was whatever I was cooking, and it was a heavy load for this chef turned farmer! I worked all day before running home to whip something up for a visiting consultant or for our weekly volunteer dinners. The day that our seminal head farm chef joined the team was a happy day for my chapped dishwater hands! I spent the subsequent months sharing with her the seasonal techniques and traditional preparations that are the keys to keeping my body and mind strong. Incredibly talented and always accommodating, our new chef tapped into her Brazilian heritage and developed this grain-free tortilla, which the whole team loved! When the quality and hydration needs began to vary significantly across brands of cassava flour, we adjusted with more or less hot water, but it still didn't completely achieve the proper dough texture. We finally settled upon adding a bit of coconut flour to the original creation to make the tortilla more pliable and to add an enjoyable sweetness! If cooking for a crowd, you can prepare and portion the dough a day in advance and store in a covered container in the refrigerator. Use a tortilla press (see Resources, page 392) if you can for achieving an even thickness, but a rolling pin and parchment paper will work in a pinch.

MAKES
32 TORTILLAS

2½ cups cassava flour

1 cup coconut flour

1½ teaspoons fine sea salt

½ teaspoon cream of tartar

½ teaspoon baking soda

½ cup cold-pressed extra-virgin olive oil

2 cups hot water (205°F to 210°F)

1. Make the dough: In a large bowl, whisk together the cassava flour, coconut flour, salt, cream of tartar, and baking soda. Drizzle in the olive oil and massage the mixture until the oil is evenly distributed and small crumbs form between your fingers. Slowly and carefully stream the hot water over the mixture. With a large spoon, fold the ingredients until the dough develops a stringy but still dry texture. Cover with a towel and let the dough rest for 5 minutes. Add up to 1 cup of cool water, 2 to 3 tablespoons at a time, and mix with your fingertips. Begin kneading the dough in the bowl until it is soft and pliable and does not stick to your hands. The consistency and texture should be like Play-Doh. Cover with a towel, and set aside to rest at room temperature for about 10 minutes.

2. Test the dough for proper hydration, according to the instructions on page 44.

3. Shape, cook, and store the tortillas: Nestle a thick cotton towel inside a serving basket or a tortilla warmer and set it next to the stovetop. Heat a cast-iron skillet, griddle, or comal over medium-high heat until very hot, about 10 minutes. Shape the remaining dough into 31 balls and cover with a towel. Press, cook, and store the tortillas according to the instructions on page 45.

CORN TORTILLAS

In our kitchen, Maria is the master tortilla maker. She has a knack for getting the texture of the dough just right, without a measuring tool in sight! She prefers using a smooth flat griddle called a comal (see Resources, page 392) to cook the tortillas and insists that this is what helps to achieve the perfect "tortilla puff." I had never heard of the legend of a "tortilla puff" before Maria, who says it has roots in Mexican superstition: if your tortillas don't billow up like little golden balloons when you cook them, you are not ready to get married.

Anytime anyone besides Maria makes tortillas in the kitchen, she secretly observes from afar, looking for this telltale sign that the tortillas are being made correctly. When they puff, she beams with pride and says, "OK, you are ready!" If the tortilla remains flat and lifeless, she shakes her head, pretends to be sad, and jokingly informs the person, "No . . . you can't get married yet." I don't know if the superstition is true, but I do know that Maria's tortillas are the best, and she somehow gets them to billow up every time without fail!

Masa harina made using the method described on page 46 is sweet and nutty and yields a wonderful floral fragrance to these tortillas. Homemade masa harina has an uneven but special texture and creates a thirstier dough; letting the dough rest after mixing allows it to evenly hydrate. Omit this step when using store-bought masa harina since it is finely and evenly ground and will require less water to mix. Use a tortilla press (see Resources, page 392) if you can for achieving an even thickness, but a rolling pin and parchment paper will work in a pinch. Use to serve tacos filled with Cinnamon and Orange-Infused Crispy Carnitas (page 285) or to make the Smoky Potato and Greens Tacos (page 150) or the Crispy Bull Meat Tacos with Romaine Slaw (page 276).

MAKES
22 TORTILLAS

2 cups masa harina

1½ to 2¼ cups hot water (about 135°F)

1½ teaspoons fine sea salt

1. Make the masa: In a medium bowl, combine the masa harina, 1½ cups of the hot water, and the salt. Mix well with both hands until there are no visible lumps remaining, adding additional hot water if necessary to bring the dough together. Cover with a damp towel and let the dough rest for 15 minutes to fully hydrate.

2. Test the dough for proper hydration: Prepare a tortilla press with two sheets of parchment paper cut to the same shape and size as your press. Pinch and roll the dough or use a 1-ounce ice cream scooper to form a ball. Press it into a disk about ⅛ inch thick and 5 inches across. If the outer edge of the dough is jagged, add 1 tablespoon of warm water to the bowl with the dough, mix, and then test again, tweaking with more water until it has a malleable and soft consistency. If, however, the dough sticks to your hands or the press and tears when tested, knead in 1 tablespoon of the masa harina to the bowl with dough, adjusting as necessary.

3. Shape and cook the tortillas: Nestle a thick cotton towel inside a serving basket or a tortilla warmer and set it next to the stovetop. Heat a 10-inch well-seasoned cast-iron skillet, griddle, or comal over medium-high heat until very hot, about 10 minutes. Divide the remaining dough into twenty-one 1-ounce round pieces, about the size of a ping-pong ball, covering with a damp towel while you work. Press each ball between the two parchment pieces in the tortilla press to ⅛ inch thick and 5 inches in diameter. Lift the handle of the press and remove the top layer of parchment paper. Using the bottom layer of parchment paper, transfer each tortilla onto the hot surface, face side down, and peel away the parchment. Cook for 1 to 2 minutes while pressing with your fingertips and moving the tortilla in a circular motion. This ensures the tortilla has full contact with the cooking surface and heats evenly. Flip and cook for an additional minute or so. The tortilla should start to puff at this point, an indication that steam is cooking the inside and making it light and fluffy. Once the tortilla has deflated, remove it from the griddle and place it in the cloth-lined basket. Repeat with the remaining dough balls, neatly stacking the cooked tortillas.

4. If not using immediately, wrap the fully cooled tortillas in a cotton cloth and place in a closed container or plastic bag for up to 1 week in the refrigerator or in the freezer for up to 6 months.

NIXTAMAL/MASA/HOMINY GRITS

Maize (corn) is a seed native to the Americas with a deep history as a nutritious food source, especially when prepared using this ancient technique. Maize began domestication in south-central Mexico, before migrating to other parts of the Americas. It evolved depending upon where it traveled, resulting in the biodiverse rainbow we enjoy today.

To soften and remove maize's tough outer coating and make the interior more malleable, you need to soak and cook it in an alkaline solution. This process and the resulting corn is called nixtamal, a Spanish word derived from the Nahuatl words *nextli* (alkaline ashes used to boil the dried kernels) and *tamalli* (unformed corn dough made from ground, cooked kernels). Nixtamal can be done in most home kitchens, but like many traditional cooking methods, it requires some mostly hands-off time to properly complete. This magical transformation results in what we describe in the English language as hominy.

To make the alkaline solution, you must prepare calcium chloride, otherwise known as pickling salt, or *cal* in Spanish. The chemical reaction between the alkalizer and the corn not only improves its digestibility and nutritional content but allows the tender kernels to form into masa (dough) for tortilla making. This recipe uses pickling lime that can be sourced online (see Resources, page 392) or from shops specializing in Latin cuisine or food preservation. Use the hominy in soups and stews, or grind it using a cast-iron hand molino (grinder) before drying it in a dehydrator or the oven. To make it into masa harina (corn flour), grind the dehydrated nixtamal using a tabletop mill (see Resources, page 392). This flour can then be rehydrated when necessary to make masa for Corn Tortillas (page 44) or Fried Dark Star Zucchini with Roasted Red Bell Pepper Sauce (page 191). Any type of dried whole organic dent corn (grain corn with a soft starch makeup) works well for this recipe, including Olotillo, Blue Hopi, or Oaxacan Green.

MAKES
5¾ CUPS GROUND FRESH NIXTAMAL OR 3½ CUPS DRIED HOMINY GRITS

4 cups dried dent corn

2 tablespoons pickling lime

1. Fill a large bowl with water and stir in the corn. Skim off any floating kernels or debris from the surface. Drain, rinse, and repeat this process, and then set the kernels aside.

2. In a 7-quart stainless steel or enamel-coated pot, combine 5 quarts of water with the pickling lime, stirring to dissolve. Stir in the corn, cover, and bring to a soft boil over medium-high heat. Remove the lid and increase the heat if needed to keep the pot at a low boil. Continue cooking until the outer skin of the corn loosens and the water thickens, 45 to 90 minutes (depending upon the age of the corn). The corn will still be firm. Remove from the heat, cover, and set aside to cool and soak for 12 hours.

3. Drain the corn in a colander and return it to the pot. Rinse with cold water while massaging the kernels to loosen the skins. Discard the skins, drain, and continue rinsing and massaging if necessary until all the skins are removed. Drain once more and set aside.

4. Set up a cast-iron hand-crank molino (see Resources, page 392) according to the manufacturer's instructions. Feed the drained corn into the molino, adjusting the grind so that it's light and fluffy. When squeezed into a clump, the ground nixtamal will resemble moist clay. Continue grinding the remaining corn. Clean the molino immediately to avoid rust.

5. Evenly spread the ground nixtamal onto four 15 × 15-inch dehydrator trays fitted with nonstick drying sheets. Set the dehydrator to 135°F and position the trays. Dehydrate until completely dry, 6 to 8 hours. Alternatively, preheat the oven to 190°F and spread the ground nixtamal over two medium sheet pans. Transfer the pans to the oven and wedge a spoon in the door, allowing moisture to escape. Dry for 4 to 6 hours, stirring every 30 minutes, until completely dry.

6. Store the dried nixtamal in a lidded container in a cool, dry location for up to 3 months.

7. Mill into hominy grits or masa harina: Feed the dried nixtamal into the hopper of a home grain mill (see Resources, page 392) that is set to a medium-to-coarse grind. Repeat as necessary, adjusting the stones to a finer setting until you achieve a coarse polenta texture for grits or a fine powder for masa harina. Store in a sealed container at room temperature for up to 3 months.

Chapter Two

FERMENTED GRAINS, VEGETABLES, FRUITS, and DAIRY

FERMENTATION IS A USEFUL TECHNIQUE FOR NOT ONLY PRESERVING the harvest but also for introducing delicious probiotics to your diet. Fermentation can also aid in the digestion of sometimes problematic foods such as wheat by breaking down gluten and helping to eliminate phytic acid. The recipes and techniques in this chapter lay the foundation for making common pantry staples from scratch, such as sourdough bread, sauerkraut, and crème fraîche.

Recipes

WHOLE-GRAIN RYE SOURDOUGH STARTER

To create a sourdough culture, all you need is some quality flour and pure water to farm the microbes responsible for fermentation. Rye flour may seem lifeless at first, but when it gets going, it will give you so much confidence! Temperature is important in the initial creation of a starter, and keeping it at 75°F encourages activity. Freshly milled, stone-ground whole-grain flour has all the delicious and nutritious parts of the original grain intact and will provide the greatest potential for an active, healthy starter. Purchase flour from a reputable mill (see Resources, page 392) and store it in the refrigerator or freezer to protect it from moisture. Starters made with whole grains, especially rye, will be thicker and pastier than those made with refined white flour, but they have more vigorous fermentation power and add a complex flavor to your bread. If you prefer a more liquid starter, you can use half whole rye flour and half sifted bread flour instead. Either way, using some rye flour makes this starter very resilient!

It is worth buying a scale, as precise measurements will help you succeed, particularly when you are getting used to the bread-making process. Set the starter in a warm spot if possible and in about 7 to 10 days of feedings, you will have a responsive culture ready to leaven bread! Store your starter in a jar with a lid that can remain loose while also covering the culture to prevent it from drying out. Regular screw-top mason jars work well or those with a flip-top lid are excellent, as you can remove the rubber gasket and allow the lid to be fully closed but still loose.

MAKES
A LIFETIME
OF BREAD

180 grams stone-ground whole rye flour (about 1½ cups)

1. Create the starter: In a lidded glass jar no larger than a quart, stir together 30 grams/¼ cup flour and 30 milliliters/2 tablespoons water to form a very thick and pasty mixture with no dry lumps remaining. With your spoon, scrape the mixture into a small lump and cover loosely with the lid. Set in a warm location (ideally 75°F) for 24 hours. Remove the lid and add 60 grams/½ cup flour and 60 milliliters/¼ cup water and stir to combine. Replace the lid and ferment at room temperature for 12 hours. The mixture will be lightly fragrant and somewhat active after this time.

2. Discard 90 grams of the starter and add 90 grams/¾ cup flour and 90 milliliters/¼ cup plus 2 tablespoons water. After this feeding, it will become more fragrant with a yeasted scent and should double in size in 8 to 12 hours. Use a rubber band or piece of tape to mark the beginning volume. When the starter has doubled in size, harvest a large spoonful, being careful not to stir or disturb the starter and release its gases. Perform a float test by gently pushing the large dollop off the spoon into a glass full of water. If it floats, the wild yeast is active enough to produce carbon dioxide gas as a by-product of fermentation and buoy the starter.

If it sinks, the starter needs to strengthen. Perform one or two additional feedings every 8 to 12 hours in equal parts by weight of starter, water, and flour, or a 1:1:1 ratio. Repeat the test, being mindful not to harvest the starter before it has doubled in volume or after it has started to exhale the gas and deflate.

3. Once your new starter passes the float test, it is ready to use! Feed it twice daily at 8- to 12-hour intervals if keeping at room temperature or move it to the refrigerator for storage after it has been fed and almost doubled in size. Each feeding should be the same 1:1:1 ratio by weight to ensure it remains healthy. When storing in the refrigerator, remove and refresh it with a feeding at least once per week, discarding some of the original when you do to make room in the jar. I like to keep at least 2 heaping tablespoons (50 to 60 grams) on hand at all times. Any more than that is excessive if you are baking only one or two times per week.

A SIMPLE SOURDOUGH SANDWICH LOAF

This rectangular loaf has delicious flavor if made with fresh, stone-ground whole wheat flour. It sports a soft, spongy, even crumb perfect for making the BLT Sandwich with Egg, Avocado, and Basil Mayonnaise (page 384) or open-faced toasts such as Avocado Toast with Tokyo Turnips, Spinach, Pastured Egg, and Bagna Cauda (page 381). Our test kitchen developed this formula using Red Fife heirloom flour for its rich and nutty flavor. It grows well in most regions, including our harsh climate, where it receives little rain. I encourage you to support your local grain economy by seeking it or a similar cultivar of high-protein, hard red wheat, such as Turkey Red or Rouge de Bordeaux, for making this delicious bread. Bread made with stone-ground whole wheat flour has become so revered in our household—my son gobbles it up!

Sustainably grown wheat from arid California and the American Southwest is considerably higher in protein and mineral content, which makes the flour thirstier than wheat grown in other locations. For this reason, I've given a range of water amounts so you can adjust according to your needs: if you are sourcing from a dry climate, use the greater amount of water. If, however, you are located in a warm and humid region such as the American Southeast, the lower amount of water is more appropriate. If you keep your starter in the refrigerator and feed it once per week, refresh it at least once before mixing this recipe and use when it has doubled in volume and is fully active. Although it is not necessary to use a baking stone, it does create beneficial, evenly distributed heat in the oven. If using, preheat it for 30 minutes on the middle rack before baking the loaf, and use an oven thermometer, if possible, to make sure the temperature matches the dial.

MAKES
1 LOAF

75 grams (3 heaping tablespoons) active Whole-Grain Rye Sourdough Starter (page 52)

10 grams (1¾ teaspoons) fine sea salt

450 grams (about 3 cups) stone-ground Red Fife whole wheat flour or hard red whole wheat bread flour

120 milliliters (½ cup) boiling water

1. Mix the dough: Combine 360 milliliters/1½ cups of water, the active starter, and salt in a medium bowl and mix with your fingers or a spoon until the salt is dissolved and the starter is well combined. Add the flour and mix with your hands until completely incorporated and no dry lumps remain. The dough should feel soft and sticky. If it feels stiff or is difficult to mix with your hands, sprinkle in an additional 15 to 45 milliliters/1 to 3 tablespoons of water and mix well to combine.

2. Cover the bowl with a plate or a reusable plastic bag and ferment until the dough has increased in size by one-third and small bubbles appear around the perimeter of the dough, about 3½ hours. During this time, stretch and fold the dough in the bowl every 30 to 45 minutes to create strength: reach to the bottom of the bowl and gently pull a handful of the dough up and over itself, folding it to the center. Rotate the bowl and repeat until all the dough has been stretched and folded to the center. Cover and repeat at least 3 more times.

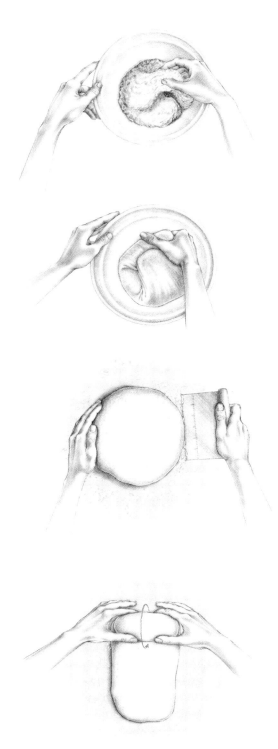

3. Generously grease an $8^{1}/_{2} \times 4 \, ^{1}/_{2}$-inch metal baking pan with butter and set aside. When the dough is puffy and has increased in volume by about one-third, preshape it into a rectangle: Transfer the dough from the bowl to a lightly floured surface and gently coax it into an even rectangular shape, about 6 by 12 inches. Position it so that the dough is facing you lengthwise. Loosely roll the dough from the top to the bottom, finishing with the seam side down. Cover with a damp towel for 10 to 20 minutes, until the dough visibly relaxes. Swiftly turn the dough over so the seam side is up, rotate a quarter turn so it is lengthwise again, and repeat the rolling motion, this time gaining more tension as you go. Using a bench scraper, release and transfer it to the baking pan with the seam side facing down and place a dry towel on top. Cover with a reusable plastic bag and refrigerate for 8 to 24 hours to improve flavor and digestibility. If you'd like to bake it the same day, however, leave the loaf, covered, at room temperature until it crests the top of the pan, 3 to 4 more hours.

4. If you refrigerated the loaf, remove it from the refrigerator and set it on the counter until it crests the top of the pan, 1 to 2 hours. The amount of time will depend upon the temperature of the refrigerator and the ambient temperature of your kitchen.

5. When the loaf has almost crested the top of the pan, place a baking stone (if using) on the middle rack of your oven and a shatterproof roasting pan on the bottom rack. Preheat the oven to 450°F for at least 30 minutes, with the fan assist turned off. When the loaf has fully proofed, place it in the oven and pour the boiling water into the preheated roasting pan. Bake for 20 minutes. Remove the roasting pan if water remains, lower the temperature to 400°F, and continue to bake for another 20 to 25 minutes. The loaf is ready when an instant-read thermometer registers 210°F when inserted into the center of the loaf and the crust is a deep, dark brown color. Do not underbake.

6. Remove the loaf from the oven. Tip the loaf out on a wire rack and let it cool completely before slicing, about 2 hours. Store wrapped in a beeswax-coated reusable linen or plastic bag for up to 1 week.

Sourdough Baking Tip Sheet

Sourdough breads made with regional, stone-ground flours are undeniably satisfying and delicious. The performance of flour is variable, depending upon the ambient temperature of your kitchen, the milling practices, and the grains that you choose. You may encounter a few hiccups along the way, and the following tips will help you troubleshoot the idiosyncrasies of naturally fermented fresh flour. No matter what you bake, it will be infinitely better than most store-bought bread, and the love and attention you give the process will only improve the results with time!

My dough isn't rising vigorously. Help!

If this is your first sourdough baking experience, it will be a wildly different process than yeasted breads. Sourdough is never "punched down" or deflated, and it's important to remember the dough will increase in size slowly. Patience is key and with repetition, you will learn the language of this ancient practice. Assuming you are using a well-fed, active starter, give the dough a chance to prove its enthusiasm.

Ambient temperature will also drastically change when the seasons shift. In winter, your dough may need an additional 30 minutes to 1 hour to ferment at room temperature before shaping, as well as additional proofing time to rise after it has been removed from the refrigerator and before it goes into the oven. Learn to watch the dough rather than the clock. Although the anticipation of warm and crusty bread may have you yearning to hurry the process, remember that slow fermentation is why it is so tasty and nutritious!

I forgot about my starter in the refrigerator and it smells like vinegar! There's also an ominous layer of murky liquid floating on the surface. Can I save it?

It cannot be overstated how important it is to maintain a well-fed, active sourdough starter. Without regular feedings (page 52), it can become imbalanced, overly acidic, and weakened in leavening power. That layer of liquid is essentially "hooch," indicating the yeast activity or leavening power has suffered, but you can, with some effort, bring it back to life. Try refreshing your starter more regularly and at a different ratio until its vigor returns. While you will typically maintain it in equal parts by weight (starter to water to flour in a 1:1:1 ratio), it is best in this instance to overfeed your starter. Try a ratio of 1:4:4 instead and harvest it for use or feed it again once it has doubled in size and smells more appealing.

The dough is a sloppy mess, and I can't seem to shape it. I'm losing my patience and my mind!

OK, take a deep breath. Shaping is one of the most challenging aspects of working with sourdough and requires practice through repetition. Make friends with your bench scraper to release sticky dough from the work surface and to avoid tearing while shaping. If you just can't seem to get the hang of it, try reducing the water in the recipe for a stiffer, easier-to-handle dough. This may lead to a drier crumb and shorter shelf life, but it will ease you into the experience so you don't lose your love for the process!

My crust is too dark or I'm not getting enough oven spring.

Home ovens can vary widely in performance, and you will likely need to adjust baking times and temperatures accordingly to achieve a proper oven spring and desirable crust. Use an oven thermometer to confirm temperature accuracy; if the temperature is too low, oven spring will be lacking. Sourdough loaves with high amounts of whole grain need long baking times and can become thick and dry in certain ovens. If your crust becomes darker than you prefer, try covering it with parchment and then securing with foil or use an inverted baking tin after the first 15 to 20 minutes of baking.

Eeep! There's a giant cave in my bread!

Assuming this is not a shaping error or that your bread is not extremely sour (overproofed), your dough may have too much water. Not all regional stone-ground flours perform the same, and this can lead to different hydration requirements for the dough. Although most sourdough should begin as slack and somewhat sticky and increase in strength and plasticity as you go, using too much water can lead to difficult-to-handle dough or cavernous holes. If this occurs, hold back 30 to 50 milliliters of water in your next batch of dough.

A CRUSTY HEARTH-STYLE SOURDOUGH BOULE

As much as I love a whole-grain sourdough bread, sometimes we crave the undeniable texture of a lighter crumb but also more rustic loaf with a thick crust. Like A Simple Sourdough Sandwich Loaf (page 54), this recipe uses stone-ground flours for both improved flavor and nutrition, and the performance of these flours will vary depending upon your source. If you keep your starter in the refrigerator and feed it once per week, refresh it at least once before mixing this recipe and harvest it for use when it has doubled in volume, smells fresh, and is fully active.

The biggest difference in this dough compared to our sandwich loaf is that only a portion of the flour is whole grain, while the rest has some of the bran sifted out to make the crumb, or the interior of the loaf, lighter. For the crunchiest crust with a robust color and flavor, I recommend a heavy enameled or ceramic Dutch oven for baking. This guarantees oven spring and traps the steam necessary for the loaf to properly expand and for the crust to become caramelized. When sourcing stone-ground bread flour, use flour that is appropriate for bread making, with 12 to 14 percent protein, and has been sifted of at least 15 percent of its bran (see Resources, page 392). This loaf requires a little more skill and practice than a sandwich loaf, and it is necessary to acquire a few more pieces of equipment, namely a 9-inch proofing basket and a scoring device (see Resources, page 392). Once you get the hang of it, though, there is no turning back!

MAKES
1 LOAF

75 grams (3 heaping tablespoons) active Whole-Grain Rye Sourdough Starter (page 52)

11 grams (2 teaspoons) fine sea salt

150 grams (scant 1¾ cups) stone-ground whole Glenn flour or hard red whole wheat bread flour

355 grams (3 cups) stone-ground sifted Edison flour or stone-ground sifted (high-extraction) bread flour

1. Mix and ferment the dough at room temperature according to the instructions on page 54 and using 430 milliliters/1¾ cups plus 1 tablespoon water.

2. When the dough is puffy and has increased in volume by about one-third, preshape it into a round loaf: Swiftly transfer the dough from the bowl to a lightly floured surface and gently coax it into a square shape. Loosely pull two sides of the dough to the center before bringing the other two sides to the center, overlapping slightly as you work. Using your bench scraper, flip the loaf over so that the seam side is facing down. Tuck the square corners underneath the loaf to create a rough

RECIPE CONTINUES

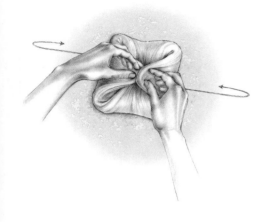

circular shape. Cover with a damp towel for 10 to 20 minutes, until the dough visibly relaxes. Swiftly turn the dough over so the seam side is up and repeat these steps, this time gaining more tension as you shape the dough. Generously flour the surface of the dough and transfer it to a 9-inch proofing basket, with the seam side facing up. Place a dry towel on top and cover with a reusable plastic bag. Refrigerate for 8 to 24 hours to improve flavor and digestibility.

3. About 1 to 2 hours before you wish to bake the loaf, remove it from the refrigerator. Set it on the counter to proof a final time, until it is soft and springy to the touch and just crests the top of the proofing basket. The amount of time will depend upon the temperature of the refrigerator, the ambient temperature of your kitchen, and the health of your starter.

4. Place a 7-quart Dutch oven with its lid (remove the knob if there is one) on the middle rack of the oven and preheat to 475°F for at least 30 minutes.

5. Prepare a piece of parchment paper to fit the size of the loaf with 2 to 3 inches of overhang to act as a sling. When the dough has fully proofed, turn it over onto the parchment paper. Score the length of the loaf with a baker's lame or a sharp razor blade to a depth of ¼ inch, using whatever design suits your fancy. Using heatproof gloves, remove the Dutch oven and place it on top of the stovetop. Using the parchment paper as a sling, lower the loaf into the hot Dutch oven and cover. Return the pot to the oven and bake for 20 minutes. Lower the oven temperature to 450°F, remove the lid, and continue to bake for another 20 to 25 minutes. The loaf is ready when an instant-read thermometer registers 210°F when inserted into the center of the loaf and the crust is a deep, dark brown color. Do not underbake.

6. Remove the loaf from the oven and cool on a wire rack before slicing, about 2 hours. Store wrapped in a beeswax-coated reusable linen bag or sealed container at room temperature for up to 1 week.

SOURDOUGH BREADCRUMBS

When making farm-style meals, we use breadcrumbs to help keep the pastured and lean ground meats tender and moist. This is an excellent pantry item to have on hand and can be used in a variety of recipes, including the Lamb Meatballs with Currants, Yogurt, and Arugula-Mint Pesto (page 267) or the Bacon-Wrapped Pastured Pork Meatloaf with Yellow Pepper Sauce (page 295). A homemade loaf of sourdough bread (page 54 or 59) or one from a reputable baker will contain more moisture and take longer to toast, so it's best to use a slightly stale or frozen and thawed loaf. Although the breadcrumbs can take a bit of time to make, they store well and the recipe can be scaled up to make an extra-large batch. Store the processed breadcrumbs in the refrigerator or freezer rather than at room temperature, as any residual moisture can cause spoilage.

MAKES
1⅔ CUPS

4½ cups sourdough bread, cut or torn into ½-inch pieces (about ½ pound bread)

1. Preheat the oven to 325°F and position a rack in the middle.

2. Nestle an ovenproof wire rack into a large baking sheet. Spread the bread over the rack, avoiding any overlap. Toast in the oven for 20 to 25 minutes, until the bread is dry to the touch and a dark golden brown.

3. Remove the pan from the oven and cool completely. Transfer to a food processor and pulse until the crumbs resemble coarse sand, about 30 seconds.

4. Transfer the breadcrumbs to a lidded container. Store in the refrigerator for up to 2 weeks or in the freezer for up to 4 months.

SOURDOUGH PIZZA AND FLATBREAD DOUGH

Homemade pizza is a favorite in our household, especially when made with stone-ground flours and tangy sourdough. We prepare this dough in large batches a few days in advance and have it ready for small weekend gatherings around the wood-fired oven. To lift our spirits during the height of the pandemic, my pod began having pizza night on Sundays, as we had plenty of time to build the fire and embrace slow foods! The texture is more complex than a typical white yeasted dough, and the flavor is worth the time invested! Pizza made with this dough is remarkably forgiving and versatile. It is excellent baked in a home oven, or you can also adapt it as a flatbread made on the stovetop! (See page 64.) If you keep your starter in the refrigerator and feed it once per week, refresh it at least once before mixing this recipe and harvest for use when it has doubled in volume and is fully active.

MAKES
TWO
10-INCH
PIZZAS

30 grams (1 generous tablespoon) active Whole-Grain Rye Sourdough Starter (page 52)

12 grams (2¼ teaspoons) fine sea salt

30 milliliters (2 tablespoons) cold-pressed extra-virgin olive oil

270 grams (2 cups) stone-ground sifted Edison bread flour

180 grams (1⅓ cups) stone-ground Sonora flour

1. Mix the dough: Combine 360 milliliters/1½ cups of water, the starter, and salt in a medium bowl, stirring until the salt is dissolved and the starter is well combined. Whisk in 15 milliliters/1 tablespoon of the oil and add the flours to the bowl. Use your hands to mix and squeeze the dough in a circular motion until no dry lumps remain. The dough should feel slightly firm but somewhat sticky. Cover with a towel and let the dough rest for 20 to 30 minutes, allowing the flour to hydrate and the gluten to relax. Uncover the dough and transfer it to a lightly floured surface. Gently knead it for 3 to 4 minutes, until it stiffens again.

2. Clean the bowl and rub with the remaining 15 milliliters/ 1 tablespoon oil. Add the dough back to the bowl, rolling to coat in the oil. Cover once more and set the bowl aside in a warm location (ideally 75°F) to ferment for 2½ hours.

3. When the dough feels slightly puffy and you see a few fermentation bubbles breaking the surface, it is time to divide and shape the dough. Lightly oil two small bowls about 8 inches in diameter. Swiftly remove the dough from the bowl and place it on a clean surface. Use a bench scraper to divide the dough in half and lightly oil your hands. Gently tuck all sides of one piece to the center, creating a ball. Flip it over and, using a circular motion, pull the ball against the clean work surface, gaining tension across the surface of the dough as you go. When you have a tight ball, use a bench scraper to release the dough from the work surface and place it in the oiled bowl seam side down. Cover with a dry cloth and

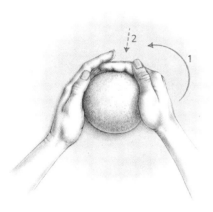

a reusable plastic bag. Repeat with the remaining piece of dough and transfer both to the refrigerator for at least 12 hours or up to 3 days.

4. Remove the dough from the refrigerator, uncover, and gently poke the surface to feel for the presence of trapped gases. If the loaf feels dense, cover and allow the dough to proof at room temperature for at least 1 and up to 3 hours before testing the dough again with your finger. If, however, the loaf feels inflated like a filled water balloon, it does not need further proofing. When ready to bake, a finger impression should linger in the dough rather than immediately bounce back. Depending upon the temperature of your refrigerator and how long the dough has retarded, it may take more or less time to proof a final time before baking.

5. Set a pizza stone on the middle rack of a cold oven and preheat to 500°F. If baking in a wood-fired oven, preheat the oven to 700°F to 750°F according to the directions on page 187.

6. If baking in a home oven, place a piece of parchment paper near your work surface and lightly dust with flour, semolina, or a little cornmeal. Gently turn the pieces of dough out onto a well-floured work surface and toss to coat. Flour your hands and begin stretching one piece of dough over your knuckles from the center outward. Lay the dough across the work surface and continue to stretch, using floured fingertips. Press from the center outward, being careful to ease off as you near the perimeter. Continue to shape the dough into a circle using your fingertips and the palm of your hand to flatten the dough outward, until the dough is 9 to 10 inches in diameter. Transfer the dough to the parchment paper. If working in a wood oven, transfer to a peel heavily dusted with cornmeal or semolina.

7. Top the pizza as desired, being careful not to use too much sauce or ingredients high in moisture, as this will contribute to a soggy bottom crust.

RECIPE CONTINUES

8. If baking in a home oven, use a pizza peel or the back of a sheet pan to slide under the parchment and transfer the pizza to the preheated pizza stone. Prepare the second pizza while the first is baking. Bake the pizza for 12 minutes before carefully checking to see if the bottom of the crust is golden brown. If you desire a crispy, slightly charred upper crust, turn the broiler to high and bake the pizza at least 8 inches from the heat for 30 to 60 seconds, depending upon your preference. Remove from the oven and repeat with the second pizza. If baking in a wood-fired oven, shake the pizza on the peel to test for sticking. If the pizza sticks to the peel, gently lift the edge and throw some additional cornmeal or semolina underneath. Follow the baking instructions on page 187. Cut and serve immediately.

SOURDOUGH FLATBREAD VARIATION

MAKES 8 FLATBREADS

Pizza dough is versatile and easy to turn into a tasty flatbread made on a griddle or in the oven. After removing the dough from the refrigerator (step 4), proof until puffy. Using a bench scraper, divide the dough into 8 equal pieces and form it into small balls. Cover with a damp towel and rest at room temperature until relaxed, 10 to 15 minutes. With a rolling pin, create round disks about 5 to 6 inches in diameter and ½ inch thick. Preheat a dry griddle on the stovetop over medium-high heat for 5 minutes. Cook on the griddle until puffy with golden brown edges, 5 to 6 minutes on each side. Alternatively, bake in a preheated wood-fired oven at 700°F to 750°F for 2 to 3 minutes on each side. Keep warm and serve immediately.

FERMENTED SUNCHOKES

The sunchoke, also called Jerusalem artichoke, is a humble-looking thin-skinned root vegetable in the sunflower family. The tuberous roots are crunchy and refreshing like water chestnuts, but with the flavor of an artichoke! Our crop was prolific the first year that we grew them, and the culinary team scrambled to invent creative recipes. The results were all delicious, until we started noticing an unfortunate recurring pattern: everyone who ate them would complain about a stomachache afterward! Thankfully with a bit of research, we discovered that fermenting the roots before cooking them can improve digestibility.

As the brined sunchokes age in the refrigerator, they continue to slowly ferment and the flavor will turn tangy. Although this nuance is delicious to some, we prefer to use them freshly fermented (after only a few days) to harness their sweet and creamy earthiness. This may seem like a large batch, but when the sunchokes are cooked, the volume shrinks to half its original size. If you do not have the space for this large jar, simply ferment the sunchokes, cook them until tender, and freeze the meat in a sealed container for up to 6 months. Alternatively, divide the recipe and ferment in smaller batches.

MAKES
8 QUARTS

8 quarts whole sunchokes (about 10 pounds)

½ cup fine sea salt

1. Rinse and brush the sunchokes clean in cold water. Drain and chop into ½-inch pieces. Arrange the pieces in a 2-gallon glass jar. Dissolve the salt in 1 quart of water and pour over the sunchokes. Pour in 5 additional quarts of water, leaving 1 to 2 inches of headspace, and position an airlock lid (see page 67). Ferment for about 4 days at room temperature (about 70°F to 75°F). By the third day, bubbles should be rising to the surface, an indication of a live and active culture with a pleasant but sour smell. As with all wild fermentation, more or less time may be needed for this to occur.

2. Replace the airlock with a nonreactive lid and store the jar in the refrigerator for up to 6 months. The brine will become slightly cloudy, but this is OK.

3. To cook, gently boil the sunchokes as necessary in twice the volume of water until tender, about 30 minutes. Once cool to the touch, squeeze the meat with your fingers to separate it from the skin. Store in a sealed container for up to 1 week in the refrigerator or up to 6 months in the freezer.

VEGETABLE LACTIC-FERMENTATION

....

Lactic-fermentation has been used by many different cultures for thousands of years to create the world's most cherished foods and beverages. These delicious traditions begin with fresh produce that is transformed by yeast and bacteria, converting sugars naturally present in the produce into by-products of carbon dioxide and flavor compounds. This gives beneficial microbes the best environment to thrive, lowering the pH of the ferment and preventing spoilage and pathogenic microbes from taking hold. Harnessing this magical, natural process not only extends the life of food but enhances its flavor, introduces probiotics, boosts the immune system, and augments the nutritive value of ingredients. The following considerations should be taken when making recipes from this book, including Jalapeño Kraut (page 68) or Fermented Sunchokes (page 65). They can also be used as a general approach to fermenting most fresh produce.

Transformation and Preservation

Commonplace condiments such as mustard, ketchup, and hot sauces, as well as pickles and relishes, traditionally began as fermented foods. With time, pasteurization became favored over fermentation to extend shelf life, and highly processed and refined additives such as corn syrup replaced more complex flavors. Artificial preservatives now make these products more shelf stable rather than acids once produced by fermentation. But these artificial ingredients have the potential to compromise our heart and gut health, dull the senses, and cancel the benefits of naturally fermented foods.

By reinstating ancient fermentation methods, we can improve the flavor of our meals and also boost our health by enhancing the bioavailability of essential vitamins and minerals. Fresh produce becomes even more nutritious when fermented, and offers a unique flavor profile you can't find in most store-bought products. The recipes in this section transform beautifully grown and harvested produce into a unique expression of place, time, and terroir that can elevate even the simplest meals.

Ingredients

The most essential ingredients of fermentation are time and patience. Choosing appropriate produce is also an equally important factor, whether from your own garden or a local farmers market. Always use produce that has been grown without chemical inputs for greatest fermentation potential. Processing and fermenting fresh produce immediately after harvest will guarantee the produce is plump with moisture and has less likelihood of spoilage. Choose these ingredients as you would for eating them raw, avoiding or removing bruises or blemishes before beginning the recipe.

Safety

When fermenting produce, follow basic food-safety protocols such as washing your hands, rinsing produce, and working on clean surfaces. Do keep in mind, however, that the beneficial microbes you are culturing are already present on the produce itself, your hands, and the surfaces around you. Rather than trying to unnecessarily "sanitize" food as with hot-water canning, we are working instead to allow the most beneficial microbes to thrive. It is an approach that encourages proliferation rather than elimination. You can ensure the safety of your ferments by providing the appropriate temperature, eliminating air exposure, and using the recommended percentage of salt. A thin milky film that develops on the surface of many ferments is common and not to be confused with mold. If this occurs, simply skim and discard the film before continuing to ferment. Although it rarely happens, if a ferment develops pink or orange fuzzy mold, discard the contents.

Temperature

The ideal temperature for most types of fermentation hovers around 70°F to 75°F. Fermenting at a lower temperature is not harmful but will slow the speed in which the recipe will be ready to store and consume. I don't advise working at a higher temperature since this may encourage the vegetables to lose their palatable crunch once fermented or for mold to occur. Temperatures above 110°F will hinder the proliferation of beneficial microbes.

Equipment

It is wise to invest in basic, reusable equipment. Choose materials that can withstand boiling water so that they can be sterilized between use if mold occurs. This includes glass, ceramic, or stone weights to keep the vegetables submerged under a brine as well as airlock lids to protect your ferments from exposure to air (see Resources, page 392) while allowing the off-gassing of carbon dioxide.

JALAPEÑO KRAUT

One of the most delicious ways to maximize the vitamin C of vegetables like cabbage is through the probiotic benefits of fermentation. We serve sauerkraut with every meal on the farm, and our team has become so accustomed to it that many now make it at home! This recipe is a spin on plain sauerkraut with a savory and spicy kick from the garlic and jalapeños. It is excellent served with Smoky Potato and Greens Tacos (page 150). To encourage a generous brine from the cabbage, use a head that has been freshly harvested.

MAKES
ABOUT
1 QUART

1 small head green cabbage (about 2 pounds)

1 cup shredded carrots (3 medium or 2 large carrots)

1 to 2 jalapeño peppers, thinly sliced (to taste)

1½ tablespoons fine sea salt

8 lightly crushed garlic cloves

1. Wash and dry the cabbage. Remove the outer 2 to 3 leaves and set aside. Using a sharp knife, quarter the cabbage and remove the heart. Using a box grater, shred the cabbage quarters or slice thinly instead.

2. In a large bowl, place the cabbage, carrots, and jalapeños. Sprinkle the salt over the top, and with a clean hand, massage the ingredients until they begin to release a brine, 5 to 10 minutes. The mixture will feel limp at first but will transform to the consistency of lightly cooked cabbage. Add the garlic cloves and toss to incorporate.

3. Pack the kraut into a clean 1-quart jar, pushing down with your fist to remove any trapped air pockets. Place the reserved cabbage leaves over the kraut and pour the remaining liquid from the bowl into the jar. Press to submerge the kraut and leaves under the brine, leaving no more than 2 to 3 inches of airspace between the top of the brine and the rim of the jar.

4. Submerge the kraut using fermentation weights and position an airlock lid (see page 66). Place the jar in a cool, dark place, about 65°F to 75°F, for 10 to 14 days. Check on the kraut every few days for small bubbles forming in the mixture, which indicates the fermentation has begun. If a thin layer of white scum appears on the surface, do not be alarmed—it is unharmful kahm yeast that can be skimmed away as it develops. If mold appears, however, remove the leaves and discard the top 1 inch layer of kraut. Fully submerge the kraut under the brine again before replacing the weights and airlock lid.

5. When the kraut has a noticeable tang and smells and tastes to your liking, replace the airlock with a nonreactive lid. Store the kraut in the refrigerator for up to 1 year.

INGREDIENT TIP: *Storing Cabbage*

Although cabbage can hold in cold storage for up to 2 months, it will lose a considerable amount of moisture if not stored properly. If you are harvesting it from your own garden or buying it from the farmers market, look for bright and shiny outer leaves and keep them intact to retain moisture. Although you can store cabbage in a plastic bag to help protect it from bruising, it is not necessary. Simply place the head in the hydrator drawer of your refrigerator, adjusted to high humidity if possible, and store until you are ready to make this beautiful sparkling green ferment!

FARMER'S CHEESE

This fresh cheese is mild in flavor and deliciously complemented by chopped herbs, sumac, lemon zest, freshly cracked black peppercorns, or smoked paprika. It is an excellent way to use raw or organic pasteurized milk that is near expiration, and it makes silky curds that are moist but spoonable. Avoid using ultrapasteurized milk. Use to sprinkle over Crispy Bull Meat Tacos with Romaine Slaw (page 276) or Hearty Ranch Chicken Soup with Crispy Cauliflower (page 224).

**MAKES
2 POUNDS**

1 gallon raw or organic pasteurized milk

¼ cup plus 1 tablespoon fresh lemon juice (1¼ large lemons) or raw apple cider vinegar

1 teaspoon fine sea salt

1. In a 4½- to 5-quart nonreactive or stainless steel pot, cook the milk over medium heat, stirring occasionally, until it reaches a soft boil. Remove from the heat and add the lemon juice. Gently stir for 30 seconds to fully distribute the acid. The milk curds will almost immediately separate from the whey, taking between 30 seconds and 5 minutes to fully form. They will resemble lumps of melted marshmallows and the whey will appear a light yellowish-green color.

2. Line a colander with a double layer of cheesecloth and strain the curds, reserving the whey for compost or to feed acid-loving plants or hungry pigs. Let the hot curds cool slightly for ease of handling, 8 to 10 minutes.

3. Wearing gloves, carefully transfer the warm curds to a nonreactive bowl. Gently break into pieces the size of shelled peas. Sprinkle the salt evenly over the curds and gently fold to mix and thoroughly distribute the salt.

4. While still warm, divide the curds into two lumps. Place each portion in a heavy nonreactive bowl. Place a smaller clean, nonreactive bowl directly on top of the hot curds and press lightly. Place the weighted bowls in the refrigerator and let them cool for 2 hours.

5. Break apart the curds and transfer to a covered container. Store in the refrigerator for up to 7 days.

VARIATIONS:

Transform the curds into a cottage cheese–like texture by stirring in ¼ cup of cream after pressing. If you prefer a firmer cheese instead, stir in at least 1 to 2 tablespoons of heavy cream while the curds are still hot and then continue to compress the cheese with a weighted bowl on top before refrigerating. After a few hours it will become a firm, sliceable cheese.

CRÈME FRAÎCHE

When I made crème fraîche for the first time, I could hardly believe how easy it was to make something that feels so fancy! This pleasantly tangy cultured cream is both delicious and nutritive when made with fresh raw dairy, but you can also substitute organic pasteurized cream. Gently heating the cream at a low temperature preserves the beneficial enzymes that are naturally present in the raw cream while encouraging the buttermilk culture to proliferate. The result is a decadent, silky texture with a rich and complex flavor. Serve it with Spring Snap Pea Salad with Spinach-Pistachio Pesto and Crème Fraîche (page 144); Potato and Butternut Squash Rösti Cakes with Chive Crème Fraîche (page 116); French Onion Potato Puree (page 111); or Pickled Deviled Eggs with Beets, Horseradish, Honey, and Crispy Chicken Skin (page 243).

MAKES
ABOUT 1 CUP

1 cup raw heavy cream

3 tablespoons cultured full-fat buttermilk

1. In a small saucepan, warm the cream over medium-low heat, stirring continuously, until it registers between 80°F and 85°F on an instant-read thermometer.

2. Pour the warm cream into a nonreactive ceramic bowl. Stir in the buttermilk and secure a cheesecloth over the bowl with a rubber band. Ferment the mixture at room temperature until the cream is thick, tastes tangy but pleasant, and smells slightly sour, about 24 hours. If the cream tastes metallic, unpleasantly cheesy, or is otherwise off-putting, it has likely spoiled and should be discarded.

3. Cover the bowl with an airtight lid or transfer the crème fraîche to a clean container with a lid. Store in the refrigerator for up to 2 weeks. The cream will thicken as it sits but will loosen once stirred.

Chapter Three

MAKE
YOUR OWN
STOCKS
and
CONDIMENTS

MAKING MEAT STOCKS AND VEGETABLE BROTHS IS AN EXCELLENT way to maximize ingredients that may otherwise be wasted; it also offers proven nutritional benefits. I turn to Chicken Stock (page 76) whenever I am run-down, and when my son, Beaudie, was little, he learned to ask for it when he wasn't feeling well! Chicken stock makes any dish go from good to great, and our family always has a quart or two in the refrigerator. The following recipes are excellent to have handy, adding complexity of flavor and nourishment to meals without unnecessary sodium, preservatives, or additives.

One of the easiest ways to personalize your pantry is by replacing processed foods with simple, homemade alternatives. The following tasty condiments use wholesome ingredients and harness seasonal flavors and healthy fats with little to no added sugar.

Recipes

CHICKEN STOCK

Walk into our kitchen on any given Monday and you will likely be greeted by the comforting aroma of simmering stock. When it's cold and dewy outside, team members from other departments will gravitate toward the bubbling pot. The vaporous warmth that hovers in the air often causes them to linger longer than they intended, uttering something like "Ugh . . . can I just stay here? It's so warm and it smells so good!"

There are many opinions about the best way to make a stock, but we like ours to be clear and gelatinous when cooled. The simple flavor of the chicken shines through and is not overwhelmed by too many herbs or one particular vegetable. Most of the time we use a combination of our mature hens and chicken feet, resulting in a gelatin-rich broth. Older chickens can sometimes be hard to source, and if you find this to be the case where you live, it's perfectly fine to use young birds. The meat of a young chicken can be shredded after the stock is cooked and used in recipes such as our Summer Orchard Shredded Chicken Salad with Dried Stone Fruit, Fresh Lemon, and Pistachios (page 217) or the Chicken Pizza with Roasted Garlic, Spinach, Toasted Pine Nuts, and Fresh Ricotta (page 218).

MAKES
4 QUARTS

7 pounds whole chicken, cut into pieces (see Breaking Down a Whole Chicken into Pieces, page 214) (about 2 medium pastured chickens)

4 chicken feet, nails and skin trimmed

3½ cups chopped carrots (about 7 medium carrots)

1 cup medium-diced celery (3 stalks)

1 cup medium-diced yellow onion, skin on (1 large onion)

6 large garlic cloves, crushed

2 bay leaves

6 sprigs fresh thyme

1. In a large stockpot (at least 8 quarts), combine 5½ quarts of water, the chicken, chicken feet, carrots, celery, onion, garlic, bay leaves, and thyme. Cover and bring to a low boil over medium-high heat and then reduce the heat to a low simmer. Cook for 5 hours, skimming and discarding any foam that rises to the surface with a slotted spoon. When it is ready to strain, the stock should have reduced by 2 to 3 inches from the original water line, the meat will be falling apart, and the liquid will be a beautiful golden brown.

2. Remove from the heat and carefully set the pot aside to cool for 20 minutes. Remove the chicken and large vegetables with a slotted spoon or spider strainer and tongs, compost the vegetables, and place the chicken on a sheet pan. Let the chicken cool for 15 minutes or until easy to handle. Shred the chicken and store in a lidded container in the refrigerator for up to 5 days.

3. Strain the stock into a large 5-quart container according to the instructions on page 80.

4. Keep the stock in the refrigerator for up to 1 week or store in the freezer for up to 6 months.

KITCHEN TIP: *Slow Cooker Chicken Stock*

As an alternative to the stovetop method, you can make chicken stock in an 8-quart slow cooker. I like the convenience of being able to make it this way overnight. This method also creates a rich, nourishing liquid that is closer to a broth than a stock and is perfect for the Bone Broth Bar (page 226). Place all the ingredients in the slow cooker and heat on high for the first hour, or until it reaches a light simmer. Reduce the heat to low and cook for 8 hours with a vented or slightly offset lid. The stock will have an amber color, and the meat will be tender.

ROASTED BEEF BONE STOCK

This fragrant stock is rich from a combination of neck and marrow bones rather than just the meat bones that are typically the main ingredient of beef stock. The neck bones hold the most gelatin and flavor, while the connective tissue of the meat dissolves slowly, adding a silky mouthfeel to the stock. Roasting the bones with vegetables and tomato paste contributes a complex and versatile flavor that can enhance some of our favorite recipes, such as Succulent Beef Short Ribs with Spring Vegetables (page 271) or the Bone Broth Bar (page 226).

The nutritional density of bones reflects the animal's diet, and it is best to purchase them from reputable sources, especially when slow cooking stock. While it can be difficult to source organic, grass-fed meat products at your local grocery store, some farms will ship frozen bones (see Resources, page 392). Neck bones add a wonderful depth of flavor to stock but are not as commonly sold as beef oxtail or shank bones (both are fine substitutions). If using these hearty cuts, remove the meat from the stock once it's tender and reserve for adding to hearty stews.

MAKES
2 QUARTS

3 pounds beef marrow bones

1¾ pounds beef neck bones with meat

3 tablespoons tomato paste

1 large onion, sliced into 6 wedges

1 large head garlic, sliced in half

5 medium carrots, sliced into 2-inch pieces

4 celery stalks, chopped into 2-inch pieces

3 tablespoons cold-pressed extra-virgin olive oil

¼ cup raw apple cider vinegar

2 bay leaves

6 sprigs fresh thyme

Salt, to taste

1. Preheat the oven to 375°F and position a rack in the middle.

2. In a large bowl, rinse the bones of debris with cold running water. Transfer the bones to a large roasting pan and place in the oven. Roast for 30 minutes and then remove the pan from the oven. Carefully smear the tomato paste over the hot bones using a small offset spatula or butter knife. Arrange the onion, garlic, carrots, and celery among the bones and drizzle the oil over the entire contents of the pan. Return to the oven and roast for an additional 30 minutes, or until the tips of the vegetables and tomato paste are blistered and deeply caramelized.

3. Remove the pan from the oven and transfer the roasted bones and vegetables to an 8-quart slow cooker. Add 1 cup of water and the vinegar to the roasting pan and let rest for 5 minutes. Pour the contents of the pan into the slow cooker, including the browned bits from the bottom of the pan. Add the bay leaves, thyme, and 2¾ quarts of water. Cook on high for 1 hour, or until the contents begin to simmer. Then, adjust the lid so it is vented or slightly offset to help the liquid reduce. Reduce the heat to low and continue cooking for 12 hours, skimming the surface occasionally with a slotted spoon to clarify.

RECIPE CONTINUES

4. Cool a few ounces, add salt to your preference, and taste. The color will be golden and the flavor robust and fragrant. The stock should be rich and silky on the tongue—a sign that enough gelatin has been extracted to thicken the liquid as it cools. Turn off the slow cooker, and using tongs, remove and compost the vegetables and discard or save the bones as pet treats. Line a large strainer with a double layer of cheesecloth and nestle over a 2½-quart or larger stainless steel bowl or container. Ladle the stock into the strainer and set aside to cool. Portion the stock into smaller containers, leaving 2 inches of headspace, and cover. Transfer the containers to the refrigerator and chill until the stock has reached at least 41°F.

5. Keep in the refrigerator for up to 1 week or transfer to the freezer for up to 6 months.

HEALING POTASSIUM VEGETABLE BROTH

MAKES
2 QUARTS

While nourishing bone stocks are often the foundation for our soups and sauces on the farm, sometimes a vegetable-based alternative like this one is more appropriate. I first learned of using potassium broths as a health-supportive food when studying at the Natural Gourmet Institute of Health & Culinary Arts in New York City, and thankfully, there are many flavorful options for using it. A traditional vegetable stock made with trimmings and aromatics can be a great backdrop for most recipes, but we wanted something versatile that can also be a potassium-rich sipping beverage.

We drew upon the flavors of dashi, a popular Japanese soup base that is made with kombu seaweed. Mushrooms impart a satisfying umami flavor, while potato skins offer additional nutrients and an almost creamy smoothness to the broth. Although you may use any type of kombu (see Resources, page 392), we have found that the Atlantic variety has a particularly pleasant and mild sweetness. Sip this broth warm or use it in place of a meat stock in your favorite recipes.

5 large yellow onions

2 tablespoons unrefined avocado or extra-virgin olive oil

¼ cup thinly sliced garlic cloves (6 large cloves)

2 cups lightly packed red potato skins (from 4 to 5 pounds potatoes)

2 cups quartered button mushrooms

1.4 ounces dried kombu (about 2 large pieces)

1¾ cups lightly packed beet leaves, sliced into 1-inch ribbons (about 12 large leaves)

½ cup dried shiitake or porcini mushrooms (about 2 ounces)

1½ tablespoons fine sea salt

GARNISH

4 teaspoons minced fresh parsley leaves

A squeeze of fresh lemon juice, to taste

1. Peel and reserve the skins of the onions and chop the flesh into ½-inch pieces. In a 4- to 5-quart pot, heat the oil over medium-high heat until shimmering, about 2 minutes. Add the garlic and chopped onions and sauté until the onions are translucent and the edges are golden, about 7 minutes. Add 3 quarts of water, the onion skins, potato skins, fresh mushrooms, kombu, beet leaves, dried mushrooms, and salt and gently stir to combine. Bring the mixture to a boil and simmer, uncovered, for 40 minutes. The vegetables will turn golden toward the end of the cooking and as water evaporates. Remove from the heat and let cool for 15 minutes before straining the broth through a sieve into a large bowl or container. Press down on the cooked vegetables to extract as much broth as possible. Compost the vegetables or add them to a pot of chicken stock to give them a second life. Taste the broth and adjust the salt as necessary. It should have a naturally sweet, earthy character but may benefit from a longer cooking time to concentrate the flavors.

2. Store in a sealed container in the refrigerator for up to 1 week or in the freezer with 2 inches of headspace for up to 6 months. The broth is delicious served warm, with the minced parsley and a squeeze of lemon to taste.

CHIPOTLE ADOBO PASTE

This recipe reflects the Mexican heritage of many members of our team and has become a staple ingredient for our communal farm meals. Chipotle en adobo is traditionally made by preserving smoky whole chile peppers in a spicy sauce, but we have adapted it to create a versatile aromatic paste instead. We toast and blend the peppers with aromatic ingredients such as onions, garlic, and herbs with a touch of honey and vinegar to bring balance and rich flavor. This condiment easily adds complexity to Smoky Potato and Greens Tacos (page 150) or Crispy Bull Meat Tacos with Romaine Slaw (page 276) and can be used to make variations of other core recipes such as Avocado Oil Mayonnaise (page 90).

MAKES
2½ CUPS

5 ounces dried chipotle chile peppers (about 35 peppers)

2 tablespoons cold-pressed extra-virgin olive oil

2 cups diced yellow onion (2 large onions)

1 teaspoon minced garlic (1 clove)

6 tablespoons tomato paste (about 3 ounces)

5 tablespoons raw apple cider vinegar, plus more as needed

2 tablespoons mild raw honey, plus more as needed

4 teaspoons fine sea salt, plus more as needed

½ teaspoon freshly cracked black peppercorns

1 teaspoon sweet paprika

½ teaspoon dried oregano

1½ teaspoons fresh thyme leaves or ¾ teaspoon dried

⅛ teaspoon ground allspice

1. Preheat the oven to 300°F and position a rack in the middle.

2. Bring 4 cups of water to a boil in a small saucepan with a lid. While the water is heating, toast the chipotles: Spread the peppers on a medium baking sheet. Transfer to the oven and toast for 5 minutes, or until they puff up and resemble little balloons. Alternatively, lightly toast the peppers in a hot pan on the stovetop, but be careful not to let them burn and become bitter.

3. Transfer the toasted chipotles to the boiling water and lower the heat to a simmer. Cover the pot and simmer the peppers until tender when pierced with a fork, 25 minutes. Remove from the heat, uncover, and let the peppers cool in the liquid until easy to handle, about 30 minutes.

4. Wearing gloves, tear into each pepper from stem end to the tip. Remove the seeds by pushing them down with your thumbs into the warm liquid. Rinse the cleaned pepper in the same water to remove any remaining seeds and transfer to a medium bowl. Repeat with the remaining peppers. Strain the liquid through a sieve, reserving 3 tablespoons of the cooking liquid. Compost the seeds.

5. In a large skillet, heat the oil over medium-high heat until it expands, about 1 minute. Stir in the onions and garlic and cook until the onion is translucent, 5 to 7 minutes. Stir in the tomato paste and continue to cook for 5 minutes. Remove from the heat and spread the mixture over a small baking sheet. Transfer to the refrigerator and chill for 20 minutes.

6. Place the cleaned chipotles in a blender. Add the cooled onion mixture, reserved cooking liquid, 1/3 cup of water, vinegar, honey, salt, pepper, paprika, oregano, thyme, and allspice. Blend until smooth and the mixture resembles tomato paste. It should smell smoky, warm, and inviting. Sample a small amount, being careful to mind the potency of the chiles. The honey should be easily detectable but not prominent. Adjust the vinegar, salt, and honey if desired.

7. Transfer the paste to a clean jar and fasten the lid. Store in the refrigerator for up to 2 months or leave 2 inches of headspace and freeze for up to 6 months.

INGREDIENT TIP: *Chipotle Chiles*

Chipotles can be made with several different chiles, but the most common ones used are overripe jalapeño peppers that are spicy and flavorful but not overpoweringly hot. The signature flavor of chipotle is the result of using smoke to dry the chiles rather than just air. Source dried chipotle chiles in bulk at Latin markets if possible, as they are typically fresher and cheaper than when prepackaged. Choose bright, leathery peppers that are fully intact, and be sure to wear gloves when handling, as the oil can easily penetrate and irritate the skin for up to a full day, even after handwashing! After working with hot chiles in New York City during culinary school, I made the mistake of wiping sweat from my forehead during a hot yoga class. I soon had pepper oils dripping into my eyes and learned the painful lesson to wear gloves from then on!

ROASTED GARLIC HOT SAUCE

At each farm lunch, we offer a tray of condiments, including our farm olive oil and avocado oil, raw apple cider vinegar, and hot sauce. We have observed with great interest that the oils and vinegar can sometimes last for months without replenishment, but the hot sauce is another story . . . let's just say that our team likes it hot!

**MAKES
2 CUPS**

This recipe has been adapted from a personal favorite made in our very first year of the test kitchen with Chef Chris Hollobaugh. We had a huge harvest of Fresno chiles that season along with a never-ending crop of cherry tomatoes. We made a hot sauce trio of flavors, but this was my favorite and has continued to evolve over the years! It is a versatile sauce for many different dishes and is especially good with eggs or tacos.

20 cloves Roasted Garlic in Oil (recipe follows)

4 cups seeded and roughly chopped fresh Fresno chile peppers (1 pound or 25 medium peppers)

1 cup cherry tomatoes (½ pound or 8 to 10 cherry tomatoes)

1 teaspoon fine sea salt

2 tablespoons apple cider vinegar

1. In the pitcher of a blender, place the garlic in oil. Add the chiles, tomatoes, salt, and vinegar. Blend to a smooth consistency, about 1 minute.

2. Transfer to a small saucepan and bring to a simmer over medium-high heat. Reduce the heat to low and continue cooking, uncovered, stirring occasionally, until the sauce thickens to your liking and smells fragrant and spicy, about 15 minutes.

3. Remove the pan from the heat and set aside to cool for about 20 minutes. Transfer the sauce to a lidded container and store in the refrigerator for up to 2 weeks.

COOKING TIP: *Roasted Garlic in Oil*

Oven-poaching garlic in oil is an easy way to add mellow sweetness to any dish, and it is a technique I use throughout this book for sauces and condiments. Preheat the oven to 350°F and position a rack in the middle. Nestle 20 peeled garlic cloves (about 2 large heads) in a 10 × 10-inch piece of parchment paper. Set the parchment over foil and partially wrap to create a small pouch. Pour in ⅓ cup extra-virgin olive oil, seal the pouch, and place on a small baking sheet. Transfer to the oven and roast until the garlic is soft and golden, about 40 minutes. Remove from the oven, carefully vent, and let cool until warm to the touch, about 20 minutes.

HARISSA

The first time I tried harissa, Alan's wife, Rose Ann, brought me a jar made with produce from their farmers market alongside fresh feta and salt-brined olives. That first jar has since encouraged us to develop our own version of this North African chile paste, made with dried Mexican chiles commonly found in Southern California. The heat from the chiles is balanced by sweet roasted red peppers, bright acidity, and warm spices. It complements the smoky character of grilled meats or roasted vegetables such as Roasted Tokyo Turnip and Nantes Carrot Medley with Carrot-Harissa Hummus (page 120). Blend this versatile paste into marinades, sauces, vegetable purees, or soups when you need a complex spice fix!

MAKES
ABOUT 1 CUP

2 medium red bell peppers

3 dried guajillo chile peppers

1 dried ancho chile pepper

1 dried cayenne pepper

1 large garlic clove

½ teaspoon fine sea salt

½ teaspoon smoked paprika

⅛ teaspoon ground cumin

2 tablespoons fresh lemon juice (½ large lemon)

1 tablespoon raw apple cider vinegar

1. Preheat the broiler to high. Place an oven rack about 11 inches from the broiler.

2. Turn a gas burner to medium-high heat. Using tongs, char the bell peppers, rotating every few minutes, until the entire surface of the pepper is blackened but not ashy white. If using the oven instead, place the peppers on a medium baking sheet and position them about 6 inches below the broiler plate. Broil on high, turning with tongs as needed until blackened, about 5 minutes per side. Turn off the heat, transfer the peppers to a plate, and cover with a kitchen towel. Let cool and steam for 15 minutes before peeling, seeding, and roughly chopping the flesh.

3. On a medium unlined baking sheet, arrange the guajillos, ancho, and cayenne pepper. Transfer to the oven for 1 to 2 minutes, until the peppers puff and inflate but before they are charred. Remove from the oven and set aside to cool. With gloved hands, seed the chiles and place in a small saucepan with 3 cups of water. Simmer the chiles over medium heat until they are hydrated and their flesh is plump, about 15 minutes. Remove the chiles with tongs and transfer to a blender. Reserve 2 tablespoons of the simmering liquid.

4. Add the bell peppers to the blender along with the garlic, salt, paprika, cumin, lemon juice, vinegar, and reserved simmering liquid. Blend until a smooth paste forms with some remaining texture from the dried chile skins, 3 to 4 minutes. Taste for salt and adjust the seasoning as needed. The harissa should taste smoky, warm, sweet, and bright.

5. Transfer the harissa to an airtight container and store in the refrigerator for up to 2 weeks or in the freezer for up to 6 months.

FERMENTED KETCHUP

Historically, many condiments were fermented and used as an aid to digestion as much as a flavor enhancer. A far cry from the original, the commercial ketchup that now graces our supermarket shelves is pasteurized and contains hefty amounts of added sugar in the form of high-fructose corn syrup. For our meal program at the farm, we created a delicious, upgraded alternative using high-quality ingredients and a bonus probiotic boost. When making this at home, consider the flavor and texture of the tomato paste you use, as brands will vary in quality, concentration, and natural sweetness. You may use a store-bought substitute in recipes throughout this book, but the flavor and consistency will not be as unique.

MAKES ABOUT 3 CUPS

1 tablespoon cold-pressed extra-virgin olive oil

3 tablespoons minced sweet yellow onion (about ½ small onion)

2 teaspoons chopped fresh garlic (about 3 medium cloves)

2 cups tomato paste (16 ounces)

¼ cup raw plain sauerkraut juice

3 tablespoons mild raw honey

2 teaspoons fine sea salt

½ teaspoon powdered yellow mustard

¼ teaspoon ground allspice

¼ teaspoon ground cayenne pepper

3 tablespoons raw apple cider vinegar

1. In a small skillet, heat the oil over medium heat. Add the onion and garlic and sauté until tender and the onion turns translucent, about 10 minutes. Remove from the heat and set aside.

2. In a food processor, place the tomato paste, sauerkraut juice, honey, salt, mustard powder, allspice, and cayenne. Transfer the onion mixture to the processor and process for 1 minute, scraping down the sides as necessary. The mixture should be thick and pourable like pancake batter. If it is too thick to blend, slowly stream in 1 to 2 tablespoons of water with the blades running.

3. Transfer the ketchup to a sterilized 1-quart mason jar, tamping the jar lightly as you work. Leave 1 to 2 inches of headspace for the mixture to expand during fermentation. Run a knife between the mixture and the jar to release trapped air bubbles. Cut a piece of clean cotton, linen, or plastic wrap to the size of the jar's interior and place over the surface of the mixture. Smooth it to release trapped air and position the airlock lid (see page 67). Label the jar with the name and date and place it out of direct sun in a location between 70°F and 75°F for 3 days. Check the jar every day, skimming the surface of any suspicious film that may form (see page 67). Depending upon your preference, increase the amount of fermentation time by a few days, allowing the flavor to develop further. When it is ready to store, it should be slightly tart with sweet honey notes and a rich tomato flavor.

4. Stir in the vinegar and fasten a nonreactive lid. Refrigerate for up to 1 month.

FERMENTED MUSTARD

When Kayla Roche first interviewed with us for the position of head chef, she was in awe of our mustard! As it turns out, mustard is one of Kayla's secret ingredients, discreetly finding its way into so many of her dressings, marinades, and sauces. This recipe has grown out of our original mustards that we used to woo Kayla into staying and is now loved so much by our farm crew that we make up to a gallon at a time! We use juice from our homemade sauerkrauts to act as a starter culture to kickstart the fermentation process, but you can also use store-bought kraut juice or pickle brine so long as it contains live cultures (this will be indicated on the labeling).

Use a small saucepan with tall sides to boil the mustard rather than a wide pot with greater surface area. If you prefer a completely smooth mustard without the graininess, soak the seeds in water overnight before boiling. You may use a store-bought substitute in recipes throughout this book, but the flavor and consistency will not be as unique.

MAKES
ABOUT
2 CUPS

⅓ cup whole yellow mustard seeds

2 tablespoons whole brown mustard seeds

1 tablespoon raw plain sauerkraut juice (optional)

10 tablespoons powdered yellow mustard

5 teaspoons fine sea salt

2 teaspoons garlic powder

1½ teaspoons onion powder

¼ cup raw apple cider vinegar

1. In a small heavy-bottomed saucepan, stir together 2 cups of water and the mustard seeds. Bring the water to a boil and cook, uncovered, until the seeds double in size and the water thickens to the consistency of syrup, about 20 minutes. Remove from the heat and let cool to room temperature.

2. Transfer the cooked mustard seeds to a blender and add the sauerkraut juice (if desired), powdered yellow mustard, salt, and garlic and onion powders. Begin blending on low, increase the speed to high, and continue blending until the mixture is smooth, about 5 minutes. Scrape down the sides and check the consistency of the mustard. Depending upon the type and age of the seed, up to 1 cup of additional water may be necessary to achieve a thin paste. There should be speckles of brown with some graininess, and the mustard will appear somewhat loose. Once cooled overnight, the mustard will thicken, and the sharp flavor will mellow.

3. Ferment the mustard according to the ketchup instructions on page 87. Between 3 and 7 days, the mustard will have thickened slightly, have a rounded flavor, and will smell spicy, like horseradish. When it smells and tastes to your liking, it is time to add the vinegar. Using a whisk or small spoon, stir the mustard and vinegar together until well combined.

4. Replace the airlock with a noncorrosive lid and store the mustard in the refrigerator for up to 6 months.

FAMILY DAY PEACH BBQ SAUCE

Family Day is an annual summer gathering for our team and their families to relax and enjoy the pleasures of the farm. This sauce became legendary at that event when served with pulled pork sandwiches! Tangy but sweet Mid Pride peaches are the stars of this recipe—when slow cooked with vinegar, honey, and spices, they create a complex but versatile BBQ sauce. If you cannot source Mid Pride, choose a peach that has a similar flavor profile with citrus notes. The flavor of this sauce is a direct reflection of the quality of the peach; it is best to use firm but ripe yellow peaches to avoid the mealy, applesauce-like texture of overripe fruit. Adding a handful of chopped dried peaches before blending can also elevate this sauce if the fresh peach flavor is dull. It is perfect slathered on Spice-Rubbed Pastured Pork Ribs (page 291), served with pulled pork or pork or chicken sliders, and for glazing chicken wings.

MAKES
3 CUPS

2 tablespoons cold-pressed extra-virgin olive oil

1 cup medium-diced red onion (about 1 large onion)

1½ tablespoons sliced garlic (2 to 3 large cloves)

2 teaspoons fine sea salt

2 teaspoons sweet paprika

1½ teaspoons onion powder

½ teaspoon ground allspice

½ teaspoon garlic powder

⅛ teaspoon ground cayenne pepper

4 cups chopped Mid Pride peaches (4 medium yellow peaches)

2 tablespoons Fermented Ketchup (page 87)

2 tablespoons mild raw honey

1 tablespoon Fermented Mustard (opposite)

¼ cup raw apple cider vinegar

¼ teaspoon freshly ground black peppercorns

1. In a 4-quart nonreactive saucepan, heat the oil over medium-high heat until it expands, 1 to 2 minutes. Stir in the onion and garlic and cook, stirring occasionally, until the onion is golden, 7 to 9 minutes. Reduce the heat to low and add the salt, paprika, onion powder, allspice, garlic powder, and cayenne. Continue to cook and stir until the onion acquires a rusty red color, 2 to 3 more minutes.

2. Increase the heat to medium and add the peaches, stirring from the bottom to release any spices that may have stuck to the pan. Add ¾ cup of water, the ketchup, honey, mustard, vinegar, and pepper. Bring to a rolling boil and then reduce the heat to low. Cook, stirring frequently, until the peaches have softened and can be easily crushed with the back of a spoon, 15 minutes. Remove from the heat and set aside to cool for 10 minutes.

3. Transfer to a blender and blend on high until smooth, about 2 minutes. Return the sauce to the pan and cook for another 30 minutes over low heat, stirring frequently to prevent scorching. The sauce will be done when it is thick, crimson, and the spices are fragrant.

4. Let the BBQ sauce cool at room temperature before transferring to a container. Fasten the lid and store in the refrigerator for up to 2 weeks or in the freezer for up to 6 months.

AVOCADO OIL MAYONNAISE

Avocado was the first unrefined oil we pressed using our popular Hass fruits. I was so proud when we received those first six 5-gallon tubs of oil and became forever hooked on its buttery texture and beautiful sparkling green color. You may not think of using avocado oil to make mayonnaise, but its pleasant flavor does not overpower the spread and is perfectly complemented by rich, pastured eggs.

MAKES ABOUT 2 CUPS

4 extra-large egg yolks

1 tablespoon Fermented Mustard (page 88)

1 teaspoon fine sea salt

1 tablespoon fresh lemon juice

2 teaspoons champagne vinegar

2 cups unrefined avocado oil

1. In a food processor, place the egg yolks, mustard, salt, lemon juice, and vinegar and pulse to combine. With the machine running, slowly stream in the oil to emulsify. The mayonnaise will begin to thicken as the second cup of oil is added.

2. When the mayonnaise is thick and holds its shape on a spoon, transfer to an airtight container and place in the refrigerator for up to 2 weeks. Once chilled, it will thicken in consistency, similar to sour cream.

CHIPOTLE MAYONNAISE VARIATION

MAKES 2¼ CUPS

This mayonnaise is hot and complex and will make the most ho-hum sandwich deeply satisfying. The vinegar creates a pourable consistency—you could also use this as a salad dressing. You can substitute canned chipotles for the Chipotle Adobo Paste (page 82), but I recommend seeding them before blending to maintain a smooth texture or if you are sensitive to heat.

2 cups Avocado Oil Mayonnaise (recipe above)

5 tablespoons Chipotle Adobo Paste (page 82)

1½ teaspoons champagne vinegar

In a small bowl, stir together the mayonnaise, chipotle paste, and vinegar. The consistency will be slightly thin, enough to be pourable or used in a squeeze bottle. Transfer to a lidded container and store in the refrigerator for up to 2 weeks.

BASIL MAYONNAISE VARIATION

MAKES 2¼ CUPS

Fresh herbs are the quintessential flavor of summer, and homemade mayonnaise is an excellent vehicle for their fleeting seasonality. Use this on the BLT Sandwich with Egg, Avocado, and Basil Mayonnaise (page 384). To best capture the essence of basil, make this variation the previous night or up to 3 days before you use it.

2 cups Avocado Oil Mayonnaise (opposite)

5 tablespoons chiffonade-cut fresh basil leaves

½ teaspoon fine sea salt

1 tablespoon champagne vinegar

In a food processor, place the mayonnaise, basil, salt, and vinegar and pulse for 5 seconds. Scrape down the sides of the bowl and pulse again twice more. Transfer to a lidded container and store in the refrigerator for up to 3 days.

FLAVORED SEA SALTS:
Citrus and Garlic, Fennel Pollen, and Fresno Chile

Salts made using seasonal ingredients such as citrus zest, herbs, or chiles provide a versatile and unique seasoning for meats and vegetables. They also give our Root Vegetable Chips (page 369) a distinct flavor. Although you can make many variations, I suggest these three for the recipes in this book. They also make great finishing salts at the table. Because these homemade salts do not contain added silica, some atmospheric moisture may cause slight clumping. To remedy this, lightly shake the jar to loosen before using.

MAKES
½ CUP EACH

CITRUS AND GARLIC SEA SALT

MAKES ½ CUP

This salt blend maximizes the fragrant oils from our organically grown Mexican, Bearss, Palestine Sweet, or Makrut limes and Lisbon, Meyer, or Pink Eureka lemons, many of which I didn't even know existed ten years ago! When John and I were living in a cramped Santa Monica apartment, I often said my dream was to live somewhere with *one* lemon tree in the backyard! This desire lived deep in my heart, where I believe anything can happen, but it evolved into a reality with more options than I had ever hoped! Use this blend to naturally complement a wide variety of fish, seafood, chicken, or vegetable dishes.

2 tablespoons lemon zest
(2 large lemons)

2 teaspoons lime zest (1 medium lime)

6 tablespoons fresh lemon juice
(about 1½ large lemons)

1 teaspoon minced garlic (1 clove)

2 teaspoons minced lemongrass
(about 1 stalk)

½ cup fine sea salt

Place the lemon and lime zests, lemon juice, garlic, lemongrass, and salt in a small bowl and stir well to combine. Evenly spread the mixture over a lined 15 × 15-inch dehydrator tray and adjust the temperature to 100°F. Dry the mixture for 12 hours, stirring occasionally. Alternatively, lightly cover with a thin cloth and place in the hot summer sun for 2 days, bringing it inside each evening before nightfall. Once the salt is dry, process small batches in a spice grinder to break apart the lumps. Transfer to a small lidded container. Store at room temperature for 2 to 3 months.

RECIPE CONTINUES

FENNEL POLLEN SEA SALT

MAKES ½ CUP

Wild fennel is native to the Mediterranean but has become widely naturalized in most of California. It is a common sight on roadsides, especially along the seashore, where it prefers well-drained soil, full sun, a warm summer breeze, and mild winters. Because of its invasive nature, be cautious when planting in your own garden if you live in an area where it may proliferate. Otherwise, you may wild harvest the beautiful golden flowers in late spring and early summer, and its dried seed heads in late summer to early autumn. We have it growing near our mixed fruit orchard where we have gathered it for years—and learned a few lessons. I was once out harvesting while in sandals (a farmer mistake for sure) when a friendly but large neighborhood snake caused me to jump and lose a shoe. It landed closer to him than me!

¼ cup fennel pollen or dried fennel florets

2 teaspoons dried fennel seed

6 tablespoons fine sea salt

With a spice grinder or mortar and pestle, crush the fennel pollen and fennel seed together until the seeds reach a coarse texture. Place the mixture in a small bowl and stir in the salt. Transfer the fennel salt to a small container and fasten the lid. Store at room temperature for 2 to 3 months.

FRESNO CHILE SEA SALT

MAKES ½ CUP

The Fresno chile pepper is a treasure of the chile world, named after Fresno County, California, where it was hybridized in the 1950s. It is easy to grow in our warm climate and is my absolute favorite pepper! These darlings are a mainstay of our garden, with their mild-mannered heat and fruity, slightly smoky but sweet flavor. You can also use them in a wide range of dishes. They look similar to red jalapeño peppers, which you can use as a substitution if necessary, although the jalapeño's thicker walls will require longer drying time. Large salt flakes (see Resources, page 392) are excellent for this method, especially for using as a finishing salt.

3 small fresh Fresno chile peppers, halved and seeded

6 tablespoons plus 2 teaspoons sea salt flakes

Place the pepper halves on a 15 × 15-inch dehydrator tray and set the temperature to 135°F. Dehydrate the peppers for 12 hours before placing on a small plate and transferring to the freezer. Freeze until they easily crumble into shards between your fingers, about 2 hours. Process in a spice grinder until the peppers become small flakes, about 3 seconds. In a small bowl, mix 4 teaspoons of the pepper flakes together with the salt. Transfer to a small container and fasten the lid. Store at room temperature for 2 to 3 months.

Part II

·········

THE
GARDEN

The garden at Apricot Lane Farms represents more than one hundred different kinds of roots, shoots, fruiting vegetables, and herbs. We cultivate the lush 2.5-acre plot that supports this diversity using rotational and cover crops as well as vermicomposting, and we plant and harvest according to the biodynamic lunar calendar. This helps us grow produce that has a unique essence and intense flavor, and ensures that it is bursting with nutrients. The recipes in this section are grouped into chapters inspired by the market seasons.

Chapter Four

ROOT VEGETABLES *and* COOL-SEASON STORAGE CROPS

THERE IS SOMETHING SO MAGICAL ABOUT THE PROCESS OF SEEING BARE EARTH transform into a lush and extraordinary abundance of food. It is creativity in its finest form: water, soil, and sunlight combined into a particularly delicious version of life tended with love and care. You can be the best chef in the world when it comes to seasoning, but having the freedom to walk barefoot into the backyard and pick fresh produce is what can make your dishes really sing! Whether it is grown in your own garden or in one stewarded by your local farmer, the attention showered on this produce makes food taste better than anything else, especially when you get to harvest and cook with fruits and vegetables right away. Now that is flavor!

Summer vegetable farming is hard and intensive work, though, and with it comes a wonderful sigh of relief when the temperatures cool and the autumn season of farming begins. The beloved staples of this chapter are the foundation of cool-weather seasons, offering reliable comfort when the nights lengthen. Hefty beets, sweet carrots, creamy sunchokes, nutty cauliflower, and crunchy jicama arrive to bid summer's dusty heat goodbye and announce a cozy transition into autumn. Hearty squashes, pungent onions, and potatoes that smell of wet earth ground us to our hearths and homes when the trees finally release their leaves to blanket the ground. These humble roots set the holiday table with fortifying dishes of savory cakes and roasted dips that carry the conviviality of gathering. When the gentle rains return once again, tender turnips plucked from the damp soil intimate the promise of spring.

The following recipes temper the sharp chill of short days with warming soups, roasted sides, and baked appetizers. Thankfully these vegetables can offer welcome variety as well, with bright salads and slaw that are a fresh luxury of the cold season.

Recipes

ROASTED CAULIFLOWER STEAKS
with Chèvre Cauliflower Cream and Almond Salsa Verde

Cauliflower is a limited crop at Apricot Lane Farms due to the shortened cool season in Southern California. When the stars do align, however, our freshly harvested cauliflower is a highly sought-after offering with a remarkable difference in flavor compared to store-bought. After a long roast in the oven, the cauliflower steaks become crispy on the exterior but remain tender through their core. The almond salsa verde finishes off the dish with a textural crunch and tanginess that cut through the creamy chèvre.

SERVES
4 TO 6

ALMOND SALSA VERDE

2 cups packed roughly chopped fresh parsley leaves (2½ bunches)

1 tablespoon minced garlic (3 cloves)

½ cup almonds

1 teaspoon nonpareil capers

2 to 3 anchovy fillets packed in oil, drained

1 tablespoon white wine vinegar

½ cup cold-pressed extra-virgin olive oil

¼ teaspoon crushed red chile flakes

¼ teaspoon fine sea salt

CAULIFLOWER STEAKS

2 medium cauliflower heads (about 3 pounds)

1 tablespoon minced garlic (3 cloves)

1 tablespoon lemon zest (1 large lemon)

¼ cup fresh lemon juice (1 large lemon)

¼ cup cold-pressed extra-virgin olive oil

1½ teaspoons fine sea salt

¾ to 1 teaspoon freshly ground black peppercorns, to taste

1. Make the almond salsa verde: Place the parsley, garlic, almonds, capers, anchovies, vinegar, oil, chile flakes, and salt in a food processor. Pulse until a thick and slightly chunky sauce forms, about 1 minute, scraping down the sides of the bowl as necessary. When the ingredients are well incorporated, set aside or transfer to a storage container and refrigerate until ready to use, up to 5 days. Bring to room temperature before serving.

2. Preheat the oven to 400°F and position a rack in the middle.

3. Make the cauliflower steaks: Line a large baking sheet with parchment paper.

4. Remove the leaves at the base of the cauliflower heads and thoroughly wash the cauliflower. Transfer the cauliflower to a cutting board, and using a large chef's knife, make four even slices through each. The outer steaks will likely crumble; reserve 4 cups of 1-inch crumbled florets for making the cauliflower cream. The three inner pieces should remain attached to the core and will be used for the steaks.

5. Arrange the cauliflower steaks in a single layer in a large baking dish. Add the garlic, lemon zest, lemon juice, and oil and massage into the cauliflower, being sure that each piece is well coated. Season both sides of each piece evenly with salt and pepper. Transfer to the prepared baking sheet and place in the oven. Roast the steaks for 1 to 1¼ hours.

RECIPE AND INGREDIENTS CONTINUE

CAULIFLOWER CREAM

½ cup whole milk

¼ cup crumbled chèvre (2 ounces)

½ teaspoon fine sea salt

¼ teaspoon freshly ground black peppercorns

After about 45 minutes, flip each steak to ensure browning of both sides. The steaks are done when the cauliflower is fork-tender and golden.

6. Make the cauliflower cream: Place the reserved florets in a medium saucepan with enough water to cover by 1 inch. Bring to a boil over medium-high heat and cook, uncovered, for 4 to 5 minutes. Lower the heat to a simmer and cook until fork tender, an additional 8 to 10 minutes. Drain the cauliflower in a colander and transfer to a food processor.

7. Pour the milk into the same saucepan and gently heat until it simmers. Transfer the warm milk to the food processor and add the chèvre, salt, and pepper. Process to a smooth and creamy puree, scraping down the sides as necessary.

8. Spread the warm cauliflower cream over a serving platter and top with the roasted cauliflower steaks. Drizzle the almond salsa verde generously over the steaks and serve immediately with any remaining salsa on the side. Store leftovers in a sealed container in the refrigerator for up to 3 days.

SEASONAL EATING
(A Transcendent Cauliflower Experience)

. . . .

Southern California has exceptional year-round growing, with many fruits and vegetables ripening before distant siblings have even sprouted. Later in the year, produce may be sown a second time or may still be ready for picking long after other growing regions have entered dormancy. Our weather shapes our distinctive growing practices, and it also creates some of the most delicious seasonal foods I've had the privilege to taste and cook. What's "in season" is constantly shifting—unpredictable weather makes it difficult for even us to predict a harvest! No matter where you live, choose what is abundantly available to you and use this book's index to find inspiration for how best to enjoy your bounty. You will be rewarded with food that not only feels good but tastes exceptional!

The experience of eating fruits and vegetables at their peak can be truly transcendent. At one of our Monday all-farm meetings, Sandra, the producer of *The Biggest Little Farm*, effusively described her "spiritual experience" with one of our cauliflowers. Like many people used to eating supermarket cauliflower, Sandra had considered it a boring vegetable that was relegated to lonely leftovers on the crudité plate. The first time she took home a head harvested from our garden and broke off a bite, she realized how nuanced the sweet nuttiness could be, even raw. After thirty-seven years of experiencing a vegetable one way, she had finally discovered its true flavor! Her enthusiasm has become legendary ever since. Our cauliflower season is always sadly short, but the walkie-talkies now chatter to life when it becomes available, so that we can alert Sandra that the staff refrigerator is full!

It's certainly important to eat produce at its peak season, but a fruit or vegetable can express its real essence best when it is grown and harvested from dynamic soil teeming with microbial life. These two things give many of our fruits and vegetables an almost Willy Wonka–like quality. Blueberries that taste so deeply like *blueberries*. Juicy citrus that is bursting with sweet and tart flavor. We have been the most surprised by a summer of eggplant that was so mild and creamy we snacked on it raw like an apple! The fun in seasonal eating is learning what shines in your region and discovering what farms near you have surprisingly exceptional crops.

KABOCHA SQUASH AND GINGER SOUP
with Chile Oil and Indian Hot Mix

Winter squash soups are a favorite comfort food at the farm, made often and with slight seasonal variations from the garden. Winter squash is superb when properly cured after picking (see Ingredient Tip, page 114) and baked to golden, caramelized perfection. If, however, the squash tastes flat after roasting, add a pinch of Powdered Green Stevia (page 160) or 1 teaspoon of raw honey to each 8-ounce serving of soup to heighten the flavor. Although we don't typically fuss with the natural complexity of our squash—its sweetness is an excellent foil for spicy condiments and garnishes, and especially hot mix! This beloved and addictive snack of India has various identities and names, depending upon how and where it is made and sold. We make ours with crispy lentils, soaked and dehydrated nuts (page 41), seeds, coconut, and plenty of warm spices for a crunchy and playful soup topping. The chile oil can be made up to 1 week in advance with either dried Fresno chiles or 1 large fruity and mild guajillo chile as a substitution. Use it as an intensely flavorful finish for many soups and savory porridges, including cooked Hominy Grits (page 239).

SERVES
6 TO 8

CHILE OIL

½ cup cold-pressed extra-virgin olive oil

2 dried Fresno chile peppers, seeded

1 tablespoon peeled and finely minced ginger (1 × 1-inch knob)

3 garlic cloves, lightly crushed

INDIAN HOT MIX

½ cup cooked red lentils

2 tablespoons unrefined avocado oil

1 teaspoon ground turmeric

1 teaspoon fine sea salt

⅓ cup chopped cashews

⅓ cup chopped pistachios

⅓ cup chopped almonds

⅓ cup dark or golden raisins

⅓ cup hulled pumpkin seeds

⅓ cup unsweetened coconut flakes

1 tablespoon garam masala

¼ teaspoon ground cayenne pepper

¼ teaspoon ground cumin

1. Preheat the oven to 375°F and position a rack in the middle.

2. Make the chile oil: In a small skillet, heat the oil over medium-high heat until it reaches 325°F on an instant-read thermometer. Remove from the heat and add the chiles, ginger, and garlic. The oil will sizzle and emit a powerful fragrance. Stir until the oil stops bubbling and then set aside to cool for 15 minutes. Transfer to a high-powered blender, blend for 2 minutes, and let the oil rest for up to 1 hour to fully infuse. Strain the vibrant oil through a fine-mesh sieve into a small jar with a lid.

3. Make the Indian hot mix: Line a large baking sheet with parchment paper. Combine the lentils, 1 tablespoon of the oil, the turmeric, and ½ teaspoon of the salt. Mix the ingredients with a spoon or clean hands to evenly coat the lentils. Roast for 45 minutes to 1 hour, rotating halfway through. Remove from the oven when the lentils split and are crispy. Cool on the baking sheet for 10 minutes and transfer to a clean bowl.

4. On the same baking sheet, combine the cashews, pistachios, almonds, raisins, pumpkin seeds, coconut flakes, garam masala, cayenne pepper, cumin, the remaining 1 tablespoon oil, and the remaining ½ teaspoon salt. Stir until evenly coated and transfer

RECIPE AND INGREDIENTS CONTINUE

KABOCHA SOUP

2 medium kabocha squash
(4½ pounds)

2 tablespoons unrefined avocado oil

1 cup medium-diced yellow onion
(1 large onion)

1 tablespoon minced garlic
(3 large cloves)

2 tablespoons peeled and finely minced
ginger (1 × 2-inch knob)

1½ quarts Chicken Stock (page 76)

3 teaspoons fine sea salt

to the oven. Roast for 5 minutes, or to a deep golden brown, being careful not to burn the coconut. Remove and cool for 10 minutes, and transfer to the bowl of lentils. Stir to combine and set aside.

5. Make the soup: Adjust two oven racks so that they are evenly spaced in the middle of the oven. Line two large baking sheets with parchment paper. Place each whole squash on its own baking sheet and roast for 1 hour, rotating the sheets halfway through. Remove the squash from the oven when it softens, appears bloated, and is easily pierced with a fork. Cool for at least 30 minutes before using a flexible knife to slice in half. Remove and compost the seeds, stem, and skin.

6. In a 6-quart Dutch oven with a lid, warm the oil over medium-high heat until it shimmers, about 2 minutes. Add the onion, garlic, and ginger. Sauté, stirring occasionally, until the onion softens and becomes translucent, about 5 minutes. Break the cooked squash into small pieces and add to the pot. Pour in the stock and season with the salt. Bring the soup to a boil and then reduce to a simmer. Cook until the squash is soft and easily breaks apart with a spoon, 15 to 20 minutes. Remove from the heat, carefully transfer the soup to a blender, and blend on high to a smooth texture. Alternatively, use a handheld immersion blender to blend to your desired consistency.

7. Serve hot, sprinkled with 2 to 3 tablespoons of the hot mix and a drizzle of the chile oil per serving. Store the cooled soup in a sealed container in the refrigerator for up to 5 days or in the freezer for up to 6 months.

FRENCH ONION POTATO PUREE

This play on French onion soup highlights the naturally complex flavor of sweet onions. We have grown several different varieties that have varied in performance by the season, but all have lower sulfur and higher water content, which results in a less pungent taste. Cooking the onions slowly and pureeing them with creamy potatoes creates a side dish that is both decadent and rich. Serve with the Tomato-Braised Pastured Chicken Thighs with Mushrooms and Bell Peppers (page 229), the Wood-Fired Rib Eye with Fermented Nasturtium Berry Sauce (page 273), or the Succulent Beef Short Ribs with Spring Vegetables (page (271). It is also an excellent recipe for any fall or winter holiday and can be made with other melty cheeses besides Gruyère or with a soft goat cheese such as chèvre.

SERVES
6 TO 8

6 cups peeled and quartered Yukon Gold potatoes (2 pounds)

¼ cup plus 2 tablespoons unsalted butter

1 cup small-diced sweet onion (1 large onion)

1 cup whole milk

1¾ to 2¼ teaspoons fine sea salt, to taste

¾ cup shredded Gruyère cheese (2 ounces)

1. In a medium pot, combine the potatoes and 2 quarts of water. Cover and bring the water to a boil over medium-high heat. Remove the lid and reduce the heat to a low boil. Cook, uncovered, until the potatoes are fork tender and cooked through, 30 to 35 minutes.

2. While the potatoes are cooking, melt the butter in a large skillet over medium heat. Add the onion and sauté slowly, stirring often, until it is caramelized and golden brown, 20 to 25 minutes. Pour in the milk and stir.

3. Drain the potatoes in a colander. Return the potatoes to the pot and steam dry for a few minutes—they should be starchy and slightly fluffy. Add the milk and onion mixture and salt to taste, and using a potato masher, mash the potatoes until smooth and creamy.

4. Fold in the cheese and serve hot. Store in a covered container in the refrigerator for up to 3 days.

SPAGHETTI SQUASH COINS
with Mascarpone and Tomato Raisins

These bite-size appetizers are deeply delicious, with a delightful texture, but their flavor hinges on the quality of the ingredients, particularly the squash and tomatoes. Spaghetti squash keeps well for about two and a half months after it is properly cured, so you have plenty of time to make and serve these crispy-edged treats! Use blue borage flowers or nasturtiums in early spring, or sprigs of rosemary, thyme, or bay leaf in the winter for a festive, seasonal plating decoration.

MAKES
35 APPETIZERS

1 small spaghetti squash (about 2½ pounds)

1 cup lightly packed thick-grated Parmigiano-Reggiano cheese (2¼ ounces)

¾ teaspoon fine sea salt

¼ teaspoon freshly ground black peppercorns

½ packed cup mascarpone cheese (8 ounces)

24 Tomato Raisins (page 35)

½ cup lightly packed edible flowers (page 140) (optional)

1. Preheat the oven to 375°F and position one rack in the middle and another 6 inches above.

2. Nestle a large ovenproof wire rack into a large baking sheet. With a sharp knife, cut the squash in half lengthwise. Scoop out the seeds and place the squash halves on the rack, cut sides down. With a fork, evenly prick the skin of each about 10 times. Transfer to the oven and half fill the baking sheet with water to gently steam the flesh while cooking. Roast for 45 minutes to 1 hour, until the skin and flesh are just fork tender. Remove the squash from the oven and let it cool until easy to handle, about 20 minutes. Remove and compost the skins and roughly chop the squash into ½-inch pieces. Reserve ¾ cup and store the rest in the refrigerator for up to 1 week or freeze in portions for later use. Hold the oven at the same temperature.

3. Line two large baking sheets with parchment paper. Place the reserved squash onto a cotton towel or paper towel and gently squeeze to extract the moisture. Transfer the squash to a large bowl and add the parmesan, salt, and pepper. Toss well with a fork to thoroughly combine; the mixture should be chunky and crumbly, falling apart easily when scooped with a spoon. Form 1 teaspoon of the squash mixture into a ball and place 1½ inches from the baking sheet corner. Repeat using the remaining mixture, allowing 3 inches between scoops. Using your fingertips, lightly flatten each ball into disks about 1½ inches in diameter and ⅛ inch thick.

4. Transfer to the oven and bake for 8 to 10 minutes, until the bottoms of the coins are nicely browned, the edges are crispy, and the centers

RECIPE CONTINUES

are fully melted. Remove the coins from the oven and let them rest for about 2 minutes. Using a flat and flexible spatula, transfer the coins to wire racks to cool completely. You can prepare the coins up to 6 hours in advance and hold them at room temperature until ready to serve.

5. Place the coins on a large serving platter. Dollop ½ teaspoon of the mascarpone onto each and gently press a tomato raisin into the center. Garnish with the edible flowers, if desired, and serve at room temperature.

INGREDIENT TIP: *Properly Curing and Storing Winter Squashes*

Curing winter squashes makes all the difference in coaxing out their mildly sweet flavor! This critical step is often overlooked by commercial growers because it requires time and ample space. Once the fruits set on the vine, they are mature and ready to harvest after 50 to 55 days. We then place them on an elevated rack or mesh frame in our greenhouse (about 80°F to 85°F) with fans for good air circulation, so they are protected from moisture and receive indirect sun. We cure our squashes for 10 to 14 days before they are ready for market. We recommend storing fully cured squash in a spot that can be kept at 50°F to 60°F with 50 to 70 percent relative humidity and good ventilation, such as a garage, root cellar, or other storage space detached from a heated home. Keeping it in a refrigerator (below 50°F) may cause chilling damage, such as sunken pits on the skin surface.

POTATO SALAD
with Preserved Lemon and Mint

Rose-skinned French Fingerling, pink-red Adirondack Red, or creamy Yukon Gold potatoes are all excellent in this brightly flavored salad. Finely mincing the onion, lemon peel, pickle, and herbs (or using a food processor to save some work!) truly makes the texture of this light, mayonnaise-free potato salad unique. It's best to use a salt-brined fermented pickle for this recipe; otherwise, cut back on the vinegar or mustard if using vinegar-brined cucumbers. The acidity of this salad pairs wonderfully with rich, slow-roasted meats such as Spice-Rubbed Pastured Pork Ribs (page 291) or alongside grilled hamburgers for a summery outdoor meal.

SERVES 6

6 cups 1-inch-sliced potatoes
(2 pounds)

½ cup minced red onion
(about ½ large onion)

3 tablespoons finely minced Preserved Lemon peel (page 34), pith removed
(5 to 6 wedges)

3 tablespoons Fermented Mustard
(page 88)

3 tablespoons rice vinegar

3 tablespoons finely minced fermented dill pickle

¼ cup cold-pressed extra-virgin olive oil

2 teaspoons fine sea salt

½ teaspoon freshly ground black peppercorns

¼ cup loosely packed finely chopped fresh parsley leaves (¼ bunch)

3 tablespoons chiffonade-cut fresh mint leaves

1. Place the potatoes in a medium pot and cover with water by 1 inch. Bring the water to a boil over high heat and then reduce the heat to a simmer. Cook, uncovered, until the potatoes are fork tender, about 20 minutes. Remove from the heat and drain the potatoes in a colander.

2. In a medium bowl, place the warm potatoes and add the onion, lemon peel, mustard, vinegar, pickle, oil, salt, and pepper. Using a large spoon, mix to fully incorporate. The potatoes should be soft and creamy but retain some small uniform chunks. Add the parsley and mint and fold to combine.

3. Transfer to a clean bowl and serve immediately or at room temperature. The mint is delicate and will begin to oxidize quickly; if making ahead, store the potato salad in the bowl and reserve the mint until ready to serve. Store in a lidded container in the refrigerator for up to 3 days.

POTATO AND BUTTERNUT SQUASH RÖSTI CAKES *with Chive Crème Fraîche*

SERVES 4

The humble potato is a modified underground stem that is used by the plant to store starches made by its leaves. The key to this recipe's success is activating that starch by first partially boiling the potatoes. Keep an eye on them as they boil so they do not completely soften; otherwise, your cakes will crumble! Yukon Gold potatoes are wonderful for this recipe, but 4 to 6 large French Fingerling, Adirondack Red, or other starchy potato works as well. For the sweetest flavor, choose a butternut squash that has been properly cured by a farmer you trust. Although red kuri or kabocha squashes tend to have drier flesh, they will work as well. Use a mild and buttery olive oil and keep the oil below 350°F so the cakes become light and crispy. If you do not have crème fraîche, serve the rösti cakes with Fermented Ketchup (page 87) or Jalapeño Kraut (page 68) instead.

⅓ cup Crème Fraîche (page 71)
(a generous 2½ ounces)

1 tablespoon finely diced fresh chives

1 teaspoon fresh lemon juice

1¼ teaspoons fine sea salt

4 medium Yukon Gold potatoes, skin on (1 pound)

1 cup packed peeled and coarsely shredded butternut squash

¼ teaspoon freshly ground black peppercorns

½ cup cold-pressed extra-virgin olive oil

1. In a small bowl, combine the crème fraîche, chives, lemon juice, and ¼ teaspoon of the salt. Mix with a spoon and refrigerate for at least 1 hour or up to 2 days before serving.

2. In a medium pot, combine 2 quarts of water and the potatoes. Cover and bring to a rolling boil over high heat. Reduce the heat to a low boil and continue cooking for 12 minutes—the potatoes should still be firm when pierced with a fork. Remove from the heat and drain the potatoes. Let them cool for 10 minutes or until easy to handle.

3. Into a medium bowl, coarsely shred the warm potatoes with a box grater. Add the squash, the remaining 1 teaspoon salt, and the pepper. Comb the lumps of sticky-warm potato gently with your fingertips to separate the strands while mixing with the squash. Make about 12 compact mounds (about 2 ounces each) and place 5 inches apart on a 13 × 13-inch piece of parchment paper. Flatten the mounds into 3½-inch circles, pressing down firmly with your palm so that the circle is compact.

4. Heat ¼ cup of the oil in a 10-inch cast-iron skillet over medium-high heat until it reaches 350°F on an instant-read thermometer. Using a flat spatula, transfer 4 rösti cakes to the skillet, leaving 1 to 2 inches in between each. Cook until dark golden brown, 7 to 8 minutes per side. Add 2 additional tablespoons of oil with each batch, as the potatoes soak up the oil. Transfer the cakes to a paper towel and blot any excess oil.

5. The rösti cakes are best served hot with chive crème fraîche on the side.

ROASTED ADIRONDACK POTATOES
with Fennel in Pastured Bacon Fat

Adirondack Blue and Adirondack Red potatoes are gorgeous, tender, oblong potato cultivars with brilliant coloring. Their respective blue or pink skin is thin and their flesh moist but firm. When roasted, they retain their striking color. In this succulent but crispy and sophisticated vegetable hash, the potato and caramelized sweetness of fennel are accentuated by the deeply savory bacon fat that is surprisingly nutty and complex when rendered from pastured pork. This recipe is excellent served with Fermented Ketchup (page 87) for an impressive side to breakfast, brunch, or dinner.

SERVES
6 TO 8

2 large fennel bulbs with their fronds

5 tablespoons strained pastured bacon fat, room temperature

2½ teaspoons fine sea salt

2 pounds Adirondack Blue and/or Adirondack Red potatoes (6 to 7 large potatoes)

1. Preheat the oven to 375°F and position one rack in the middle and another rack just below.

2. To prepare the fennel, cut away the stems and fronds and set aside the fronds to use as garnish. Cut each bulb in half from stem end to the base. Using the tip of your knife, remove the core from each of the four halves. Slice the bulb into ¼-inch-thick pieces and scatter over an unlined medium baking sheet. Massage 2 tablespoons of the bacon fat and 1 teaspoon of the salt into the fennel to evenly coat the slices.

3. Carefully slice the potatoes on a mandoline to a ¼-inch thickness. Transfer to an unlined medium baking sheet and massage the remaining 3 tablespoons bacon fat and the remaining 1½ teaspoons salt into the potatoes, making sure each slice is separated and coated with fat.

4. Place the potatoes on the middle rack and the fennel on the lower rack of the oven. Roast for 20 minutes, rotating halfway through. Remove them from the oven and stir well. Transfer any potatoes and fennel that are already crispy to separate plates, and return the baking sheets to the oven, rotating the position of the fennel and potatoes. Continue roasting for an additional 10 to 15 minutes. Remove the golden and crispy fennel from the oven, combine with the other fennel, and cover to keep warm. Continue roasting the potatoes if necessary for another 10 minutes, until the edges are crisp and the potatoes are cooked through. Remove from the oven.

5. Nestle the warm potatoes onto a shallow serving platter. Mound the roasted fennel on top of the potatoes and garnish with a pinch of sea salt and a few sprinklings of the reserved fennel fronds. Serve hot.

ROASTED TOKYO TURNIP AND NANTES CARROT MEDLEY
with Carrot-Harissa Hummus

Monday-morning garden walks have always been a time when we check on what is ready to harvest. We'll pluck carrots straight from the ground, wipe them on our jeans, and enjoy! Nantes carrots have become our staple crop because of their consistently sweet flavor and pleasant crunch. They really shine in this recipe, but other varieties of tender carrots cut to a uniform size will work. If you are soaking and cooking your own chickpeas (see Cooking Tip, page 137), save ½ cup of the cooking liquid to make the hummus, and add more if you need it to reach the right consistency.

SERVES 6

ROASTED TURNIPS AND CARROTS

1 pound small Tokyo turnips, cut into ½-inch wedges (4 cups)

4½ tablespoons unrefined avocado oil

1½ teaspoons fine sea salt

½ teaspoon freshly ground black peppercorns

2½ pounds small Nantes carrots

2 tablespoons chopped fresh parsley leaves

¼ teaspoon sumac

HUMMUS

3 cups cooked chickpeas (see Cooking Tip, page 137)

¼ teaspoon smoked paprika

½ teaspoon sumac, plus more for garnish

2 tablespoons raw tahini

¼ cup Harissa (page 86)

2 teaspoons fine sea salt

1. Preheat the oven to 375°F and position one rack in the middle of the oven and another 6 inches above.

2. Make the roasted turnips and carrots: Line two large baking sheets with parchment paper. In a large bowl, toss the turnips with 2 tablespoons of the oil, ½ teaspoon of the salt, and ¼ teaspoon of the pepper. Spread the turnips onto one of the prepared baking sheets and set aside. In the same bowl, combine the carrots, the remaining 2½ tablespoons oil, the remaining 1 teaspoon salt, and the remaining ¼ teaspoon pepper. Toss to coat and spread over the second baking sheet. Place the turnips on the middle rack and the carrots on the upper rack. Roast the turnips for 30 to 35 minutes, until tender and golden, and the carrots for 45 to 55 minutes, until slightly blistered, stirring both halfway through. Remove from the oven and set aside in a warm place. Hold the oven at the same temperature.

3. Make the hummus: Transfer about one-third of the roasted carrots to a food processor. Add the chickpeas, paprika, sumac, tahini, harissa, ½ cup of water (or chickpea cooking liquid), and the salt. Process until a thick and slightly textured hummus forms, 1 to 2 minutes, scraping down the sides and adding more water if needed.

4. Spread the hummus over a large serving platter. Combine the remaining carrots and turnips onto one baking sheet and return to the oven to warm, about 5 minutes. Remove from the oven and toss with the chopped parsley. Gently mound the medley over the hummus. Sprinkle with sumac and serve immediately.

CARROT AND BEET SLAW
with Pistachios and Golden Raisins

This dish is bright and irresistibly delicious when made with farmers market carrots and beets, a perfect example of how freshly harvested produce can improve even the simplest recipes. Accentuated by warm spices, fresh herbs, bright lemon zest, and the honeyed essence of raisins, this sweet slaw sparkles with vibrant colors and lively flavors! It's possible to make this in advance, but reserve the herbs until ready to serve.

SERVES
4 TO 6

4½ cups julienned carrots
(about 5 medium carrots)

4 cups julienned beets
(5 medium beets)

½ cup golden raisins

½ cup chopped toasted pistachios

¾ cup lightly packed finely chopped fresh parsley leaves (about ¾ bunch)

¼ cup lightly packed finely chopped fresh mint leaves (about 9 stems)

1 tablespoon lemon zest (1 large lemon)

¼ cup fresh lemon juice (1 large lemon)

¼ cup cold-pressed extra-virgin olive oil

2 teaspoons fine sea salt

½ teaspoon freshly ground black peppercorns

¼ teaspoon ground cumin

⅛ teaspoon ground green cardamom

GARNISH

A small handful of whole fresh parsley leaves or mint sprigs (optional)

1. In a large bowl, place the carrots, beets, raisins, pistachios, parsley and mint leaves, lemon zest and juice, oil, salt and pepper, cumin, and cardamom, mixing well to combine.

2. Arrange the salad on a large platter, tossing again a few minutes before serving. Garnish with a few sprigs of fresh herbs if desired.

CLASSIC CURTIDO SLAW

This Salvadoran-inspired relish is delicious as an accompaniment to Cinnamon and Orange-Infused Carnitas (page 285) and Spice-Rubbed Pastured Pork Ribs (page 291) or as a substitution to coleslaw. Although curtido is typically lightly fermented, I love serving it fresh, crunchy, and made with Mexican oregano (*Lippia graveolens*) from our garden. This aromatic shrub in the verbena family is native to the southwestern United States, Mexico, and Central America and brings a bright lemony oregano flavor to savory dishes. If you cannot source it online or from a Latin market, Mediterranean oregano is a fine substitution.

SERVES
4 TO 6

6 cups finely shredded green cabbage
(1 small head)

2 cups shredded carrots
(4 large carrots)

2 large jalapeño peppers, seeds
removed and sliced into rings

1 tablespoon fine sea salt

4 teaspoons dried Mexican oregano

½ cup raw apple cider vinegar

2 tablespoons unrefined avocado oil or
cold-pressed extra-virgin olive oil

I. In a large nonreactive bowl, combine the cabbage, carrots, jalapeños, salt, oregano, vinegar, and oil. Toss and set aside to marinate for 10 to 15 minutes before serving.

2. Store in a lidded container in the refrigerator for up to 2 days. Alternatively, prepare and store the vegetables separately up to 2 days in advance of tossing with the dressing and serving.

SIMPLE JICAMA SALAD
with Sumac, Bearss Lime, and Ancho Chile

I love a good summer cucumber, but we really struggled to grow them the first few years and almost gave up! We stayed the course, though, trying different cultivars until we landed on one that wouldn't succumb to powdery mildew. And I'm so glad that we did! Our cucumbers have a natural and unexpected sweetness that pairs well with crunchy jicama and ripe peaches in this refreshing salad. Over the years, some of my teammates have introduced me to the fruity-hot combinations commonly found in Latin American foods, and this recipe deliciously riffs on those flavors. Make sure to core the cucumber before slicing if the seeds are large or tough. Mid Pride peaches are excellent in this recipe, but you can choose any firm but ripe variety that has a nicely balanced sweet-tart flavor. Serve as a garnish for tacos or as a side to a light meal.

SERVES 6

1 large jicama

1½ cups ¼-inch-thick sliced English cucumber, cut into half-moons (about 1 medium cucumber)

¼ cup thinly sliced red onion (about ¼ medium onion)

½ cup peeled and crushed peach flesh (about 1 large peach)

5 tablespoons fresh lime juice (about 2½ medium limes)

2 teaspoons fine sea salt

1½ tablespoons unrefined avocado oil or cold-pressed extra-virgin olive oil

1 cup ¼-inch-thick sliced yellow peaches (1 small peach)

GARNISH

2 pinches ground ancho chile powder

2 pinches sumac

1 pinch ground cayenne pepper

1. Peel the jicama, slice it in half from stem to root end, and lay each half on a cutting board, cut side down. Slice into ¼-inch-thick planks. Stack the planks into small piles and cut into triangles. You should have about 4½ cups.

2. In a large bowl, place the jicama, cucumber, onion, crushed peach, lime juice, salt, and oil. Stir to combine, and fold in the sliced peaches.

3. Transfer the salad to a serving bowl. Sprinkle the ancho, sumac, and cayenne just before serving to avoid their color bleeding into the vegetables.

4. Transfer leftovers to an airtight container and store in the refrigerator for up to 2 days. The spices will bleed into the vegetables but will not affect the taste.

CREAMY BAKED SUNCHOKE DIP
with Vegetable Crudité

This rich and satisfying dip is the perfect appetizer for a small party, but it can easily be doubled for larger gatherings. Ferment the sunchokes (page 65) for up to six months in advance and enjoy this dip with tender seasonal vegetables. The longer the sunchokes have been fermenting, the sharper the dip will be. A good way to judge the flavor before preparing the dip is to taste one sunchoke before or after it is roasted and adjust the lemon juice according to your preference.

SERVES
6 TO 8

SUNCHOKE DIP

10 peeled garlic cloves
(about 1 large head)

¾ cup cold-pressed extra-virgin olive oil

3 cups Fermented Sunchokes (page 65), rinsed (to make 2 cups roasted sunchokes)

1 cup diced yellow onion (1 large onion)

¼ cup diced shallot (1 large shallot)

1½ teaspoons fine sea salt

2 tablespoons fresh lemon juice

¼ cup Greek yogurt

CRUDITÉ

Fresh raw seasonal vegetables of choice, such as carrots, peas, young turnips, radishes, summer squash, or tender kohlrabi

1. Preheat the oven to 350°F and position a rack in the middle.

2. Roast the garlic in ½ cup of the oil according to the instructions on page 84. Remove from the oven, set aside to cool, and strain and reserve the roasted garlic oil.

3. Pat the sunchokes dry with a paper towel and evenly spread them over a large unlined baking sheet. Drizzle with 2 tablespoons of the olive oil and toss to coat. Transfer to the oven and roast for 50 to 60 minutes, until the sunchokes have evenly browned; some sunchokes will be firm but cooked through, while others will soften considerably—this range of texture is normal. Remove from the oven and set aside to cool for 20 minutes.

4. Heat 2 tablespoons of the roasted garlic oil in a medium skillet over medium heat. Add the onion and sauté until it is translucent and slightly golden, about 7 minutes. Remove the pan from the heat and let cool for 10 minutes.

5. Place the roasted garlic cloves in the pitcher of a blender. Add the cooled sunchokes, the remaining 2 tablespoons olive oil, the sautéed onion, shallot, salt, lemon juice, and yogurt. Blend on low and then increase the speed to high, processing until the dip is thick and slightly textured. If necessary, add up to ¼ cup of water to assist with blending or to achieve your desired dip consistency.

6. Scoop the dip into a serving bowl and serve immediately or store, covered, in the refrigerator for up to 3 days, stirring well before plating with the vegetables of your choice.

FERMENTED SUNCHOKE SOUP
with Crispy Sunchoke Chips

This irresistible soup highlights the natural sweetness of Fermented Sunchokes (page 65), especially when you make it shortly after preserving them. The creamy soup is a pleasing contrast to the crisp and crunchy fried sunchoke chips—it's like having a double feature of this unique seasonal treat. Use a mandoline to shave the sunchokes to a consistent 1/16 inch for best results when frying.

SERVES 6

SUNCHOKE CHIPS

3 cups cold-pressed extra-virgin olive oil or virgin coconut oil

1 cup drained and thinly shaved Fermented Sunchokes (page 65) (1 large 1½ × 3-inch sunchoke)

A few pinches fine sea salt

SOUP

12 cups drained Fermented Sunchokes (page 65)

2 tablespoons unrefined avocado oil

1½ cups small-diced sweet yellow onion (about 1½ large onions)

2 teaspoons minced garlic (about 2 cloves)

1 quart Chicken Stock (page 76)

1 teaspoon chopped fresh rosemary leaves or ½ teaspoon dried

2 teaspoons fine sea salt

2 tablespoons diced fresh chives

1. Make the sunchoke chips: Nestle a wire rack into a baking sheet and set next to the stovetop. In a 2-quart saucepan, heat the olive oil over medium-high heat to 325°F on an instant-read thermometer. With a spoon, lower 10 to 15 sunchoke slices into the oil and stir gently to separate the slices. Fry until golden brown, 3 to 4 minutes. With a slotted spoon, remove the chips and transfer to the wire rack to drain. Sprinkle with a pinch or two of salt and repeat with the remaining chips. Set the cooled chips aside in a small bowl until ready to serve with the soup.

2. Make the soup: Place the sunchokes in a large stockpot and cover with 1 gallon of water. Cover and bring to a low boil. Cook until mostly tender but not falling apart, about 30 minutes. Drain the sunchokes in a colander and set aside to cool until easy to handle, about 15 minutes. Squeeze the meat from the softened sunchokes into a large bowl and compost the skins. You should have about 2⅔ cups sunchoke meat. Set aside.

3. In a 4-quart pot, heat the avocado oil over medium-high heat until it expands and shimmers, about 2 minutes. Stir in the onion and garlic and cook until the onion is soft and translucent, about 7 minutes. Add the cooked sunchoke meat and stir until the mixture becomes a thick paste. Remove from the heat and transfer to the pitcher of a blender. Add the stock, rosemary, and salt and blend on high until smooth and slightly frothy. Return the soup to the pot and warm over medium heat, stirring occasionally until it reaches a low boil.

4. Ladle the hot soup into bowls and garnish each bowl with 2 tablespoons of crispy sunchoke chips and a sprinkling of chives. Serve immediately. Store in a covered container in the refrigerator for up to 1 week or freeze for up to 6 months.

AUTUMN KURI SQUASH BARS

Red kuri is an orange-fleshed, dense winter squash that resembles a teardrop-shaped pumpkin. It's one of my all-time favorites! If you cannot source it, kabocha or Hubbard squashes are good substitutes. Ground squirrels love these sweet squash as much as we do, and one season we lost a whole crop to those rascals! This lightly sweet bar, which combines the roasted squash with blended soaked cashews, resembles a cheesecake. Use the same method for roasting as described for the Kabocha Squash and Ginger Soup (page 108), and remove the skin before measuring the squash for this recipe. The texture and flavor will keep improving once you've baked and refrigerated the bars.

MAKES
20 BARS

FILLING

2 cups soaked and dehydrated cashews (page 41)

2 cups hot water (about 180°F)

2¼ cups roasted, peeled, and cubed red kuri squash

⅓ cup maple syrup

2 teaspoons vanilla extract

1 teaspoon ground cinnamon

⅛ teaspoon ground nutmeg

2 large eggs, room temperature

CRUST

1½ teaspoons cold-pressed extra-virgin olive oil or virgin coconut oil

2 cups finely chopped walnuts

2 cups finely chopped pecans

¼ cup maple syrup

2 tablespoons raw tahini

½ teaspoon fine sea salt

1. Place the cashews in a medium bowl and pour in the hot water. Soak for 1 hour.

2. Preheat the oven to 350°F and position one rack in the middle and another 6 inches below it.

3. Make the crust: Grease a 9½ × 12-inch baking sheet with the oil. In a medium bowl, combine the walnuts, pecans, maple syrup, tahini, and salt and stir to coat. Transfer to the prepared baking sheet and spread evenly over the entire surface. Using the bottom of a large measuring cup, evenly and firmly compress the crust and set aside.

4. Make the filling: Drain the cashews in a colander or fine-mesh sieve. Transfer to the pitcher of a blender and add the squash, ½ cup of water, the maple syrup, vanilla, cinnamon, nutmeg, and eggs. Puree on high until smooth and creamy, 1 to 2 minutes, scraping down the sides as necessary. The filling should be silky, smooth, and thick.

5. Place the crust in the oven on the middle rack and bake for 5 minutes, or until slightly set. Remove from the oven, pour in the filling, and with an offset spatula, smooth to evenly distribute. Fill a 2-quart casserole dish with 1½ quarts of water and place on the bottom rack of the oven. Transfer the baking sheet to the middle rack and bake for 20 minutes, rotating halfway through. Remove from the oven when the filling is set and let cool at room temperature for at least 30 minutes. Transfer the baking sheet to the refrigerator and chill thoroughly for at least 1 hour before cutting into 20 squares.

6. Serve cold. Store, covered, in the refrigerator for up to 1 week.

Chapter Five

TENDER SPRING VEGETABLES, LEAFY GREENS, *and* CULINARY AND MEDICINAL HERBS

SPRING IS FULL OF INVIGORATING SUNSHINE AND A FEELING OF NEW BEGIN-
nings. It is my favorite time of year, and it always reminds me of the first morning I spent on
the farm, eager to engage in the many possibilities of cooking. It was an April day, and dew
made the leaves of the calla lilies that were blooming everywhere iridescent in the shimmering early light. John was away for work and it was just me and Todd, roaming through dozens
of acres of lemons and avocados. My excitement for being on the farm shielded me from truly
seeing how ramshackle the orchards were. Thinking about them today through the lens of
regenerative agriculture brings into focus how far we needed to come. But back then, it was
just the greatest thing in the world to be here! I remember making tea from lemon peels to
soothe a sore throat that morning and greeting the grumpy resident rooster with gusto.

Now that we've been here for over a decade, I still experience those sensations of wonder
and awe. Each spring reminds me that there is more deliciousness to experience and even
more to love than I had ever anticipated about this crazy life. After the months of winter, delicate leaves and an abundance of fortifying herbs emerge to restore the spirit. The body awak-
ens, with tender salads, cleansing tonics, and savory sauces that increase our vital energy. We
savor the return of greens, my favorite tender peas, and radishes at this time, using ingredients that are fresh and taste alive!

Recipes

KALE SALAD
with Crispy Chickpeas and Parmesan

Produce that is grown with care and harvested at its peak needs little effort to make it enjoyable, and this simple recipe is another perfect example. Although kale is now available at most grocers year-round, it is best during the colder months of autumn, winter, and early spring, when frigid temperatures sweeten the tender leaves. For tasty, perfectly crispy chickpeas, drain them well after soaking and cooking and blot dry on a towel before tossing in the oil and seasonings.

SERVES 4

CRISPY CHICKPEAS

2 cups cooked chickpeas (see Ingredient Tip)

2 tablespoons cold-pressed extra-virgin olive oil

1 tablespoon fresh lemon juice

1 teaspoon fine sea salt

½ teaspoon freshly ground black peppercorns

½ teaspoon smoked paprika

SALAD

5 cups packed chopped kale, stems removed (about 2 bunches)

2 teaspoons minced garlic (2 cloves)

3 tablespoons fresh lemon juice (1 medium lemon)

¼ cup cold-pressed extra-virgin olive oil

1 cup shaved Parmigiano-Reggiano cheese (4 ounces)

1 teaspoon fine sea salt

Freshly cracked black peppercorns, to taste

1. Preheat the oven to 375°F and position a rack in the middle.

2. Make the crispy chickpeas: Line a large baking sheet with parchment paper. Place the chickpeas in a small bowl and drizzle with the oil and lemon juice. Sprinkle with the salt, pepper, and smoked paprika and toss well to combine. Spread the chickpeas over the prepared baking sheet and transfer to the oven. Roast for 45 minutes to 1 hour, stirring occasionally, until the chickpeas are crispy and browned. Remove from the oven and set aside to cool.

3. Make the salad: In a large bowl, combine the kale, garlic, lemon juice, oil, Parmesan, salt, pepper, and crispy chickpeas. Toss well to combine and serve immediately.

4. Store the dressed kale in a covered container in the refrigerator for up to 2 days. If possible, store the chickpeas separately to maintain their texture or roast and toss them just before serving.

COOKING TIP: *Chickpeas*

Beans are treated like any other seed in our kitchen and soaked well before cooking. This not only makes them more digestible but also improves their texture! If you are cooking your own chickpeas in advance of making this recipe, about ⅔ cup dry chickpeas will yield 2 cooked cups. Cover the amount that is needed in twice the volume of water and soak at room temperature for 12 hours. Drain, rinse well, and bring the chickpeas to a simmer in plenty of water salted to taste like the sea. Cook until they yield to a nice and creamy texture, 30 to 45 minutes.

RED LENTIL SOUP
with Sausage and Greens

When the days are chilly, we turn to this lightly creamy soup to warm and fortify ourselves on the farm. It is a favorite of our head chef, Kayla, who likens it to a comforting split pea soup. It is also adaptable: you can use a braised ham hock instead of the sausage or make it vegetarian and substitute a vegetable stock. It can be enjoyed as a meal in itself, especially when served with generously buttered slices of A Crusty Hearth-Style Sourdough Boule (page 59). Depending on the pork, the sausage may release ¼ to ½ cup of fat when cooked; to lighten the soup, strain and save this delicious fat in a small container for future cooking projects. Although hearty kale works well in this composition, spinach or Swiss chard are tasty substitutes.

SERVES
6 TO 8

2 cups dried red lentils

1 pound Apricot Lane Farms Pork Sausage (page 298)

1 cup small-diced yellow onion (about 1 large onion)

1 cup small-diced carrots (about 3 medium carrots)

1 cup cored and small-diced fennel bulb (½ large bulb)

1 cup minced celery (about 3 stalks)

1½ tablespoons minced garlic (4 to 5 large cloves)

1 quart Chicken Stock (page 76)

1 cup full-fat coconut milk

2½ teaspoons fine sea salt

½ teaspoon ground black peppercorns

1 bay leaf

1 tablespoon chopped fresh dill fronds

2 cups loosely packed chopped kale, stems removed (1 small bunch)

1 tablespoon raw apple cider vinegar

1. Place the dried lentils in a medium bowl and cover with water in excess of 2 inches. Soak overnight, or 8 to 10 hours in advance of preparing the soup. Drain through a fine-mesh sieve, rinse well, and set aside.

2. Place the sausage in a 3-quart saucepan and set over medium-high heat. Cook, stirring occasionally, until crumbled and crispy, about 10 minutes, then transfer to a clean bowl. To the same pan, add the onion, carrots, fennel, celery, and garlic. Cook over medium-high heat, stirring occasionally, until the vegetables soften, about 10 minutes. Stir in the drained lentils, stock, coconut milk, salt, pepper, and bay leaf. Bring the mixture to a boil and then reduce to a low simmer. Cook, uncovered, until the lentils are tender, 20 to 25 minutes.

3. Remove the bay leaf. If using an immersion blender, puree the soup in the pan by pulsing 2 or 3 times until thick but still chunky, or transfer the mixture to a blender and puree before returning to the pan. Stir in the dill, kale, sausage, and vinegar, and cook until the greens begin to soften but remain bright green, 5 minutes. Remove from the heat.

4. Serve the soup immediately. Store in a covered container in the refrigerator for up to 5 days or in smaller portions in the freezer for up to 6 months.

SUGAR SNAP PEA SALAD
with Shaved Radish, Carrot, and Preserved Lemon Vinaigrette

There is a moment after the end of winter and before spring fully arrives that the earth takes one last long and deep breath. Daylight has already triggered germination of our seedlings, and yet the pervasive chill and occasional late frost keep our salad greens, herbs, and tender root vegetables from filling our market stall. When the garden finally picks up momentum, our team knows we've passed the threshold of winter and that the abundance of summer isn't far behind! This salad is our crunchy, lemony reward for waiting patiently while the soil warms and the trees burst into bloom. If making in advance, prepare the dressing and salad components separately and store, covered, in the refrigerator for up to 2 days before serving.

SERVES 4

PRESERVED LEMON VINAIGRETTE

3 tablespoons minced Preserved Lemon peel (page 34), pith removed (5 to 6 wedges)

2 tablespoons Fermented Mustard (page 88)

¼ cup fresh lemon juice (1 large lemon)

¼ teaspoon fine sea salt

¼ cup cold-pressed extra-virgin olive oil

SALAD

5 cups sugar snap peas, stemmed and thinly sliced on the bias (1 pound)

1½ cups thinly sliced carrots (about 4 medium carrots)

1¾ cups thinly sliced common or breakfast radishes (8 medium radishes)

¼ cup minced red onion (about ¼ large onion)

½ teaspoon fine sea salt

¼ teaspoon freshly cracked black peppercorns

¼ cup chiffonade-cut fresh basil leaves

2 tablespoons chopped fresh mint leaves

I. Make the dressing: In the pitcher of a blender, combine the preserved lemon peel, mustard, lemon juice, and salt. Pulse the mixture several times until incorporated. With the machine running, slowly stream in the oil to emulsify. Turn off the blender and set aside.

2. Assemble the salad: In a large bowl, combine the peas, carrots, radishes, onion, salt, and pepper. Pour the dressing over the vegetables and toss evenly to coat. Just before serving, add the basil and mint and gently toss. Serve immediately. Store in a covered container in the refrigerator for up to 3 days.

THE EDIBLE FLOWERS
of Apricot Lane Farms

....

Beautiful flowering wild and cultivated plants play an important role in the health of our vegetable garden, orchards, and even our pastures. They add biodiversity to our land, provide forage for pollinators in the off season, and cover the soil when we are not intentionally cultivating food crops. Though there are some common wildflowers, such as the shortpod mustard (*Hirschfeldia incana*), that are nonnative invasives, we try to keep them in check even though they are pretty! The cheerful flowers of the shortpod mustard were one of the first plants our son, Beaudie, learned to pick and eat himself, and they never seem to suffer from diligent weeding.

Until we began the farm, edible flowers were not part of my wheelhouse as a chef, and I rarely considered their specific flavors when composing a dish. Over the years, though, our talented garden team has introduced edible flowers into our beds, and with this exposure, I discovered a new palette of flavors and textures and learned a true whole-plant approach to eating vegetables. We now grow very specific edible (and some ornamental) plants with the benefit of tasty flowers, many of which you will see used as garnish throughout the photographs of this book. These beautiful adornments are packed with potent antioxidants that protect our cells from disease and may significantly improve immune responses. Many are also used for their medicinal properties and may aid in relaxation, sleep, and cognitive function, among other benefits. (See Therapeutic Uses of Plants on the Farm, page 162.) Plus, they bring beauty and life to our dishes!

Below is a list of twenty of our favorites that can grow in a diverse range of climates or in small spaces, such as on a stoop or even a fire escape. Always check to see what common garden plants are invasive in your region before seeding freely, and note that the flowers of many are bonus gifts from plants typically grown for other uses. By allowing these plants to mature and flower, you will attract and feed pollinators such as European honeybees, hummingbirds, and butterflies, and in many cases, you can also harvest their edible green seedpods, best picked when the seeds are green and tender. Playful but spicy radish pods, fragrant cilantro seed heads, or peppery nasturtium "berries" are excellent when pickled or added in small amounts to ferments such as Jalapeño Kraut (page 68). If you have space, consider identifying and growing native plants in your region to help encourage and feed the native bees that are equally important to a healthy environment.

If you cannot grow your own edible flowers, source from a farmer who does not use chemical sprays. Never gather roadside flowers, and always positively identify both the species and edible parts of the plant before ingesting. With the exception of the feijoa and German chamomile, always remove the inner reproductive parts (pistil and stamen) and outer sepals, or use the petals only, to avoid a bitter or off-putting aftertaste. As with all plants, including those listed here, wild species and their domesticated cultivars can produce a wide array of natural compounds that may cause adverse effects in some people. Always assess your personal risk before consumption.

SCIENTIFIC NAME	COMMON NAME	COLOR		FLAVOR, TEXTURE, AND USE
Abelmoschus esculentus	okra	Large cream-colored to buttery yellow petals with a dark red eye.		Crisp, succulent, and mild. Best used in fresh vegetable salads.
Acca sellowiana	feijoa or pineapple guava	White to pink or red petals with bright red stamens.		Bright and fruity with hints of pineapple, mint, kiwi, and marshmallow. Wonderful with fruit salads or as a beverage garnish.
Allium schoenoprasum	garden chives	Umbels of lavender-purple florets.		Savory and slightly sweet with a chive fragrance. Best used as a garnish for savory dishes.
Allium tuberosum	garlic chives	Umbels of white florets with faint green stripes.		Savory and slightly sweet with a garlic aroma. Best used as a garnish for savory dishes.
Borago officinalis	borage	True vivid blue star-shaped flowers.		Sweet, with a slight cucumber flavor. Wonderful for both savory and sweet applications.
Calendula officinalis	pot marigold	Bright buttery yellow and orange petals or lighter, creamy-colored cultivars.		Sweet and mild with hints of citrus and tarragon. Great for both savory and sweet dishes as well as fresh or dried in teas.
Centaurea cyanus	bachelor's button	Cornflower-blue, pink, white, and magenta flowers.		Straw-like, sweet, and mild. Use for both sweet and savory applications as well as fresh or dried in teas.

SCIENTIFIC NAME	COMMON NAME	COLOR		FLAVOR, TEXTURE, AND USE
Clitoria ternatea	butterfly pea flower	Deep but bright royal-blue pea flowers with a flush of yellow and white.		Best used fresh or dry for steeping to create a beautiful blue hue in teas or cocktail syrups. Use an acidifier such as lemon to produce a pinkish-lavender color.
Coriandrum sativum	cilantro and coriander	Lacy umbels of elegant white florets.		Flowers are bright and somewhat soapy tasting. Use for both sweet and savory recipes. Tender green seed heads are excellent for pickling or fermenting.
Eruca vesicaria ssp. *Sativa*	arugula	Veined pale yellow to cream-colored flowers.		Peppery, zesty, and verdant flowers and buds. Best used for savory vegetable salads or for garnishing meat dishes.
Helianthus tuberosus	sunchoke	Cheery golden-yellow flowers.		Nutty and sweet. Use for both savory dishes and garnishing desserts.
Hemerocallis fulva and some but not all cultivars (properly identify edibility before consumption)	daylily or ditch lily	Rusty to bright orange flowers.		Buds and flower petals are crunchy with a sweet artichoke or asparagus flavor. Wonderful raw in salads or battered and fried.
Hirschfeldia incana	shortpod mustard or Greek mustard	Bright yellow flowers.		Flower buds are tender and good in stir-fries or ferments. Flowers are spicy and mustard flavored and best for garnishing savory dishes.

SCIENTIFIC NAME	COMMON NAME	COLOR		FLAVOR, TEXTURE, AND USE
Lobularia maritima	sweet alyssum	Carpets of tiny white, pink, or purple flowers.		Honey-scented, subtle, and delicate texture to garnish sweet or savory meals.
Matricaria chamomilla	German chamomile	Daisylike flowers with white petals and a yellow eye.		Subtle honey flavor used fresh or dried in teas. Garnish both sweet and savory meals.
Raphanus sativus	garden or wild radish	Veined white, pink, purple, pale yellow, or rusty-orange flowers.		Spicy flowers are tasty in savory vegetable salads. Tender and young green seedpods are excellent for pickling or fermenting.
Salvia elegans	pineapple sage	Deep red flowers.		Tropical fruit flavor with an uncanny pineapple fragrance. Excellent garnish for fruit salads or iced beverages.
Tropaeolum majus	garden nasturtium	Pale to bright yellow, orange, or red flowers.		Crisp and succulent, these peppery flowers are excellent to cut through rich meals of roasted meats or to garnish vegetable salads.
Tulbaghia violacea	society garlic	Umbels of delicate, star-shaped lavender florets.		Savory, with hints of garlic. Use to garnish meats and vegetable salads.
Viola tricolor var. *hortensis*	garden pansy	Cheerful animated flowers that range in colors from white to yellow, orange, pink, and purple—or a combination.		Lettuce-like flavor with hints of licorice. Whimsical in salads or to garnish desserts.

SPRING SNAP PEA SALAD
with Spinach-Pistachio Pesto and Crème Fraîche

When I was a child, my gramma lived on my uncle's farm in Ford City, Pennsylvania, where I would visit and first fall in love with the sights and smells of farmland. With this exception, I spent my elementary years in the suburbs of Pittsburgh without much exposure to cultivated plants, except for a neighbor who would share his freshly picked garden peas. I snacked on them eagerly, and always looked forward to more, but never knew why they tasted so different! Later, when I met John, he indulged my curiosity for nature with his love for the outdoors. He taught me how to camp and garden, and our first crop of sugar snap peas returned my senses to those childhood memories. I learned that you really could taste the earth and the sun when produce is eaten straight from the garden. This salad is crunchy, refreshingly creamy, and naturally sweet, especially when you can use young sugar snap peas straight from the vine.

SERVES 2

SPINACH-PISTACHIO PESTO

3 cups chopped spinach (3 ounces)

½ cup lightly packed fresh mint leaves

½ cup cold-pressed extra-virgin olive oil

½ cup pistachios

½ teaspoon fine sea salt

1 tablespoon fresh lime juice
(½ medium lime)

SEASONED PEAS

3½ cups sugar snap peas, stemmed and sliced (8 ounces)

A handful of young pea tendrils

2 tablespoons thinly sliced shallot
(1 shallot)

2 tablespoons cold-pressed
extra-virgin olive oil

1 tablespoon fresh lime juice
(½ medium lime)

¼ teaspoon fine sea salt

GARNISH

½ cup Crème Fraîche (page 71)
(4 ounces)

¼ cup finely chopped pistachios

1. Make the spinach-pistachio pesto: Combine the spinach, mint, oil, pistachios, salt, and lime juice in a food processor. Process until the pesto is thick and smooth, scraping down the sides as necessary, and set aside. This recipe yields about 1 cup.

2. Make the seasoned peas: In a medium bowl, combine the peas, pea tendrils, shallot, oil, lime juice, and salt. Toss to combine.

3. Using the back of a spoon, smear about ¼ cup of the crème fraîche over the center of each of two small plates. Dollop half the pesto over the crème fraîche. Divide the seasoned peas evenly between the plates and garnish with the pistachios. Serve immediately.

RADISH-TOP SALAD
with Mustard Dressing and Crispy Lentils

Tender radishes plucked fresh from the ground have the added benefit of lush, leafy green tops that are so often underappreciated in the kitchen. Radishes are also useful to the gardener as a versatile quick-growing companion to slower-growing crops. This salad uses the whole vegetable and is delicious with even the spiciest radishes since they will lose a little of their heat when salted and drained. Choose firm, brightly hued common or breakfast radishes with full and vibrantly green stems and leaves. Avoid yellow leaves that are often found on radishes that have been harvested and stored for long periods of time. It is best to prepare this dish the day it is served, and if you do not have Crème Fraîche (page 71), substitute a thick Greek yogurt instead.

SERVES
4 TO 6

1¼ cups dry beluga lentils

2 bay leaves

3 teaspoons fine sea salt

7 tablespoons cold-pressed extra-virgin olive oil

¼ cup finely chopped shallot (about 1 large shallot)

3 cups loosely packed chopped radish greens (2 bunches)

3 cups loosely packed chopped spinach (3 ounces)

2 bunches common or breakfast radishes

2 tablespoons plus 1½ teaspoons Fermented Mustard (page 88)

1 tablespoon mild raw honey

¼ teaspoon freshly ground black peppercorns

¼ cup plus 2 tablespoons fresh lemon juice (1½ large lemons)

½ cup Crème Fraîche (page 71) (4 ounces)

1. Soak the lentils: At least 12 hours before cooking, place the lentils in a 2-quart container and cover with 1½ quarts of water.

2. Preheat the oven to 350°F and position a rack in the middle.

3. Drain the lentils in a fine-mesh sieve and discard the soaking liquid. Transfer the lentils to a 3-quart pot and cover with 2 quarts of fresh water. Add the bay leaves and stir in 1 teaspoon of the salt. Place the pot over medium-high heat and bring to a boil. Reduce the heat to a simmer and cook the lentils, uncovered, until tender, about 15 minutes. Remove from the heat and drain the lentils in a fine-mesh sieve, discarding the cooking liquid and bay leaves. Rinse the lentils with cool water and drain completely.

4. Transfer half the lentils to a large baking sheet. Drizzle 3 tablespoons of the oil over the lentils and sprinkle with ½ teaspoon of the salt. Toss to coat and transfer to the oven. Bake for 25 minutes, stir well, and continue baking for an additional 5 to 10 minutes, until crispy. Remove from the oven and set aside.

5. In a 10-inch cast-iron skillet, heat 1 tablespoon of the oil over medium heat until shimmering, about 2 minutes. Stir in the shallot, radish leaves, and spinach and sauté until any moisture from the greens has evaporated, about 5 minutes. Remove from the heat and set aside.

RECIPE CONTINUES

6. Slice the radishes into ¼-inch wedges and place in a small bowl. Add ½ teaspoon of the salt and toss to coat. Set aside for at least 5 minutes before draining any accumulated water from the bowl. Pat the radishes dry with a paper towel and set aside.

7. In a small bowl, whisk together the mustard, honey, pepper, lemon juice, the remaining 3 tablespoons oil, the remaining 1 teaspoon salt, and the pepper until well combined and set aside.

8. In a large bowl, combine the cooked greens, radishes, and all the lentils. Drizzle the dressing over the top and stir well to combine. On a large serving platter, spread the crème fraîche with the back of a spoon to create attractive ripples. Mound the lentil salad on top and serve immediately.

BEET KVASS

This earthy, salty, sour, and slightly effervescent medicinal beverage of eastern European and Slavic origins has been heralded as a blood and liver tonic with remarkable probiotic benefits. At the farm, we sometimes share it in small shot glasses. It is a bold, acquired taste, but even Beaudie asks for it regularly, and we almost always have it in our fridge. Red beets are best, as they are sweet and impart a beautiful dark-red wine color to the kvass. The warmer the days, the faster the fermentation. If you make this in a cooler season, the kvass will need more time to create its deeply complex flavor.

MAKES
ABOUT
5 CUPS

5 cups unpeeled 1-inch diced red beets
(6 medium beets)

1½ tablespoons fine sea salt

1. Place the beets in a sterilized 2-quart mason jar. Add the salt and 5 cups of water and tightly fasten the lid. Shake the jar to dissolve the salt, then remove the lid. Wipe the mouth of the jar clean and position an airlock lid (see page 67). Label the jar with the date and recipe name and store the kvass in a cool, dark place for 3 to 7 days. Shake and observe the jar once daily, noting signs of increased bubbling. If mold occurs on the surface of the liquid, skim, discard, and continue fermenting. When the fermentation subsides, the kvass should have a bold but refreshing beet flavor and a somewhat viscous character. It should taste tart, slightly effervescent, and salty like the sea. If it does not, continue fermenting until it tastes to your liking.

2. Strain the contents of the jar into a flip-top bottle suitable for high-pressure liquids, leaving 2 inches of headspace. Compost the spent beets. Seal the bottle and label it clearly, lest it be mistaken for red wine! Ferment the kvass at room temperature in a dark location until the kvass exhibits increased effervescence when the top is popped, an additional 1 to 2 days.

3. Although the color may eventually oxidize, the kvass can be stored for up to 6 months in the refrigerator. Serve cold or over ice if you prefer a diluted flavor.

SMOKY POTATO AND GREENS TACOS

These meatless tacos are deliciously savory and fulfilling, especially when eaten for breakfast smothered with Lazy Salsa (page 369) and Roasted Garlic Hot Sauce (page 84). Homemade Corn Tortillas (page 44) lend a sweet and nutty bite to this recipe, complementing the hearty greens, golden brown and crispy-edged potatoes, melty cheese, and smoky aroma. Make them vegan friendly by replacing the bacon fat with avocado oil and by omitting the cheese and sprinkling with Mineral Gomasio (page 159) instead. Although not a typical cheese for tacos, mozzarella is an excellent choice for hearty greens such as kale or collards and holds up well under the broiler. French Fingerling, Adirondack, or Yukon Gold potatoes all work well. To keep your tortillas warm, heat them until pliable and hot in a preheated skillet and wrap them in a cotton towel–lined basket, preferably one with a lid, until ready to use.

MAKES
8 TACOS

4 cups medium-diced potatoes
(1¾ pounds)

3 tablespoons strained pastured bacon fat or unrefined avocado oil

2 teaspoons fine sea salt

¾ teaspoon smoked paprika

½ teaspoon chili powder

½ teaspoon ground cumin

5 cups chopped kale, stems removed
(2 bunches)

1 teaspoon finely chopped garlic
(1 clove)

1 cup shredded mozzarella (6 ounces)

8 Corn Tortillas (page 44), warmed

GARNISH

¼ cup Roasted Garlic Hot Sauce
(page 84)

½ cup Lazy Salsa (page 369)

8 lime wedges (2 limes)

3 tablespoons cilantro leaves

1. Preheat the oven to 375°F and position a rack in the middle.

2. In a medium bowl, combine the potatoes, 2 tablespoons of the bacon fat, 1½ teaspoons of the salt, the smoked paprika, chili powder, and cumin. Toss until evenly seasoned, spread the potatoes in an even layer over a large unlined baking sheet, and transfer to the oven. Bake for 20 minutes. Using a spatula, flip the potatoes to encourage even browning and bake for an additional 10 to 15 minutes, until golden brown and slightly crispy. Remove from the oven and set aside.

3. In a 10-inch cast-iron skillet, melt the remaining 1 tablespoon bacon fat over medium-high heat. Add the kale, garlic, and remaining ½ teaspoon salt. Sauté the kale until it wilts and the water has evaporated from the pan, about 5 minutes.

4. Set the broiler to high and position a rack 6 inches below the broiler.

5. Spread the kale over the potatoes in an even layer and top with the shredded mozzarella. Broil for 2 minutes, rotate the pan, and broil for an additional minute. When the cheese is fully melted, bubbly, and golden brown with crispy edges, remove the baking sheet from the oven.

6. Assemble the tacos: Scoop the cheesy filling into each warm tortilla. Serve warm with the hot sauce, salsa, lime, and cilantro on the side.

MULTI-SEED HERB CRACKERS
with Thyme and Rosemary

This recipe combines a flavorful mixture of seeds with abundant fresh garden herbs to create a versatile, filling cracker. They are excellent for snacking or to serve as appetizers with your favorite spread. We always keep a large supply on hand in the refrigerator, and we often serve them for special dinners. Try them with Classic Chicken Liver Pâté with Gordon Apples (page 329), Creamy Baked Sunchoke Dip (page 126), or Carrot-Harissa Hummus (page 120), or smear with butter and a spoonful of salty salmon roe for a delicious and nutrient-dense treat! Note that I recommend soaking the seeds in this recipe for 12 hours before you make this recipe.

MAKES
30 TO 40 LARGE CRACKERS

2 cups raw golden or brown flaxseeds

2 cups raw white or black sesame seeds

2 cups raw hulled pumpkin seeds

2 tablespoons fine sea salt

½ cup minced shallot (about 2 large shallots)

1 tablespoon minced garlic (3 cloves)

¼ teaspoon ground cayenne pepper

2 teaspoons minced fresh thyme leaves or 1 teaspoon dried

2 teaspoons minced fresh rosemary leaves or 1 teaspoon dried

A few pinches flaked sea salt, to garnish

1. In a medium bowl, combine the flaxseeds with 4 cups of water. Stir, cover with a cloth or lid, and set aside for 12 hours, or until the flaxseeds are suspended in the thickened liquid. In a separate large bowl, combine the sesame seeds, pumpkin seeds, 1 tablespoon of the salt, and enough water to cover the seeds by 2 inches. Stir, cover with a cloth or lid, and set aside to soak for 12 hours.

2. Drain the sesame and pumpkin seeds in a fine-mesh sieve and rinse well. To the bowl with the flaxseeds, stir in the shallot, garlic, the remaining 1 tablespoon salt, and the cayenne. Place half the mixture in a food processor and process until some of the seeds are broken, about 1 minute. Transfer to a large bowl and repeat with the remaining flaxseeds. To the bowl, add the sesame and pumpkin seeds, thyme, and rosemary and stir to combine.

3. Line five 15 × 15-inch dehydrator trays with nonstick sheets and spread about 2 cups of the seed mixture onto each tray. Using an offset spatula, spread the seed mixture into a ¼-inch-thick patty. Sprinkle with flaked sea salt and set the temperature to 150°F. Dehydrate for 12 hours. Carefully peel away the liner from each tray and flip the crackers. Continue to dehydrate until completely dry and crunchy, about an additional 6 hours. Alternatively, spread the mixture over a large, Silpat-lined sheet pan and bake at 175°F for 4 to 5 hours, until crispy and set.

4. Break the crackers into large pieces. Place in a well-sealed, airtight container and store at room temperature for up to 1 week, in the refrigerator for up to 2 months, or in the freezer for up to 6 months.

FRESH ELDERBERRY SYRUP

MAKES
ABOUT 1 CUP

Elderberries cooked into a syrup are deeply delicious and are used to boost immunity, especially during cold and flu season. At Apricot Lane Farms, we integrate California native western blue elderberries (*Sambucus nigra* ssp. *Caerulea*) into our riparian habitat, an area important for balancing wild plants and animals with the cultivated soil and pastureland of the farm. It includes twenty-four acres of a natural habitat buffer throughout and has grown from just 60 species of native plants when the farm began in 2011 to now over 250! The riparian habitat is critical to the life cycles of monarchs, amphibians, barn owls, and badgers; provides stopping points for egrets and other birds on migration routes; and nurtures native trees and shrubs. Ruby and Lucas, of our habitat restoration team, collect ripe elderberries from this area with our culinary team to turn into elderberry syrup.

This recipe is best made using native western blue elderberries (*Sambucus nigra* ssp. *Caerulea*), black elderberries (*Sambucus nigra*), or the native eastern elderberry (*Sambucus canadensis*). If you are collecting sustainably from the wild, be sure to correctly identify this woody shrub that can be confused with poisonous imposters. Elderberries should be harvested when they are fully ripe, and cooked before being consumed. They will have a very dark purple to black color, or in the case of the western blue species, they will develop a naturally occurring dusty yeast coating when ripe. To harvest the berries, clip the whole cluster from the shrub in the morning. Soak the clusters briefly in cool water, drain, and then freeze the whole clusters to make it easier to destem the berries—or simply pluck them fresh if you have a small amount. Use immediately, store in the refrigerator for up to 3 days, or dehydrate them at 95°F for 12 to 14 hours. The syrup is delicious poured over a snow cone, stirred into club soda, blended into smoothies, or eaten by the spoonful.

2 cups fresh elderberries

¼ cup mild raw honey

1. In a 2-quart pot, heat the elderberries and 1 cup of water over medium heat until the berries burst. Raise the heat to bring the mixture to a boil, and then reduce the heat to a simmer. Cook, uncovered, until the berries turn an opaque purple and the cooking liquid is the color of red wine, about 20 minutes. The aroma will be fragrant and floral.

2. Remove from the heat and strain the mixture through a fine-mesh sieve into a heatproof measuring cup. There should be about ⅔ cup of strained liquid. Compost the cooked berries or blend them into a smoothie. Let the liquid cool to at least 110°F to preserve the integrity of the raw honey before adding and stirring to dissolve.

3. Pour the syrup into a clean, lidded glass container. Store in the refrigerator for up to 6 months. The syrup may ferment in the refrigerator over time, but this should not cause alarm. Consume 1 tablespoon per day for adults or 1 teaspoon of unfermented syrup per day for kids during flu season.

DRIED ELDERBERRY SYRUP

This version of elderberry syrup can be made in any season. The dried berries lend a concentrated flavor when cooked over a low boil, and the yield will vary depending upon the species and quality of the berry.

MAKES
¾ TO 1 CUP

1 cup dried elderberries

¼ cup mild raw honey

1. Cook the elderberries in 4 cups of water according to the instructions on page 154.

2. Remove from the heat and strain the berries through a fine-mesh sieve into a heatproof measuring cup, pushing on them to extract all the liquid. There should be ½ to ¾ cup of strained liquid. Compost the cooked berries or blend them into a smoothie. Let the liquid cool to at least 110°F to preserve the integrity of the raw honey before adding and stirring to dissolve.

3. Store and serve according to the instructions on page 154.

INFUSED HONEYS

Raw honey (page 27) is a living food with many health-enhancing properties. Its color, taste, aroma, and texture vary greatly and are unique to the type(s) of flowers a honeybee frequents to collect nectar. The intricate process of converting this sugary liquid into a thick, golden, and bioactive food teeming with microorganisms is nothing short of fascinating! It is a cooperative effort that begins with worker bees that extract flower nectar using their long, tube-shaped tongues. The outcome is a concentrated wonder of nature that, when harvested sustainably, also makes our lives a little sweeter.

Years ago, I was given a special jar of raw honey that was packed with the concentrated essence and medicinal benefits of lemon balm. It made such an impression that I have been making versions of it ever since, using fragrant dried herbs grown on our farm. You can collect lavender and lemon balm and dry it yourself or purchase it in bulk from herbal apothecaries (see Resources, page 392). Both of these variations are strongly flavored and excellent when stirred into hot teas, blended into yogurt or smoothies, drizzled over buttered toast, or made into Almond Avocado Oil Cake with Meyer Lemon Curd (page 359). Use a mild honey such as clover or a wildflower blend as your base. The mixture can crystalize during the colder months, which can make it difficult to strain. To remedy this, pour warm water into a deep bowl and place the jar inside the bowl, making sure the lid stays above the water line. Set aside for 15 minutes and then stir to break up the honey crystals. For a more delicate infusion, dilute the strained honey by adding ½ cup of additional plain raw honey and stirring to combine.

LEMON BALM–INFUSED HONEY

MAKES A GENEROUS ¾ CUP

Fresh lemon balm (*Melissa officinalis*) has a pleasantly bright, slightly minty, and citrus-forward aroma and flavor. When dried, however, it can become brittle and more subtle in fragrance. This recipe uses a generous amount of dried leaves to flavor the honey. Because the leaves break easily when stirred, fine leaf particles may slip through the sieve into your strained honey. For me, the leaves are barely noticeable and worth the trade-off! But if it troubles you, use a fine muslin or cheesecloth to line the sieve and allow plenty of straining time. This honey can be used to sweeten teas and desserts but is a wonderful addition to roast chicken or pork or savory sauces.

¾ cup lightly packed dried lemon balm leaves

1 cup mild raw honey

Infuse, strain, and store the honey according to the instructions on page 158.

RECIPE CONTINUES

LAVENDER-INFUSED HONEY

MAKES A GENEROUS ¾ CUP

Lavender is a beautiful landscape plant that grows easily in our climate and thrives in our well-drained soil. It is an excellent bee attractor, and thanks to the generous sunny weather, our Goodwin Creek and French lavender (*Lavandula dentata*) are often in bloom. In the early days of the farm (and still today), I pick the brightest purple and heavily scented fresh lavender flowers and bring them inside to make cheerful bouquets, or I rinse and dry them to store. Although we don't grow it, the hardy English lavender (*Lavandula angustifolia*) is a more common species in colder climates. This infusion captures the calming effect of lavender.

½ cup dried lavender flowers   **1 cup mild raw honey**

In a 1-pint jar, stir together the lavender and honey until combined. Cover and place in a cool place away from sunlight to infuse for a minimum of 2 weeks. Strain through a fine-mesh sieve or cheesecloth into a clean half-pint jar. Cover and store at room temperature.

MINERAL GOMASIO

Gomasio is a Japanese low-sodium seasoning blend that is traditionally used to enhance the flavoring of rice dishes. It is always made with sesame seeds, salt, and sometimes seaweed, but we love to incorporate our stinging nettle too. Stinging nettle is a common wild plant that grows in damp, fertile areas and is especially tender in the spring. It has been used medicinally since ancient Egyptian times and likely adds health benefits, in addition to a flavor twist, to this umami-packed seasoning. Sustainably harvest and dry your own nettles by following the instructions for Powdered Green Stevia (page 160). Using thick gloves, harvest about twenty-four 8-inch nettle stems for this recipe and dry at 125°F for 6 hours, until the leaves are brittle. You can also purchase organic whole-leaf dried nettle online (see Resources, page 392) or look for it along with the kelp and dulse in health food stores. One of my favorite snacks is to cut creamy-ripe avocados in half, remove the pit, and fill the hole with avocado oil before sprinkling with a generous amount of Mineral Gomasio and a pinch of flaked sea salt. Spoon it right out of the skin, or as John likes to do, add a squeeze of lemon.

MAKES
¾ CUP

½ cup raw white sesame seeds

1 tablespoon dried organic onion flakes

½ cup loosely packed dried nettle leaves

1 teaspoon kelp granules

2 teaspoons dulse flakes

½ teaspoon flaked sea salt

1. In a small skillet, lightly toast the sesame seeds and onion flakes over medium heat, stirring occasionally, until the sesame seeds become golden, about 5 minutes. Remove from the heat and set aside.

2. In a spice grinder, process the nettle leaves to a coarse powder, 2 to 5 seconds, and transfer to a small bowl. Add the warm sesame seeds and onion flakes, kelp, dulse, and salt to the grinder cup, and pulse 2 or 3 times. The mixture will be coarse with some whole sesame seeds. Combine with the powdered nettle and stir until combined. Let the gomasio cool completely.

3. Store in an airtight container at room temperature for up to 6 months. It is best used as a finishing salt and can live in a small shaker on your table.

POWDERED GREEN STEVIA

MAKES
ABOUT
3 CUPS

When I eliminated refined sweeteners from my diet, I discovered stevia, a natural but intensely sweet-tasting plant that has been used to flavor teas and beverages for hundreds of years. Sometimes affectionately referred to as "sweet leaf," it is up to three hundred times sweeter than sugar but does not affect blood sugar levels. Most store-bought stevia products are off-putting to my palate since they have a synthetic, chemical undertone. The pure, vibrant flavor of this magical fresh herb is much different, however, and I was excited to try growing it. *Stevia rebaudiana* originates from Brazil and Paraguay and contains the most intensely flavored leaves. Once dried and made into a powder, it has a dark green color. I like to use it in smoothies, to help sweeten granola or pancake batter, to balance acidity in tomato sauces, or even to add complexity to taco meat seasoning.

If you'd like to grow stevia in your own garden, check with your local garden center or look for plants online. They overwinter in zones 8 or higher but will act as an annual in colder climates. Stevia plants require full sun and well-drained soil, both of which are abundant here in California. We must supplement dry summers with additional water, though, since stevia appreciates consistent moisture. Stevia is one of our favorite things to share when showing people around the garden, as they are so surprised at how sweet a leaf can be! Beaudie and most kids love to know where the plant is for the occasional sweet treat. It is best to harvest and dry before it flowers and bitterness sets in during autumn—you can store the whole leaves in jars. To keep fresh, process the leaves into a powder as necessary using a spice grinder or a food processor, and sift lightly before transferring to a container. This method is also excellent for processing other culinary and medicinal herbs!

3 pounds fresh stevia stems, about 9 inches long

1. Remove any dried, off-colored, or dead leaves from the stevia and compost them. Submerge the stems in a shallow pan of water and gently massage, releasing any soil or small insects. Drain the water and spread the stems over a clean towel to drain completely.

2. To avoid mold, gather the stems into small, ¼-inch bundles. Make sure the ends of the stems align and tie the bundle together with a piece of twine using a tight knot. Leave about 4 inches on each end of twine.

3. Tie each bundle to a drying rack or line placed in a well-ventilated location out of direct sun. Leave 5 to 6 inches between bundles for airflow. Dry the bundles until the leaves crumble between your fingers and are no longer pliable, 7 to 10 days. Alternatively, dehydrate at 95°F for about 12 hours.

4. Once the stevia is fully dry, remove the bundles from the rack and reserve the twine for another use. Lay the stems on a baking sheet and remove the leaves. Save the stems for steeping in tea if desired and place the dried leaves in a jar.

5. Working in small batches, fill a spice grinder or food processor with some of the dried leaves and pulse a few times to reduce the volume. Add a second batch of leaves and pulse to a fine powder; a good rule is to process double the volume of the grinding cup. If the stevia feels warm to the touch, let the grinder cool before continuing, to preserve the herb's delicate flavor. Transfer the powder to a clean glass jar. Store the remaining leaves in a sealed jar at room temperature until you're ready to process the next batch of stevia powder.

6. Store for up to 6 months at room temperature.

THERAPEUTIC USES
OF PLANTS ON THE FARM

·········

There is written evidence that for at least five thousand years, humans have relied upon the therapeutic value of plants for promoting health and preventing and treating illness. The art and science of this traditional practice is known as herbal medicine. Although there are many unique practices within one country or region, their shared principle is using herbs to stimulate the body's innate healing power in combination with lifestyle and dietary considerations. Ayurveda and Traditional Chinese Medicine are just two well-known examples of practices that use herbs to prevent disease, heal the body, and nourish the spirit. Up to 75 percent of the world's population currently uses traditional healing practices like these to address their primary health needs.

I've used herbs to boost my immune and digestive systems and treat inflammation for decades, and so when we moved to the farm I was excited about the potential of the native and nonnative plants growing here. Now we collect chamomile (*Matricaria chamomilla*) each summer and enjoy using it to calm our body and mind in an evening tea—it is especially delicious when used fresh. In the spring, we gather dandelion root (*Taraxacum officinale*) so that we can use it in a tea after a large meal or a day of indulgence. We turn to thyme leaf tea (*Thymus vulgaris*) when any of us begin showing signs of a cold. Tea made from the narrowleaf plantain (*Plantago lanceolata*) helps with respiratory challenges and can be crushed and applied to a cut while in the field to relieve insect bites, swelling, or redness. When I was pregnant, I used to make raspberry leaf tea to strengthen the uterus. And come autumn, I look forward to collecting native rose hips that grow by the pond for a boost of vitamin C in the colder months. All these plants have strengthened my relationship to the land and fortified my spirit through our unique seasonal changes.

Our team has since welcomed and integrated more wild and ornamental species that not only have medicinal properties but also contribute to the overall diversification and harmonization of the farm. For example, we have a vigorous patch of nettles (*Urtica dioica*); they're delicious and fortifying in Mineral Gomasio (page 159), but we also steep them in an insect-repelling "tea" that is applied to the foliage of our vegetables and herbs grown for the farmers market or fermented and used as a fertilizing supplement when incorporated into our compost. Just as herbal medicine considers the body in totality, plants used in a biodynamic system are not always intended for culinary harvest. These are integrated into our market garden, hedgerows, and orchard pollinator rows, and amplify the health of the farm as a whole organism. Chamomile, valerian, chrysanthemum, borage, butterfly pea flower, lemon balm, and lavender have the potential to provide health-supportive medicinal attributes to the farm's stewards and customers, and boost the health of our natural environment by attracting beneficial pollinators and building soil health and its microbiome in unique ways.

Using plants and herbs to nurture the overall health of a farm is a core principle of biodynamics and central to our method of farming. In 1924, Rudolf Steiner pioneered biodynamics to bring chemically treated, depleted soils back to life. Like herbal medicine, this alternative practice is based upon both physical and spiritual principles. Biodynamic herbal preparations use fermented plants and other natural methods to enliven the soil and compost, supplement plant health, and improve food quality. Some of the benefits include increased disease, pest, and drought resistance; more complex fruit flavors; and tastier leafy greens—and where there is flavor, nutrition is sure to follow! It is a science both ancient and also in its infancy, and we are continuously improving through observing what works and learning all we can about microbiology. Thanks to these biodynamic strategies, our organic and chemical-free approach, managed intensive grazing, cover cropping, a full-scale vermicomposting facility, and a native habitat restoration project, the farm is buzzing with life more than ever before!

Our soil health is carefully stewarded by Shawn Greenbaum, director of Soil and Plant Fertility. He uses biodynamic practices that nurture the totality of the farm, similar to how herbal medicine boosts connections between the human mind, body, and spirit. Treating the ecosystem as a whole is what makes biodynamics an alternative agriculture, much in the same way as herbal medicine is considered by most to be an unorthodox approach to health care. Although at times it seems like the more we discover, the less we know, we keep striving to provide a farming system that both enriches our land and supports the delicious and nutritious food that we grow and cook.

Chapter Six

SUMMER
SUN'S
ABUNDANCE

WHEN DAYLIGHT LINGERS WELL INTO THE EVENING, WE CELEBRATE THE SPOILS of summer with outdoor meals at the farm. The rewards are plenty for the long days leading up to this time that our team has spent weeding, watering, and tending. And the work continues—the lengthy list of tasks that accompanies summer amplifies our appetites! We enjoy the pleasure of eating sun-warmed tomatoes from our hand like apples. Twilight is an invitation to light the grill or wood-fired oven and savor the primal smokiness of plump eggplant and its tender, creamy flesh. The brightness of gazpacho spiked with the sweetness of loquat is a fresh and welcome distraction from our plentiful zucchini crop. Summer squashes find their way into savory fritters and piquant salads, with nary a dent in our stash! Together with okra, peppers, and green beans, the ingredients of this season are an endless source of creativity as we hustle to offer this extravagant abundance to an eager market.

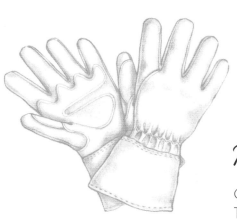

Recipes

Ginger-Buttered Tomatoes with Turmeric

Roasted Picnic Pepper and Tomato Panzanella Salad

Corn Chowder with Jalapeño Pork Crumble

Summer Corn Salad with Tomato Raisins, Basil, and Chèvre

Marinated Picnic Peppers Stuffed with Chorizo and Manchego Cheese

Zucchini Fritters with Lemon-Cucumber Yogurt Sauce

Blistered Okra with Ginger Vinaigrette and Fresno Sea Salt

Prosciutto-Wrapped Crostini with Eggplant Caponata and Fresh Farmer's Cheese

Wood-Fired Eggplant Puree with Crispy Spiced Lamb, Raisins, and Almonds

Fried Dark Star Zucchini with Roasted Red Bell Pepper Sauce

Grilled Green Chopped Salad with Pine Nuts and Chèvre

Blistered Haricots Verts and Fennel Salad with Chopped Egg Vinaigrette

Zucchini Salad with Tahini and Date Dressing

GINGER-BUTTERED TOMATOES
with Turmeric

Although sun-ripened cherry tomatoes need little to heighten their juicy-sweet character, this simple recipe provides a quick way to elevate your enjoyment of them just a bit more. Use firm but ripe cherry tomatoes in an assortment of colors and shapes—they will look like little jewels on the plate! The butter is best heated shortly before serving. You can cook down any leftovers and make a delicious sauce or blend them into a flavorful tomato soup.

SERVES 4

4 tablespoons unsalted butter

1½ teaspoons peeled and finely minced ginger (½-inch knob)

1 tablespoon minced garlic (3 cloves)

2 tablespoons minced shallot (1 small shallot)

2 teaspoons minced jalapeño pepper (1 small pepper)

¼ teaspoon ground turmeric

3 cups halved cherry tomatoes, room temperature (about 2 pounds)

1½ teaspoons fine sea salt

2 tablespoons chopped fresh parsley leaves

½ teaspoon champagne vinegar

8 slices A Crusty Hearth-Style Sourdough Boule (page 59), cut into triangles

1. In a medium skillet, melt the butter over medium heat and add the ginger, garlic, shallot, jalapeño, and turmeric. Cook, stirring occasionally, until the mixture simmers, 3 to 4 minutes.

2. Add the tomato halves to the skillet and continue cooking until a thick and chunky sauce forms, about 12 minutes. Sprinkle with the salt, parsley, and vinegar, and fold to combine. Turn off the heat but leave the skillet on the burner to keep warm.

3. Toast the bread and top the slices with a large spoonful of the warm buttered tomatoes. Serve immediately.

ROASTED PICNIC PEPPER AND TOMATO PANZANELLA SALAD

This Tuscan-style salad with red wine vinaigrette and toasted sourdough is a wonderful way to showcase summer abundance. Though this particular iteration is delicious, it is a loose formula that can be adjusted seasonally. Have fun using a variety of seasonal vegetables, cheeses, and herbs! If you cannot source picnic peppers, substitute chopped roasted red peppers instead. In the winter, we like roasted beets and butternut squash with shaved pecorino and fried sage. Come spring, try baby carrots, artichoke hearts, and shaved radishes with goat cheese. Or when summer squash is abundant, grill it with sweet red onions and combine with dollops of lemon ricotta and fresh mint! Although you may prepare the dressing a few days in advance, this salad is best served at room temperature and tossed just before serving.

SERVES
6 TO 8

VINAIGRETTE

2 tablespoons minced shallots
(about 1 small shallot)

1 tablespoon Fermented Mustard
(page 88)

¼ cup red wine vinegar

1 teaspoon mild raw honey

2 teaspoons chopped fresh oregano
leaves or ¾ teaspoon dried

½ teaspoon fine sea salt

¼ teaspoon freshly ground black
peppercorns

3 tablespoons cold-pressed
extra-virgin olive oil

1. Make the vinaigrette: In a small nonreactive bowl, combine the shallot, mustard, vinegar, honey, oregano, salt, pepper, and oil. Whisk until well combined and set aside at room temperature or cover and place in the refrigerator for 1 to 2 days. The dressing will naturally separate and should be whisked again before tossing with the salad.

2. Make the salad: Place the tomatoes in a colander and set over a bowl. Sprinkle with ½ teaspoon of the salt and set aside to drain.

3. Preheat the oven to 375°F and position one rack in the middle and another 6 inches above.

4. Line two large baking sheets with parchment paper. In a medium bowl, toss the peppers with 3 tablespoons of the oil, 1 teaspoon of the salt, and ½ teaspoon of the pepper. Spread the peppers over one of the prepared baking sheets. Using the same bowl, combine the bread, the remaining 3 tablespoons oil, the remaining 1½ teaspoons salt, and the remaining ½ teaspoon pepper. Toss until the bread is thoroughly coated and spread evenly over the other baking sheet.

RECIPE AND INGREDIENTS CONTINUE

SALAD

2 cups cherry tomatoes, halved if small or quartered if large (about 1 pound)

3 teaspoons fine sea salt

2 pounds picnic peppers (about 30 peppers)

¼ cup plus 2 tablespoons cold-pressed extra-virgin olive oil

1 teaspoon freshly ground black peppercorns

5½ cups 1-inch-cubed sourdough bread (pages 54 or 59) (about ¾ pound)

8 large basil leaves

1 cup fresh mozzarella, diced or torn into ¾- to 1-inch pieces (8 ounces)

5. Place the bread on the middle rack and the peppers on the rack above. Toast the bread for 15 to 20 minutes, stirring at least once, until an even golden brown. Remove from the oven and set aside to cool. Bake the peppers for 25 minutes, or until they are slightly blistered. Remove from the oven and let them cool to room temperature. Remove the stems if desired.

6. In a large bowl, combine the tomatoes, roasted peppers, toasted bread, and dressing and tear the basil leaves over top. Mix thoroughly and transfer to a large serving bowl or platter. Garnish with the fresh mozzarella and serve.

CORN CHOWDER
with Jalapeño Pork Crumble

SERVES
4 TO 6

This chowder perfectly highlights the fleeting sweet summer corn, but it also begs to be enjoyed in the colder months. When farmers markets are spilling with freshly picked plump ears, stock your freezer to make this hearty recipe any time of the year. You can also freeze the shucks and naked corn cobs to add to broth later, like Chicken Stock (page 76), or compost or feed them to the chickens. Blending some of the kernels into the soup base intensifies the flavor for a sublime, corn-y experience! We grow a variety of delicious potatoes, including German Butterball and jewel-colored Adirondack Red, that can be substituted for the fingerlings. Once refrigerated, the chowder will gel and become easily scoopable but will liquify again once reheated. The Apricot Lane Farms Pork Sausage (page 298) or spicy Chorizo (page 297) are excellent substitutions for the ground pork!

PORK CRUMBLE

1 pound ground pork

¼ cup minced jalapeño pepper (2 large peppers)

2 teaspoons minced garlic (2 cloves)

1½ teaspoons fine sea salt

½ teaspoon freshly ground black peppercorns

½ teaspoon garlic powder

½ teaspoon onion powder

½ teaspoon ground coriander

SOUP

3 tablespoons strained pastured bacon fat or unrefined avocado oil

2 cups small-diced yellow onion (2 large onions)

2 tablespoons minced garlic (6 cloves)

¼ cup small-diced fresh Fresno chile pepper (about 3 peppers)

5 cups fresh or frozen sweet corn kernels (6 to 7 ears corn)

1. Make the pork crumble: Line a plate with paper towels. In a medium bowl, combine the pork, jalapeño, garlic, salt, pepper, garlic powder, onion powder, and coriander. Mix with a spoon until thoroughly combined. In a 10-inch cast-iron skillet over medium-high heat, cook half the pork, breaking up large pieces with a spoon until crispy, 7 to 10 minutes. Drain on the lined plate and repeat with the remaining pork.

2. Make the soup: In a 3-quart pot, melt the bacon fat over medium heat. Sauté the onion, garlic, and chile peppers, stirring occasionally, until the onion is translucent, 5 to 7 minutes. Add 4 cups of the corn kernels and cook until fragrant, about 10 minutes. Reduce the heat to low and add the salt, pepper, garlic powder, onion powder, and thyme. Stir until well combined and remove from the heat.

3. Add the coconut milk and cooked vegetables to the pitcher of a blender. Blend on high until the mixture is smooth, 2 to 3 minutes. Return the mixture to the pot and set over medium-high heat. Add the stock, potatoes, bell pepper, celery, and the remaining 1 cup corn kernels and bring the mixture to a boil, stirring frequently, until it thickens and coats the back of a wooden spoon. Reduce the heat to low and continue cooking until the potatoes are tender, about 15 minutes.

RECIPE AND INGREDIENTS CONTINUE

5 teaspoons fine sea salt

1 teaspoon freshly ground black peppercorns

2 teaspoons garlic powder

2 teaspoons onion powder

2 teaspoons fresh thyme leaves or 1 teaspoon dried

1 (13.5-ounce) can full-fat coconut milk

2 cups Chicken Stock (page 76)

1 cup small-diced French Fingerling potatoes (about ½ pound)

1⅔ cups small-diced red bell pepper (about 1⅔ medium peppers)

1⅔ cups small-diced celery (5 stalks)

GARNISH

¼ cup sliced fresh chives

¼ cup minced fresh cilantro leaves

6 lime wedges (1 lime)

4. To serve: Ladle the chowder into bowls and serve hot topped with the sausage crumble, chives, cilantro, and the lime wedges on the side. Let the chowder cool and store, covered, in the refrigerator for up to 1 week or portion into individual servings and freeze for up to 6 months.

SUMMER CORN SALAD
with Tomato Raisins, Basil, and Chèvre

Our fresh corn is known for its sweetness and begins arriving at the market when the days are long and the sun is hot! The corn harvest feels like it passes in a blink, but Beaudie makes fun use of the growing season while chasing his friends up and down the corn rows! Since every corn silk thread must be pollinated to fill the cob, the kids serve as human pollinators by shaking the pollen, all while having a good time! Source tender ears that have been picked shortly before being sold to avoid any starchiness that may otherwise dull the flavors of this salad. Use vacuum-packed or oil-cured and drained sundried tomatoes if you do not have Tomato Raisins (page 35). Pair with Spice-Rubbed Pastured Pork Ribs (page 291) and Potato Salad with Preserved Lemon and Mint (page 115).

SERVES
6 TO 8

BALSAMIC VINAIGRETTE

1 teaspoon minced garlic (1 clove)

1 tablespoon Fermented Mustard (page 88)

¼ cup balsamic vinegar

1¼ teaspoons fine sea salt

⅛ teaspoon freshly cracked black peppercorns

¼ cup cold-pressed extra-virgin olive oil

CORN SALAD

7 cups fresh corn kernels (about 9 ears corn)

1½ cups minced green bell pepper (about 2 small peppers)

½ cup small-diced red onion (about ½ large onion)

1 cup Tomato Raisins (page 35) (about 30 raisins)

¾ cup pitted and halved Kalamata olives

3 tablespoons finely chopped fresh parsley leaves

3 tablespoons chiffonade-cut basil leaves (6 to 8 large leaves)

¼ cup crumbled chèvre (2 ounces)

1. Make the balsamic vinaigrette: In a small food processor, combine the garlic, mustard, vinegar, salt, and pepper. Pulse to combine for 10 seconds. With the blades running, slowly stream in the oil to emulsify.

2. Make the salad: In a large bowl, combine the corn, peppers, onion, tomato raisins, olives, parsley, basil, and vinaigrette and mix with a spoon. Transfer the salad to a large serving platter and garnish with the crumbled chèvre. This salad is best eaten at room temperature the day it is made, or cover and chill for up to 2 hours before serving.

MARINATED PICNIC PEPPERS
Stuffed with Chorizo and Manchego Cheese

Stuffed picnic peppers are bite-size party pleasers in a festive spectrum of orange, yellow, and red. The pepper's sweet and fruity flavor is a huge hit with children at the Farm School, our one-room schoolhouse, and is also a perfect pairing with our spicy Chorizo (page 297)! When combined with Manchego cheese and baked, the peppers' blistered appearance and savory aroma ooze with temptation. Choose a young Manchego (aged three months) for a soft melt and avoid the drier, saltier, and more piquant flavor of an aged cheese. Firm peppers that are uniform in shape and size are best and should appear slightly inflated for ease of stuffing. If preparing and refrigerating a day in advance, bake just before serving and add an additional 10 minutes to the cooking time.

MAKES
ABOUT 15
APPETIZERS

1 pound assorted picnic peppers (about 15 medium peppers)

¾ cup shredded young Manchego cheese (3½ ounces)

1⅓ cups cooked and crumbled Chorizo (page 297)

1 tablespoon plus 1½ teaspoons chopped fresh oregano leaves or 2 teaspoons dried

2 tablespoons cold-pressed extra-virgin olive oil

1 teaspoon lime zest (½ medium lime)

2 tablespoons fresh lime juice (1 medium lime)

½ teaspoon fine sea salt

1. With a paring knife, slice off and compost the stem end of a pepper. Slice the pepper from the top to the pointy end and gently open it with your fingers. Remove and compost the white spongy membrane along with any seeds. Place the cored pepper in a bowl and repeat with the remaining peppers.

2. In a small bowl, toss together the cheese and cooked chorizo until well combined. Fill each pepper with 1½ to 2 tablespoons of the mixture, pressing firmly to close the pepper. To prevent a messy bake, do not overstuff. Place the stuffed peppers in an 8 × 10-inch shatterproof casserole dish.

3. In a small bowl, whisk together the oregano, oil, lime zest, lime juice, and salt. Drizzle over the peppers and massage each pepper to coat. Arrange the peppers seam side up and transfer to the refrigerator. Marinate for 2 hours before baking.

4. Preheat the oven to 375°F and position a rack in the middle.

5. Place the cold casserole dish in the preheated oven and bake for 30 to 35 minutes, rotating halfway through, until the peppers sizzle, soften, and blister. Remove from the oven and let them cool for 10 minutes. Serve immediately.

ZUCCHINI FRITTERS
with Lemon-Cucumber Yogurt Sauce

These satisfying fritters carry the delicate and nutty scent of virgin coconut oil, which is complemented by a chunky and refreshing yogurt, cucumber, and herb sauce.

MAKES
12 FRITTERS

LEMON-CUCUMBER YOGURT SAUCE

½ cup Greek yogurt

½ cup seeded finely diced English cucumber (about ¼ cucumber)

1½ teaspoons lemon zest (½ large lemon)

1½ teaspoons fresh lemon juice

2 tablespoons finely minced shallot (1 small shallot)

1 tablespoon finely chopped fresh dill fronds, stems removed (about 4 sprigs)

¼ teaspoon minced garlic (about ½ small clove)

½ teaspoon fine sea salt

⅛ teaspoon freshly ground black peppercorns

ZUCCHINI FRITTERS

3 cups lightly packed shredded zucchini (2 to 3 small zucchini)

1 teaspoon fine sea salt

1 large egg

¼ cup finely minced red onion (about ¼ large onion)

1 tablespoon minced fresh chives

1 tablespoon minced fresh mint leaves

1 tablespoon minced fresh parsley leaves

½ teaspoon minced garlic (about ½ large clove)

3 tablespoons sprouted wheat flour

3 cups virgin coconut oil

1. Make the lemon-cucumber yogurt sauce: In a small bowl, combine the yogurt, cucumber, lemon zest, lemon juice, shallot, dill, garlic, salt, and pepper. Mix until well combined, cover with a plate or plastic wrap, and chill until ready to serve.

2. Make the zucchini fritters: Place a colander inside a medium bowl. Scoop the shredded zucchini into the colander and spread it in an even layer. Sprinkle the salt over the zucchini and set aside for 10 minutes. Firmly squeeze the zucchini in your hands over the colander to remove the water. The zucchini will be limp and only slightly damp when you are finished squeezing. Transfer to a bowl and add the egg, onion, chives, mint, parsley, and garlic. Combine with a fork until the egg is evenly distributed. Sprinkle the flour over the mixture and fold the batter until combined—do not overwork.

3. In a 2-quart pot, heat the oil to between 315°F and 325°F, using an instant-read thermometer. Place a clean baking sheet next to the stovetop and nestle a wire rack inside. Carefully scoop four or five 1-tablespoon portions of the zucchini mixture, form them into an oval shape with your fingers, and carefully dunk into the hot oil. Fry each fritter until the surface is golden brown and the inside is cooked through, about 2 minutes on each side. Remove from the oil with tongs or a slotted spoon and transfer to the wire rack. Sprinkle with salt and repeat with the remaining batter.

4. Serve the fritters immediately with the cold yogurt sauce.

INGREDIENT TIP: *Virgin Coconut Oil*

Virgin coconut oil is an unrefined fat with a low smoke point that is best heated between 315°F and 325°F to avoid discoloration and off flavors. After you use the oil to make these fritters, strain it through a fine-mesh sieve, discard the browned bits, and cool it to use for another round of fritters or a small batch of Root Vegetable Chips (page 369).

BLISTERED OKRA
with Ginger Vinaigrette and Fresno Sea Salt

I lived much of my adolescent and young adult life in Atlanta, where okra is a popular vegetable, and so I appreciate a recipe that highlights its unique but often polarizing flavor and texture. Roasting the pods whole to a blistered finish will convert even the most suspicious eaters, especially when the okra is dressed and served in a tangy, gingery vinaigrette. Although the dressing can be made in advance and stored in the refrigerator, the okra should be roasted the day of serving. Okra does not keep well once harvested and is best cooked right away. Choose small, tender pods with bright taut skin. You should be able to easily snap fresh okra in half.

SERVES
4 TO 6

2 pounds whole okra, 2 to 4 inches long

¼ cup cold-pressed extra-virgin olive oil

1 teaspoon fine sea salt

1 tablespoon peeled and finely minced ginger (1 × 1-inch knob)

1 tablespoon minced garlic (3 cloves)

2 teaspoons lime zest (1 medium lime)

1 tablespoon lime juice (½ medium lime)

1 tablespoon chickpea or white miso

2 tablespoons rice vinegar

¼ cup fresh orange juice

1 teaspoon mild raw honey

3 tablespoons torn or chiffonade-cut fresh basil leaves

2 tablespoons torn or chiffonade-cut fresh mint leaves

½ teaspoon Fresno Chile Sea Salt (page 95)

1. Preheat the oven to 375°F and position a rack in the middle.

2. In a medium bowl, toss the okra with the oil and salt. Spread onto a large baking sheet and place in the oven. Roast for 30 to 40 minutes, until the okra blisters and turns an olive green. Remove from the oven and let cool for 10 minutes.

3. In the pitcher of a blender, place the ginger, garlic, lime zest, lime juice, miso, vinegar, orange juice, and honey. Blend on high until the dressing appears creamy but thin and slightly chunky, 30 to 45 seconds.

4. In a medium bowl, combine the warm okra and vinaigrette and toss to coat. Add the basil, mint, and flavored salt and stir to combine. Transfer to a serving bowl and serve warm.

PROSCIUTTO-WRAPPED CROSTINI
with Eggplant Caponata and Fresh Farmer's Cheese

One evening while prepping dinner, I sliced into the first of our recent crop of eggplants and threw a raw piece in my mouth. For the first time in all my years, I tasted a sweet eggplant and was floored! Eggplant is typically so bitter it can't be eaten raw, and I certainly had never experienced it as sweet—such is the difference that healthy soil can make! Try it alongside over-easy eggs and use the crostini to soak up the yolky goodness, or try the caponata solo as a topping for a wood-fired pizza. The caponata will last 3 to 4 days in the refrigerator or up to 6 months in the freezer.

MAKES
10 CROSTINI

CAPONATA

3 tablespoons cold-pressed extra-virgin olive oil

2 cups peeled small-diced eggplant (½ medium eggplant)

¾ teaspoon fine sea salt

½ cup small-diced yellow onion (about ½ large onion)

½ cup small-diced red bell pepper (½ medium pepper)

1 teaspoon minced garlic (1 clove)

¼ teaspoon freshly ground black peppercorns

1 tablespoon tomato paste

1½ tablespoons balsamic vinegar

1½ tablespoons dried currants

1½ tablespoons lightly toasted pine nuts

1½ tablespoons finely chopped fresh parsley leaves

CROSTINI

Five 5½-inch-long × ½-inch-thick slices A Crusty Hearth-Style Sourdough Boule (page 59), cut in half lengthwise

Ten 2½ × 3-inch slices aged prosciutto

6 tablespoons plus 2 teaspoons crumbled Farmer's Cheese (page 70)

1. Make the caponata: In a medium pot, heat 2 tablespoons of the oil over medium-high heat until it expands and shimmers, about 2 minutes. Add the eggplant and ½ teaspoon of the salt and sauté, stirring frequently, until the eggplant is tender, soft, and lightly caramelized, about 15 minutes. Transfer to a bowl and set aside. In the same pot, heat the remaining 1 tablespoon oil over medium-high heat and add the onion, bell pepper, garlic, the remaining ¼ teaspoon salt, and the pepper. Sauté, stirring frequently, until the onion turns translucent, about 7 minutes. Combine the eggplant with the onion mixture and stir in the tomato paste. Cook until the tomato paste evenly coats the eggplant, about 1 minute. Deglaze the mixture with the balsamic vinegar and cook for another 2 to 3 minutes, stirring frequently. Remove from the heat; stir in the currants, pine nuts, and parsley; and set aside.

2. Preheat the oven to 375°F and position a rack in the middle.

3. Make the crostini: Line a large baking sheet with parchment paper. Wrap one slice of bread snugly with one slice of prosciutto and place on the baking sheet, seam side down. Repeat with the remaining bread and prosciutto slices. Transfer to the oven and bake for 12 to 15 minutes, until the bread is lightly toasted and the prosciutto is crisp.

4. Remove from the oven and top each crostini with about 2 tablespoons of the caponata. Place the crostini on a serving platter and garnish each with 2 teaspoons of the cheese. Once assembled, these appetizers are best served warm.

COOKING *with* FIRE

....

Cooking over a fire brings a depth of flavor and an elemental connection to foods and the outdoors that is both thrilling and fun! At the farm, we have a wood-burning grill that we love using for small gatherings or during weekends when it is too hot to cook inside.

Below are some tips for building a bed of hot coals for the grill to make the Wood-Fired Rib Eye with Fermented Nasturtium Berry Sauce (page 273) or Wood-Fired Eggplant Puree with Crispy Spiced Lamb, Raisins, and Almonds (page 189). It takes about 40 minutes from when you first build the fire until it will be ready for cooking. You'll need about six 3½ × 14-inch dried logs, 2 medium pine cones, a fistful of small twigs, and a few small mounds of dried grass, but adjust this according to the size and build of your grill. If you have a wood oven, use the same method to build heat for making Sourdough Flatbreads (page 64) or the Chicken Pizza with Roasted Garlic, Spinach, Toasted Pine Nuts, and Fresh Ricotta (page 218).

Fire risk is a serious consideration in our area, and we have included safety measures to set you up for success! It helps to have a set of metal tools handy, including a shovel and a prod, as well as heavy gloves, sand, and a fire extinguisher or water hose to use if the fire gets out of bounds. When choosing wood, use what is most abundant in your region, and make sure it is well cured and dry. Avocado and oil-rich eucalyptus wood are not ideal for grilling and lend a stronger flavor to food than we prefer. However, citrus wood from orange and lemon trees, as well as the dense hardwood from coastal oaks, burns longer and hotter, and we prefer using these when they are available from expired trees on the farm.

1. Clear your area of flammable debris.

Sweep the surrounding patio of dry leaves. Remove any clutter, especially items that could easily catch fire or cause someone to trip. Place a fire extinguisher nearby for emergency use.

2. Build a log frame.

Lay 3 logs 3 inches apart on the floor of the grill. The first should be about 2 inches from the back of the grill and about 4 inches from either side of the grill. Center the pine cones in the middle of the stack between the logs. Stack the last 3 logs perpendicular to the bottom layer, about 2 inches apart from each other. Around the pine cones, nestle some bunches of dry grass and twigs.

3. Start and watch the fire.

Light the kindling and watch as the pine cones quickly catch. The fire will engage with small flames, and clouds of dark smoke will be produced. As the logs catch fire, the flames will extend to about a foot high and smoke will continue billowing. Once the flames have subsided, adjust the grill top to sit about 6 inches above the burning logs. As the fire mellows, the surface of the logs will turn white and, when prodded with a fire rod, will crumble into glowing embers with gentle flames. Move your hand about a foot above the fire and scan the top of the grill to find the hot and cool spots for cooking. You should have about 1 square foot of grill space that is very hot, with the edges better used for holding cooked foods. This fire lasts for about 1 hour without additional fuel.

4. Cook with the fire.

Place the ingredients that take the longest to cook onto the hot grill first, with the thicker parts angled directly over the hotter part of the grill. Cook according to the recipe instructions.

5. Remove the ashes.

Once you have finished cooking, allow the fire to fully cool, or douse it lightly with water to extinguish. Clean the grill with a wire brush. Using a metal scoop, transfer the ashes into a metal bin and clean the grill area. Sprinkle water over the ashes to ensure they are fully extinguished, and transfer to the compost. Hardwood charcoal is especially high in minerals, and as an alternative to composting, small amounts can be used to supplement the diets of pigs as a preemptive tool for digestive health. When given as a free-choice supplement, this charcoal can act as an immunity boost similar to biochar that assists with parasite resistance.

Wood-Fired Pizza Oven Adaptation for Sourdough Pizza and Flatbreads (pages 62 to 64):

To make a similar fire in a pizza oven, make sure all debris and any leftover ashes are swept clean. Build your log frame in the middle of the oven, where you can easily light the fire. Once the wood has caught, the flames have died down, and the embers are glowing, push the fire to one side, spreading it along the wall with a shovel. Add 3 additional logs of similar size to the embers. Allow the logs to catch and burn until the black smoke has cleared. If you have an infrared surface thermometer, the floor of the oven should read between 700°F and 750°F before you attempt to cook a pizza. If the oven is not hot enough, add a few more logs, allow them to catch, and when the smoke clears again, retake the floor temperature. Once the target temperature is achieved, transfer the prepared pizzas to the center of the oven and bake for about 5 minutes, rotating a few times with the peel until the crust is evenly browned and the cheese is golden. If you are baking flatbreads, bake until they are puffy, flipping halfway through.

WOOD-FIRED EGGPLANT PUREE
with Crispy Spiced Lamb, Raisins, and Almonds

Irresistibly smoky and yet perfectly balanced between sweet and savory, this lush Mediterranean-inspired appetizer or tapas-style plate builds layers of flavors through various ingredient preparations. The eggplant puree is almost custard-like, the lamb brings another rich taste, and the pop of almonds and raisins adds a crunch and sweetness to finish. It is best to char the vegetables over a wood fire (see instructions, page 186), but use a gas flame as an alternative.

SERVES 6

EGGPLANT PUREE

2 medium globe eggplants
(about 2 pounds)

4 vine-ripened tomatoes
(about 1½ pounds)

2 tablespoons unrefined avocado oil

¾ cup minced yellow onion
(about ¾ large onion)

2 teaspoons minced garlic (2 cloves)

2 tablespoons minced jalapeño pepper
(1 large pepper)

3 tablespoons almond butter

1 tablespoon fresh lemon juice

½ teaspoon ground cumin

½ teaspoon ground coriander

2 teaspoons yellow curry powder

1½ teaspoons fine sea salt

1. Prepare the wood-fired grill according to the instructions on page 186.

2. When the smoke from the wood fire has subsided, the flames are short, and the embers are glowing, the grill is ready to char the vegetables.

3. Make the eggplant puree: Place the whole eggplants and tomatoes onto the hot grill plate. Cook the tomatoes for 12 to 15 minutes, turning every 5 minutes, until the skin is blackened and blistered and the flesh is soft. Cook the eggplant for 20 to 25 minutes, turning every 7 to 8 minutes, until the skin is blackened and charred and the inner flesh is soft and tender. Transfer the cooked vegetables to a baking sheet and let them cool for 15 minutes, or until easy to handle. Remove the stems and some of the charred skins, slice in half, and remove any fibrous membranes or dark seeds from both the tomato and eggplant. Roughly chop the vegetables into large chunks and set aside for 10 minutes. Drain any accumulated liquid.

4. In a medium pot, heat the oil over medium-high heat until shimmering, about 2 minutes. Add the onion, garlic, and jalapeño and sauté until the onion is translucent, 3 to 4 minutes. Add the chopped eggplant and tomato, almond butter, lemon juice, cumin, coriander, curry powder, and salt. Continue cooking, mashing the vegetables with the back of a spoon, until the vegetables have softened and the eggplant is custard-like, 8 to 10 minutes. Transfer the mixture to the pitcher of a large blender. Beginning on low speed and increasing to high, puree

RECIPE AND INGREDIENTS CONTINUE

SPICED LAMB

1 tablespoon unrefined avocado oil

1 pound ground pastured lamb

1 cup minced yellow onion
(1 large onion)

1 tablespoon minced garlic (3 cloves)

1½ teaspoons fine sea salt

1 teaspoon ground cinnamon

1 teaspoon chili powder

1 teaspoon ground cumin

½ teaspoon ground coriander

¼ cup chopped almonds

¼ cup chopped raisins

GARNISH

1½ tablespoons toasted sesame seeds

2 tablespoons finely chopped fresh
mint leaves

until smooth and creamy, about 1 minute. Pour the dip into a large, shallow bowl and spread the mixture with the back of a spoon to create deep ripples.

5. Make the spiced lamb: In a large cast-iron skillet, heat the oil over medium-high heat until shimmering, about 2 minutes. Add the lamb and sauté, breaking up the meat with the back of a spoon, until just barely cooked through, about 5 minutes. Add the onion, garlic, salt, cinnamon, chili powder, cumin, and coriander. Continue cooking, stirring frequently, until brown and crispy, another 8 to 10 minutes. Remove from the heat and stir in the almonds and raisins.

6. Sprinkle the crispy lamb over the dip and garnish with the sesame seeds and chopped mint. Serve with warm grilled Sourdough Flatbread (page 64). Store any leftovers in a covered container in the refrigerator for up to 3 days.

FRIED DARK STAR ZUCCHINI
with Roasted Red Bell Pepper Sauce

SERVES 4

When I was a child growing up in Pennsylvania, my mom would often fry zucchini at the peak of summer. I loved to help dip the zucchini and would lick my sticky, doughy fingers! No matter how much she made, it felt like there was never enough. This childhood recipe needed a nourishing upgrade, so we created a delicious version with less-refined ingredients to properly honor those memories. Floral but earthy masa harina is worth making for this recipe (page 46), or you can find it sold organically in many health food stores, online (see Resources, page 392), or in most Latin American markets. The pleasant texture of masa harina combines with egg and moisture from the squash to make a sticky but light and crunchy breaded coating that is peppered with shards of bright green parsley. When choosing the zucchini, small and bright-skinned varieties are best. Dark Star is a common cultivar, but most others, including Goldy and Costa, will work as well. This dish is best served hot, so prep the sauce in advance and fry when ready to serve.

PEPPER SAUCE

2 large red bell peppers, sliced in half lengthwise, stems and seeds removed

½ medium red onion, cut into quarters

6 whole garlic cloves, unpeeled

1 tablespoon cold-pressed extra-virgin olive oil

½ teaspoon fine sea salt, plus more to taste

¼ teaspoon freshly ground black peppercorns

1½ teaspoons Fermented Mustard (page 88)

1 tablespoon sherry vinegar

2 tablespoons cashews

1. Preheat the oven to 375°F and position a rack in the middle.

2. Make the pepper sauce: Line a large baking sheet with parchment paper and place the peppers, cut side down, onto the parchment along with the onion. Scatter the garlic cloves throughout. Drizzle with the oil, sprinkle with the salt and pepper, and massage the seasonings into the vegetables to evenly coat.

3. Place the baking sheet in the oven and roast for 15 minutes, until the peppers have some char and the onion quarters are translucent. Remove the onion and garlic from the pan and set aside to cool. Return the sheet to the oven and continue to roast the peppers for an additional 15 minutes. Remove and let the peppers cool until easy to handle.

4. Peel the garlic and place the cloves along with the onion into a large food processor. Peel and discard the pepper skins and add the flesh to the food processor along with the mustard, vinegar, and cashews. Process, scraping down the sides as necessary, until the sauce is mostly smooth with some texture from the cashews, about 2 minutes. Taste and adjust for salt—it should be tangy but somewhat sweet. Transfer to a serving dish and set aside or cover and store in the refrigerator for up to 3 days before serving at room temperature.

RECIPE AND INGREDIENTS CONTINUE

FRIED ZUCCHINI

1 pound Dark Star zucchini, sliced into ½-inch-thick rounds (2 to 3 medium squash)

1 teaspoon fine sea salt

½ cup masa harina

¼ cup almond flour

¼ cup loosely packed finely chopped fresh parsley leaves (¼ bunch)

2 teaspoons lemon zest (¾ large lemon)

1 teaspoon garlic powder

¼ teaspoon freshly ground black peppercorns

2 large eggs

3 cups virgin coconut oil

5. Make the fried zucchini: Line a medium baking sheet with a paper towel or dry linen towel and spread the zucchini rounds on top, about ½ inch apart. Sprinkle with ½ teaspoon of the salt and let rest for 10 minutes so that they absorb the seasoning and release moisture.

6. In a shallow container, whisk together the masa harina, almond flour, parsley, lemon zest, garlic powder, pepper, and remaining ½ teaspoon salt. In a separate small container, whisk the eggs until well combined. Arrange a station near your cooktop, placing the zucchini, egg, dry mix, and a plate in an assembly line. Bread 4 or 5 slices at a time, dipping the zucchini into the egg, shaking off any excess, and then resting on the dry mix. Turn to coat the slices with the dry mix and shake off the excess. Allow the breaded zucchini to rest on the plate while you continue to work.

7. Nestle a wire rack into a baking sheet and place it close to the stovetop. In a cast-iron skillet, melt the coconut oil over medium-low heat until it reaches 315°F to 330°F on an instant-read thermometer. Carefully lower 4 or 5 pieces of the battered zucchini into the hot oil using a slotted spoon. Cook the zucchini until the breading is golden brown, the parsley resembles bright green shards of glass, and the squash is tender, about 2 minutes per side. Drain the zucchini on the wire rack and repeat with the remaining squash.

8. Plate the zucchini and serve immediately with the sauce. If serving as appetizers, place the zucchini on a small platter and spoon a small amount of sauce on top.

GRILLED GREEN CHOPPED SALAD
with Pine Nuts and Chèvre

This lightly grilled salad is delightfully crunchy, simple to assemble, and celebrates the verdant abundance of summer. Beaudie was our most enthusiastic recipe tester, and he went back for thirds on this one! Once stirred into the salad, the avocado contributes a silkiness to the creamy dressing, while the chèvre and lemon amplify the smokiness with a little tang. If you prefer an extra-creamy dressing, toss the chèvre with the vegetables instead of using it as a garnish. This salad is best enjoyed at room temperature the same day it is made to avoid the avocado oxidizing. If making in advance, prepare up to 4 hours ahead, cover, and keep in the refrigerator, allowing it to come to room temperature for at least 20 minutes before serving.

SERVES
4 TO 6

1 bunch asparagus, woody ends trimmed (about 1 pound)

1 medium red onion, sliced into ¼-inch-thick rounds

2 medium green zucchini, sliced into ½-inch-thick planks

3 tablespoons cold-pressed extra-virgin olive oil

1½ teaspoons fine sea salt

1½ teaspoons freshly ground black peppercorns

2 cups seeded and ½-inch-diced English cucumber
(1 medium cucumber)

1¼ cups ½-inch-diced Hass avocado
(1 medium avocado)

½ cup toasted pine nuts

2 teaspoons lemon zest
(¾ large lemon)

2 tablespoons fresh lemon juice
(½ large lemon)

¼ cup loosely packed finely chopped fresh parsley leaves (¼ bunch)

¼ cup loosely packed finely chopped fresh basil leaves

½ cup crumbled chèvre (4 ounces)

1. Preheat a cast-iron grill plate to high heat over a charcoal or wood fire for 10 minutes according to the instructions on page 186.

2. Place the asparagus, red onion, and zucchini into separate medium bowls. Dress each bowl with 1½ teaspoons of the oil, ¼ teaspoon of the salt, and ¼ teaspoon of the pepper and toss to coat. Lightly cook each vegetable on the grill plate in batches for 2 minutes on each side. Dark grill marks will form, but the vegetables should remain crunchy. Transfer the vegetables to a cutting board and let them cool until easy to handle. Cut each vegetable into ½-inch pieces and place in a large bowl.

3. To the bowl, add the remaining ¾ teaspoon salt, ¾ teaspoon pepper, and 1½ tablespoons oil, along with the cucumber, avocado, pine nuts, lemon zest, lemon juice, parsley, and basil. Stir to combine thoroughly. Taste for salt and adjust as desired. Transfer to a serving dish and garnish with the crumbled chèvre. Serve immediately.

BLISTERED HARICOTS VERTS AND FENNEL SALAD
with Chopped Egg Vinaigrette

Haricots verts are long and thin French green beans harvested young, before the seeds mature. Since becoming a farmer, I realize that it is more effort to grow haricots verts than regular beans, since it takes more picking labor to harvest the same weight. I now prepare them with even more appreciation! This recipe can be served as a hearty and filling lunch or with a simple protein such as broiled chicken or fish. To preserve the bright colors, serve soon after the beans are broiled to avoid discoloration in the refrigerator, and avoid overcooking the eggs, as they will impart a dull gray color. You can certainly omit the anchovies, but an additional sprinkle of salt or some capers would work well in the vinaigrette instead.

SERVES 6

VINAIGRETTE

2 teaspoons minced garlic (2 cloves)

3 tablespoons pitted and minced green olives

1 tablespoon Fermented Mustard (page 88)

1 teaspoon lemon zest

2 tablespoons plus 1 teaspoon fresh lemon juice (1 medium lemon)

1 tablespoon champagne vinegar

1½ tablespoons creamed raw honey

2 tablespoons minced fresh parsley leaves

3 tablespoons cold-pressed extra-virgin olive oil

1 teaspoon fine sea salt

¼ teaspoon freshly ground black peppercorns

1 teaspoon minced salted anchovies

SALAD

1½ pounds haricots verts or tender green beans, stem ends removed and sliced in half on the bias

2 tablespoons strained room temperature or warm pastured bacon fat or unrefined avocado oil

½ teaspoon fine sea salt

2 cups cored and thickly shaved fennel bulb (1 large bulb)

Scant ¾ cup small-diced hard-boiled eggs (3 medium eggs)

RECIPE CONTINUES

1. Make the vinaigrette: In a small bowl, combine 2 tablespoons of water, the garlic, olives, mustard, lemon zest, lemon juice, vinegar, honey, parsley, olive oil, salt, pepper, and anchovies. Mix vigorously with a spoon or small spatula until the honey is dissolved and the mixture is emulsified. Set aside.

2. Preheat the broiler to high and position a rack 6 inches below it.

3. Make the salad: In a large bowl, combine the haricots vert, bacon fat, and salt. Spread the beans over two large baking sheets in a single layer. Blister one tray at a time, 5 to 6 minutes each, until the beans are bright green and tender. Remove from the oven and set aside to cool for 5 minutes.

4. In a large bowl, toss together the cooked beans and shaved fennel and transfer to a serving platter. Gently fold the egg into the vinaigrette and generously spoon over the green beans and fennel. Serve at room temperature.

COOKING TIP: *Slicing and Storing Fennel*

To prepare and store fennel in advance of cooking or using in salads, core and slice or shave it on a mandoline, and place it in a lidded container filled with ice water. Store the container in the refrigerator for up to 5 days, then drain and dry completely before tossing into salads or coating in oil and roasting or sautéing. This storage method will dilute the flavor of fennel somewhat, but it's very convenient and makes the fennel extra crisp and crunchy! The slightly milder taste will also please those who find fennel's character too assertive or competitive with other ingredients.

ZUCCHINI SALAD
with Tahini and Date Dressing

Zucchini are some of the most generous plants you can grow, and they can inspire new creative heights by the end of summer. The nutty and slightly sweet dressing in this recipe will convince even the most fatigued squash eaters of its lasting virtues. It's a great side to most any summertime meal. Prepare the dressing and salad separately up to 3 days in advance, and allow the dressing to sit at room temperature for 20 minutes before mixing; the salt will draw out the water from the zucchini and loosen the dressing. Choose a tahini that is mellow, sweet, and creamy, and use fresh, small zucchini with tight skin and dense flesh. If you are using large zucchini, slice them in half or quarters (depending upon the size), seed, and then slice into ⅛-inch-thick pieces. You can also use a mandoline or spiralizer to cut the zucchini into "noodles," but be aware that the increased surface area of the squash will draw out more water and dilute the texture and seasoning of the dressing.

SERVES
6 TO 8

TAHINI AND DATE DRESSING

½ cup raw tahini

6 tablespoons fresh lemon juice (1½ large lemons)

½ teaspoon grated garlic (1 small clove)

1 teaspoon mild raw honey

3 Medjool dates, pitted and chopped

1 tablespoon fine sea salt

SALAD

12 cups ⅛-inch-thick oblong rounds zucchini (about 3 pounds)

¾ cup diced red onion (about ¾ large onion)

2 tablespoons finely diced fresh chives

2 tablespoons chopped fresh mint leaves

1 cup coarsely chopped walnuts

1. Make the tahini and date dressing: In a food processor, combine the tahini, lemon juice, ¼ cup of water, garlic, honey, dates, and salt. Pulse 5 or 6 times to incorporate and then process for 1 minute. Scrape the sides of the bowl and process again until smooth. The dressing should be assertive and salty. Once combined with the zucchini, it will mellow.

2. Make the salad: In a large bowl, combine the dressing, zucchini, onion, chives, mint, and walnuts. Mix thoroughly and serve immediately.

Part III

THE
PASTURE

Our animals are of course endearing, but their husbandry plays an integral role in the soil health at Apricot Lane Farms. The menagerie of poultry, cows, sheep, and pigs that live among the rolling hills cycle nutrients and bioactivity to the earth through managed intensive grazing, rotational grazing, and cover crop foraging. For example, the carefully choreographed dance of responsibly managing our cow herd begins with their nibbling of fresh grass while simultaneously trampling and fertilizing it. When the pasture has reached its threshold, we must recognize this as the right time to move them on to fresh grass. This rotational style prevents overgrazing, enhances grass regrowth, and builds the rich humus that ultimately creates water- and carbon-sequestering topsoil. These grazing practices have contributed to an increase in our levels of soil organic matter by 50 to 100 percent farm-wide in under eight years!

....

It took many years before we developed breeding lines that fit our climate and farming methods, a process that is ongoing. Contemporary animal breeds are very different from the original animals they were derived from. During the process of domestication, people began to select better animals for breeding, ultimately with the intention of developing improved livestock. Agriculture has more recently undergone tremendous changes, and technology has been used to breed animals for large-scale farming operations and to maximize cost and efficiency. The cramped conditions away from pasture and the quick turnover that these animals are bred to withstand come at the sacrifice of the animals' welfare as well as the nutritional benefits we gain from their meat.

Alongside unhealthy living conditions, the decline of health in conventional livestock can be attributed to the lack of diversity in their diet. To achieve balance in a grass-grazed system, careful attention is given to which plants are grown in the fields. A healthy pasture system embraces plant diversity that nurtures soil fertility. It is the symphony of grasses, legumes, and forbs (an herbaceous flowering plant that is not a grass) that encourages a soil ecosystem to thrive, due to the different roles each plant plays. For example, legumes are nitrogen fixers, whereas grasses help to build the soil aggregate (structure) of the soil. The result is nutrient-dense forage that acts as preventative health care for the animals.

When our first animals arrived at the farm, they had various respiratory illnesses and digestive disruption due to a conventional upbringing. A champion conventional ewe that we brought to the farm in the early days garnered the nickname Wheezy due to how she sounded walking up hills. She remained Wheezy to us, but thankfully in name only! It took time on grass, mineral supplementation, and increasing the health of our forage to stabilize her and the other animals' immune systems before we could successfully breed them into stronger animals. Eventually, through careful selection of offspring, desired traits have appeared, such as better adaptation to our hot and arid summers. Over time, our herds and flocks have developed into hardy breeds thanks to humane, preemptive, and hormone- and chemical-free nurturing. This labor- and resource-intensive approach means the cost to the consumer is higher, but the rewards are unparalleled in flavor, fat quality, and the general well-being of the animal.

When we cook our vegetables and fruit, we use techniques and flavors that complement the ingredients' inherent traits. We do the same with our meat dishes. For example, beef from Akaushi cattle is very different from our Highland cows. Likewise, we have tested several different heritage breeds of roaster chickens to settle on what we like best, and we can absolutely tell the differences in flavor and tenderness between each. The following recipes embrace the distinct qualities of pastured heritage-breed livestock versus their conventional, store-bought counterparts. With a few approachable techniques, you can maximize flavor, tenderness, and fat quality of pastured animals, regardless of the breed available to you.

Chapter Seven

PASTURED CHICKEN
and
EGGS

THE ROOM TO ROAM MAKES OUR HENS HAPPY AND OUR EGGS remarkably nutritious! They are the "cleanup crew" that rotates into our pastures after our cows are done grazing, pecking away at protein-rich larvae and insects. As a result of this rotation, our eggs have higher levels of omega-3 fatty acids compared to store-bought, along with other beneficial nutrients. But the challenge is that it's not easy to wrangle these birds! John's running joke on the farm is "How do you catch a chicken?" with the honest punch line being: "You have to *want* to catch a chicken." It is not unusual to see a hilarious performance by our team and volunteers as they stalk and cajole our playful birds in the field. The following recipes celebrate the remarkable flavor of truly farm-fresh eggs and guide you through the sometimes-special considerations of cooking pastured birds.

Recipes

Curried Coconut Soup with Chicken and Yellow Squash Noodles

Slow-Roasted Pastured Chicken with Lemon-Fennel Crust

Summer Orchard Shredded Chicken Salad with Dried Stone Fruit, Fresh Lemon, and Pistachios

Chicken Pizza with Roasted Garlic, Spinach, Toasted Pine Nuts, and Fresh Ricotta

Braised Pastured Chicken Thighs with Lemon, Spring Onion, and Honey

Hearty Ranch Chicken Soup with Crispy Cauliflower

Bone Broth Bar

Tomato-Braised Pastured Chicken Thighs with Mushrooms and Bell Peppers

Spring Frittata with Fresh Peas, Arugula, Artichokes, Chèvre, and Pesto

Summer Frittata with Tomato Raisins, Zucchini, Shallots, Rainbow Chard, and Cheddar

Autumn Frittata with Kale, Potato, Garlic, and Breakfast Sausage

Winter Frittata with Butternut Squash, Leeks, Collard Greens, and Bacon

Roasted Fennel, Green Olive, and Manchego Omelets

Sunny-Fried Eggs with Bacon, Kale, and Hominy Grits

Baked Eggs in Tomato Sauce with Chickpeas and Feta

Pickled Deviled Eggs with Beets, Horseradish, Honey, and Crispy Chicken Skin

CURRIED COCONUT SOUP
with Chicken and Yellow Squash Noodles

This Thai- and Indian-inspired recipe highlights the best of our summer ingredients in a delicious curry with cooling lemongrass, warm spices, and playful squash noodles—yet another use for all that summer squash! This is a dish that only improves in flavor if made in advance. Store the noodles separately from the soup until serving to ensure they remain fresh and with some bite. The heaps of fresh herbs for the garnish create a beautiful presentation and also add a remarkable aroma!

SERVES 8

CURRY PASTE

2 tablespoons unrefined avocado oil

2 cups small-diced sweet yellow onion (about 2 large onions)

2 tablespoons peeled and finely minced ginger (1 × 2-inch knob)

2 tablespoons minced lemongrass (1 stalk)

2 tablespoons minced garlic (6 cloves)

2 tablespoons minced jalapeño pepper (1 large pepper)

4 cups small-diced red bell pepper (about 4 medium peppers)

2 tablespoons lime zest (3 medium limes)

½ teaspoon freshly ground black peppercorns

1 teaspoon ground coriander

1 teaspoon ground cumin

1 teaspoon ground turmeric

1 teaspoon fine sea salt

2 tablespoons creamed raw honey

1 (13.5-ounce) can full-fat coconut milk

SOUP

2½ quarts Chicken Stock (page 76)

2 tablespoons fish sauce

2 teaspoons ume plum vinegar (see Ingredient Tip)

1 teaspoon fine sea salt

2 tablespoons fresh lime juice (1 medium lime)

5 cups finely shredded roasted or boiled chicken, skin removed

4 cups yellow squash noodles, cut or spiralized into ⅛ × ⅛ × 6-inch noodles (4 small squash)

GARNISH

½ cup packed fresh cilantro leaves

1 cup loosely packed fresh Thai or sweet basil leaves

½ cup loosely packed fresh mint leaves

2 jalapeño peppers, sliced into rounds

8 lime wedges (2 limes)

RECIPE CONTINUES

1. Make the curry paste: In a 4-quart heavy-bottomed pot, heat the oil over medium heat until shimmering, about 2 minutes. Add the onion, ginger, lemongrass, garlic, jalapeño, bell pepper, lime zest, pepper, coriander, cumin, turmeric, salt, and honey. Sauté until the onion is translucent and the bell peppers are soft, 8 to 10 minutes. Remove the pot from the heat and set aside to cool, about 10 minutes. Transfer the mixture to the pitcher of a blender and add the coconut milk. Blend on high, scraping down the sides of the bowl as necessary, until the mixture is smooth and thick, about 3 minutes.

2. Make the soup: Return the curry paste to the pot and place over medium-high heat. Stir the paste to prevent it from burning and add the stock, fish sauce, vinegar, and salt. Bring to a boil, then lower the heat to a simmer. Cook, uncovered, for 15 minutes before adding the lime juice and shredded chicken. Stir to break apart the chicken and heat through, about 5 minutes.

3. Portion the yellow squash noodles into serving bowls and ladle the hot soup over top. Garnish with the fresh cilantro, basil, mint, and jalapeño and serve with the lime wedges on the side. Store separately from the squash noodles for up to 5 days in the refrigerator or portion the soup into individual servings without the noodles and freeze for up to 6 months.

INGREDIENT TIP: *Ume Plum Vinegar*

Ume plum vinegar is the pickling brine made from preserving umeboshi plums with salt and red shiso leaf. It is a gorgeous ruby color! You can source it in Japanese groceries or most health food stores, but if you can't find it, you may substitute ½ teaspoon of sea salt dissolved in 1½ teaspoons rice vinegar.

SLOW-ROASTED PASTURED CHICKEN
with Lemon-Fennel Crust

If you have ever eaten a pastured chicken, you will have noticed a remarkable difference in the flavor quality over conventional poultry. The cooking challenge, however, lies in the toughness of the meat, a result of the chicken living an active lifestyle scratching and pecking for bugs, seeds, grasses, and worms. To produce a succulent and juicy bird with a golden, crispy skin, we must use a low and slow cooking technique. When cutting up the chicken for this recipe, please refer to Breaking Down a Whole Chicken into Pieces (page 214). Total cooking time may vary by 20 to 30 minutes depending on the quality and size of the chicken and your oven.

SERVES
4 TO 6

1 whole chicken, cut into 5 pieces
(5 to 6 pounds)

1½ tablespoons Fennel Pollen Sea Salt
(page 94)

1 teaspoon freshly ground black
peppercorns

⅓ cup ghee or cold-pressed
extra-virgin olive oil

1½ tablespoons minced garlic
(about 5 large cloves)

1 tablespoon lemon zest (1 large lemon)

2 tablespoons fresh lemon juice
(½ large lemon)

1. Preheat the oven to 300°F and position a rack in the middle.

2. Line a large baking sheet with parchment paper and lay a wire rack over the paper. Arrange the chicken pieces on the rack and sprinkle with the fennel salt and pepper. Turn each piece to ensure both sides are well coated, leaving them skin side up on the rack. Set aside.

3. In a small saucepan over medium-high heat, melt the ghee with the garlic, lemon zest, and lemon juice. Using a brush, cover each piece of chicken generously with the seasoning mixture, coating the inside cavity of the breast meat as well. Set the remaining seasoning mixture aside.

4. Transfer the baking sheet to the oven. After 1 hour, brush the chicken with the remaining seasoning mixture and return to the oven for another 1½ to 2 hours, depending upon the size of the chicken. After cooking for 2½ to 3 hours total, remove the breast meat from the oven. Confirm the internal temperature has reached 165°F using an instant-read thermometer, cover with a piece of parchment paper and foil to keep warm, and set aside. The leg and wing pieces should continue cooking for an additional 30 to 45 minutes. The leg meat and wings are done when they are golden brown and crispy and the joint between the thigh and leg can be pulled apart easily.

5. Allow the chicken to cool slightly. Transfer the breast to a cutting board and separate the meat from the ribs. Transfer the legs to the cutting board and cut at the joint to separate the drumsticks from the thighs. Arrange the chicken pieces on a platter and serve immediately. Store, covered, in the refrigerator for up to 5 days.

Breaking Down a Whole Chicken into Pieces

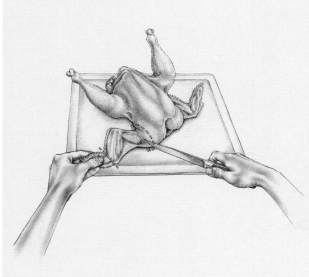

Learning to cut up a whole chicken into parts has several benefits: you can adjust cooking times to avoid drying out leaner cuts or undercooking others, the rest can be saved for preparing Chicken Stock (page 76), and whole birds are always less expensive pound for pound than their already-cut-up counterparts.

To butcher a chicken, you will need a large cutting board, a sharp knife, and two medium containers. One container will be for the wings, legs, and breasts and the other for the scrap pieces (such as the wing tips and backbone).

1. Remove the wings.

Place the chicken, breast side up, on a large cutting board. Using a knife, remove the wing tips and put in the scrap container. Pull one wing out and away from the chicken. At the joint where it connects to the breast, use the tip of the knife to pierce the taut skin and then separate the wing from the body. Put the wing in the nonscrap container. Repeat this process for the other wing.

2. Separate the legs.

Cut the skin on the diagonal where the leg meets the breast. As you cut downward, flip the chicken onto its side and continue to run the knife up, over, and along the back until it releases from the body; the leg and thigh will be intact as one piece. Repeat this process with the other leg. You can separate the thighs from the drumsticks if you'd like at this point by cutting through the joint that attaches them. Place these pieces in the container with the wings.

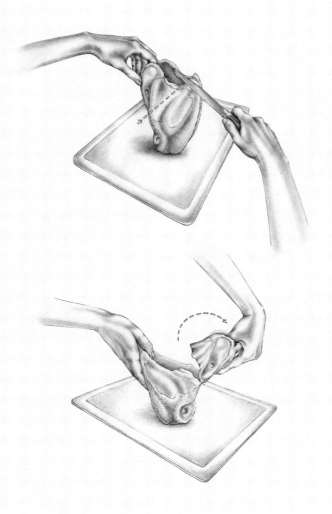

3. Separate the breast from the body and remove the lower portion of the backbone.

Stand the chicken upright so the neck is resting on the cutting board. Remove the breast piece with part of the backbone and ribs attached using short, downward strokes of the knife or kitchen shears on both sides of the backbone. Snap the backbone toward the cutting board. Finish separating the two pieces by slicing through any remaining skin and flesh with a knife and transfer the backbone to the scrap container. You will now be left with the two breasts intact and attached to the rib bones. Transfer the whole breast piece to the container with the legs and wings.

4. Store.

The chicken pieces can be used immediately or put in an airtight container or plastic bag. Package up the scraps, too, if keeping. Store in the refrigerator for up to 2 days or in the freezer for up to 9 months.

SUMMER ORCHARD SHREDDED CHICKEN SALAD

with Dried Stone Fruit, Fresh Lemon, and Pistachios

Chicken salads are a staple meal throughout the year on our farm, and the ingredients change slightly with the season. Although the dried summer fruit adds brightness, try substituting crisp apples in the winter or crunchy snap peas in the spring. If the salad thickens beyond your liking once chilled, let it sit at room temperature for 15 minutes or add sliced room-temperature avocado before serving to complement the Avocado Oil Mayonnaise (page 90).

6 cups shredded roasted or boiled chicken

1 cup Avocado Oil Mayonnaise (page 90)

1 cup chopped pistachios

½ cup diced yellow onion (about ½ large onion)

2 tablespoons minced fresh chives

¼ cup loosely packed finely chopped fresh parsley leaves (¼ bunch)

2 tablespoons Fermented Mustard (page 88)

2 teaspoons fine sea salt

¼ teaspoon freshly ground black peppercorns

1 tablespoon lemon zest (1 large lemon)

3 tablespoons fresh lemon juice (¾ large lemon)

2 tablespoons chiffonade-cut fresh basil leaves

½ cup golden raisins

½ cup chopped Dried Summer Stone-Fruit Medley (page 36)

1 teaspoon grated garlic (about 1 large clove)

1. In a large bowl, stir the shredded chicken and mayonnaise until thoroughly combined. Add the pistachios, onion, chives, parsley, mustard, salt, pepper, lemon zest, and lemon juice. Massage the mixture with your fingers, breaking apart the larger pieces of chicken. Stir in the basil, raisins, stone fruit, and garlic until evenly combined.

2. Cover and chill the salad for 1 hour in the refrigerator. If making the day before, you may need to stir in extra mayo before serving. Serve on a large platter with lettuce or grilled sourdough bread (pages 54 or 59) for making sandwiches.

CHICKEN PIZZA
with Roasted Garlic, Spinach, Toasted Pine Nuts, and Fresh Ricotta

Several years ago, a beautiful wood-fired pizza oven was built at the farm. I had visions of using it to roast our pastured chickens to golden perfection and for making whole-grain sourdough pizzas bubbling with cheesy goodness. Sadly, my first go on a roast chicken turned out completely charred on the outside while the internal cooking temperature registered only 92°F! As my beloved ballet teacher Dennon says, *"Repetition, repetition, repetition, rinse and then repeat!"* Repeat we have, resulting in this chicken pizza redemption! Although we love a good saucy pizza, this recipe uses creamy and sweet roasted garlic (page 84) as the base instead. You can use roasted chicken, but after experimenting, we found we prefer juicy boiled chicken here. Place it under the mozzarella while the pizza cooks to prevent the chicken from drying out in the oven. For best crust flavor, prepare the dough at least a day in advance of baking.

MAKES
2 PIZZAS

1 recipe Sourdough Pizza Dough (page 62)

2 tablespoons cold-pressed extra-virgin olive oil

10 cups packed fresh spinach leaves (about 10 ounces)

1 teaspoon fine sea salt

6 cloves Roasted Garlic (page 84) (about 2 tablespoons)

½ cup fresh ricotta (4½ ounces)

4 strips Simple Salt and Pepper Bacon (page 38), cooked and crumbled

⅔ cup shredded boiled chicken (page 76 or 77)

⅔ cup shredded mozzarella (5¼ ounces)

4 teaspoons toasted pine nuts

1. At least 15 hours and up to 3 days before baking the pizza, prepare the dough according to the instructions on page 62. Remove the dough from the refrigerator at least 1 hour before baking the pizza. It is ready to shape when it reaches room temperature, feels inflated, and when you gently press the dough with a floured finger, an impression remains. This may take more or less time depending upon the refrigerator and room temperature.

2. If you are using a home oven, place a pizza stone on the middle rack and preheat to 500°F. If you are using a wood-fired pizza oven, prepare the fire 40 to 60 minutes before baking the pizzas (see Wood-Fired Pizza Oven Adaptation, page 187). The oven is ready when the floor temperature reads between 700F° and 750F° on an infrared surface thermometer.

3. In a large skillet, heat the oil until shimmering, about 2 minutes. Stir in the spinach and sprinkle with the salt. Cook until the spinach is tender, about 7 minutes. Remove from the heat and drain the spinach through a fine-mesh sieve, pushing lightly to remove any remaining moisture. Blot the spinach with a paper towel until dry and set aside.

RECIPE CONTINUES

4. Shape the dough according to the instructions on page 63. Smear each circle of dough with 1 tablespoon of roasted garlic, leaving a ¾-inch cornicione (outer crust rim). Using an offset spatula, spread ¼ cup of the ricotta over each pizza and evenly top with 1 cup drained spinach, 2 tablespoons of the bacon, and ⅓ cup of the chicken. Sprinkle each pizza with ⅓ cup of the mozzarella.

5. If you are using a home oven, slide a peel under the parchment paper of the prepared pizza and transfer it to the preheated pizza stone. Bake for 8 to 10 minutes, until the edges are golden brown and puffed and the cheese is crispy and golden. Repeat with the remaining pizza. If baking in a wood-fired oven, transfer both pizzas to the center of the oven and bake for about 5 minutes, rotating a few times with the peel, until the crust is evenly browned and the cheese is golden.

6. Place the cooked pizzas on a cutting board and sprinkle each with 2 teaspoons pine nuts. Slice and serve immediately. Store any leftovers in a covered container in the refrigerator for up to 3 days. Reheat in a preheated 350°F oven for about 7 minutes.

BRASED PASTURED CHICKEN THIGHS
with Lemon, Spring Onion, and Honey

This is one of my favorite ways to showcase our happy pastured chickens—pairing them with tender spring onions (or sweet yellow onion in other seasons). Slow cooking at a low temperature tenderizes the meat and brings out the rich flavor a natural diet imparts. This dish is wonderful for sharing and can be easily multiplied by three to feed a crowd—just use a larger pot! If you do not have homemade Chicken Stock (page 76), use a low-sodium chicken stock instead.

SERVES 4

4 bone-in, skin-on chicken thighs (1¼ to 1½ pounds)

1 tablespoon fine sea salt

1½ teaspoons ghee

2 cups 1-inch-sliced leek bulb and leaves (2 large leeks)

¾ cup chopped spring onions or sweet yellow onion (about ¾ large onion)

1 tablespoon roughly chopped Preserved Lemon peel (page 34), pith removed (about 2 wedges)

2½ tablespoons fresh lemon juice (about ½ large lemon)

2½ cups Chicken Stock (page 76)

1 tablespoon mild raw honey

1. Thirty minutes before cooking the chicken, place the thighs on a baking sheet and sprinkle evenly on all sides with 2 teaspoons of the salt. Cover with plastic wrap and let it rest at room temperature while you continue to work.

2. Preheat the oven to 300°F and position a rack in the middle.

3. In a wide 2¼-quart ceramic or enamel-coated pot, melt the ghee over low heat. Adjust the heat to medium-high and sear the chicken, skin side down, until the skin contracts and turns an even, golden brown, about 10 minutes. Use tongs to gently remove the chicken thighs from the pot and return them to the baking sheet. The chicken will have slowly rendered its fat, leaving a large amount in the pot. Remove all but about 1 tablespoon and reserve the excess fat for future cooking projects.

4. Place the leeks, spring onions, and preserved lemon in the same pot and sauté over medium heat until the leek leaves have turned bright green, about 2 minutes. Add the lemon juice, stock, honey, and the remaining 1 teaspoon salt. Stir the mixture until the honey is fully dissolved and evenly coats the vegetables.

5. Nestle the chicken thighs in the braising liquid, skin side up. Bring the braise to a simmer over medium heat. Remove from the heat and cover the pan with the lid or parchment paper and then foil. Bake for 2 hours, until slightly tender but not falling off the bone.

RECIPE CONTINUES

6. After 2 hours of cooking, remove the lid from the pot. Return the uncovered braise to the oven and cook an additional 50 minutes, or until the chicken easily falls off the bone. The sauce will have reduced by half and will appear a deep golden brown. Turn the broiler on high and broil for an additional 8 to 10 minutes on the middle rack, keeping an eye on the skin, as broiling intensity will vary by oven. This will ensure a crispy skin without sacrificing the juicy tenderness of the meat.

7. Remove the pot from the oven and let cool for 15 minutes. Using a slotted spoon, transfer the chicken and vegetables to a rimmed, deep, wide serving platter. Skim the pan sauce for excess fat, leaving a small amount to flavor the dish. Spoon the skimmed liquid into the serving platter, drizzling some of the liquid over the crispy chicken skin to give it a nice sheen. Serve immediately.

8. Store any leftovers in a covered container in the refrigerator for up to 5 days.

HEARTY RANCH CHICKEN SOUP
with Crispy Cauliflower

When the autumn air takes on a frosty chill that sinks into the bones, this nourishing soup is perfect for creating warmth and comfort. If prepared in advance, it tastes even better the next day served with crumbled tostadas or crispy fried tortillas for a little extra crunch. The toppings are versatile and, when used generously, help to fortify this brothy soup. If you prefer a mild flavor or heartier soup, stir one can of full-fat coconut milk into the stock to tone down the spice and enrich the consistency. For more of a chicken chili, try adding cooked pinto or Peruano beans near the end of the cooking time.

SERVES 8

CRISPY CAULIFLOWER

1 medium cauliflower (about 2 pounds), core removed and cut into ½- to ¾-inch florets

1 teaspoon chili powder

1 teaspoon ground cumin

2 teaspoons fine sea salt

1 teaspoon freshly ground black peppercorns

¼ cup unrefined avocado oil

SOUP

3 tablespoons unrefined avocado oil

2 cups small-diced red onion (2 large onions)

2 tablespoons minced garlic (6 cloves)

1 tablespoon seeded minced jalapeño pepper (1 medium pepper)

2 tablespoons chili powder

1 tablespoon ground cumin

4 teaspoons fine sea salt

1 (18.3-ounce) jar crushed tomatoes

2½ quarts Chicken Stock (page 76)

2 bay leaves

1 tablespoon dried oregano

4 cups finely shredded roasted or boiled chicken, skin removed

GARNISH

½ cup packed chopped cilantro leaves

2 cups diced avocado (about 2 large avocados)

1½ cups crumbled Farmer's Cheese (page 70)

2 limes, sliced into quarters

1. Preheat the oven to 375°F and position a rack in the middle.

2. Make the crispy cauliflower: Line a large baking sheet with parchment paper. Place the cauliflower florets, chili powder, cumin, salt, and pepper in a large bowl and toss to evenly coat. Add the oil and stir until thoroughly combined. Spread the cauliflower on the prepared baking sheet and bake for 25 to 30 minutes, until the cauliflower is golden with dark brown edges. Remove from the oven and set aside to cool.

3. Make the soup: In a 4- to 5-quart pot, heat the oil over medium-high heat until shimmering, about 2 minutes. Add the onion, garlic, jalapeño, chili powder, cumin, and salt. Cook until the onion becomes translucent and the spices fragrant, 5 to 7 minutes. Add the crushed tomatoes, stock, bay leaves, oregano, and shredded chicken and stir to combine. Cover and bring the mixture to a boil. Reduce the heat to a simmer and cook, uncovered, for 15 minutes before removing the bay leaves. The soup will have a high stock-to-meat ratio and taste warm and spicy with a slight acidity. When ready to serve, stir in the crispy cauliflower.

4. Ladle the soup into bowls and garnish with the cilantro, avocado, farmer's cheese, and lime wedges. Store the cooled soup in an airtight container in the refrigerator for up to 5 days, or portion into individual servings and freeze for up to 6 months.

BONE BROTH BAR

Our farm meal program often offers this nourishing choose-your-own-adventure-style meal. It begins with a pot of seasoned stock or broth and a big bowl for stuffing with seasonal vegetables, soft-boiled eggs, and meats. Although Roasted Beef Bone Stock (page 79) certainly works, the Chicken Stock (page 76) is a lighter alternative and can be prepared with extended cooking time in a slow cooker to make it a true broth. You can omit the bay leaf and thyme and add herbs and spices of your choice, such as thinly sliced Makrut lime leaf and lemongrass for a more Thai-inspired version. Coconut aminos is a low-sodium savory sauce that is a soy- and wheat-free alternative to saltier soy sauce, but if tolerated, the latter may be used in a lesser amount. Other ramen noodles will work, but we love the flavor, appearance, and texture of those made with wheat-free black or forbidden rice.

SEASONED BROTH

2 quarts Chicken Stock (page 76)

1 cup sliced yellow onion (1 medium onion)

1 tablespoon minced ginger
(1 × 1-inch knob)

1 tablespoon minced garlic (3 cloves)

½ teaspoon crushed red chile flakes

2½ teaspoons Citrus and Garlic Sea Salt (page 93)

3 tablespoons coconut aminos or soy sauce, to taste

1 tablespoon ume plum vinegar (see Ingredient Tip, page 211)

1 tablespoon mild raw honey

TOPPINGS

3 large eggs, cold

5 ounces black or forbidden rice ramen noodles

2 cups finely shredded roasted or boiled chicken

1½ cups shredded or julienned carrot (3 medium carrots)

¼ cup thinly sliced toasted nori (one and a half 7½ × 10-inch sheets)

¼ cup sliced scallions (about 2 scallions)

1. Season the stock: In a medium pot, combine the stock, onion, ginger, garlic, chile flakes, salt, coconut aminos, vinegar, and honey. Cover and bring to a boil over medium-high heat, about 20 minutes. Remove the lid, reduce the heat to medium-low, and simmer the stock, adjusting the heat if necessary, until it's robustly flavored, about 30 minutes. Remove from the heat and strain the broth through a fine-mesh sieve positioned over a large bowl. Transfer the seasoned broth back into the pot and set over low heat.

2. Make the toppings: In a medium bowl, prepare an ice bath and set aside. While the broth is simmering, boil 1 quart of water in a small saucepan. Add the eggs and cook, uncovered, at a low boil for 8 minutes for a soft center, or 10 minutes for a slightly firmer center. Ladle the eggs into the ice bath and let them cool until easy to handle, about 5 minutes. Peel and set the eggs aside until ready to serve.

3. Bring 1 quart of fresh water to a boil. Add the ramen noodles and cook until tender but al dente, 3 to 4 minutes. Drain the noodles in a colander, rinse with cold water, and drain again.

4. Set up the broth bar by assembling the dishware and ingredients in order of serving: large bowls, broth pot with a ladle, and the toppings in small individual bowls with appropriate utensils. Slice the eggs in half with a sharp paring knife and serve them yolk side facing up. Store any leftover broth and toppings in covered containers in the refrigerator for up to 5 days.

TOMATO-BRAISED PASTURED CHICKEN THIGHS

with Mushrooms and Bell Peppers

After first being served this chicken dish at a dinner party with dear friends, John talked about his love for it for the next week or two, and we knew it had to go in the book! This saucy dish is warm and deeply gratifying, especially for a cozy dinner served with French Onion Potato Puree (page 111). The bell peppers and ground fennel add a sweetness that balances the tomatoes, and the pastured chicken enjoys a long, slow braise to become succulent and tender. Use a large Dutch oven for even cooking or, in a pinch, a heavy-bottomed stainless steel pot with a lid, making sure to stir often while the sauce reduces.

SERVES
3 TO 4

6 bone-in, skin-on chicken thighs (about 2 pounds)

2½ teaspoons fine sea salt

1 teaspoon freshly ground black peppercorns

2 tablespoons strained pastured bacon fat or unrefined avocado oil

1 cup diced yellow onion (1 large onion)

1 tablespoon minced garlic (3 cloves)

1¾ cups stemmed and thinly sliced cremini mushrooms (8 ounces)

1 teaspoon ground fennel seed

1 teaspoon fresh thyme leaves or ½ teaspoon dried

½ teaspoon crushed red chile flakes

2 cups julienned red bell peppers (about 2 medium peppers)

3 cups Chicken Stock (page 76)

1 (18.3-ounce) jar crushed tomatoes

3 tablespoons chopped fresh parsley leaves (optional)

1. On a large baking sheet, place the chicken and sprinkle with 1½ teaspoons of the salt and ½ teaspoon of the pepper.

2. In a large enameled Dutch oven, heat the bacon fat over medium heat until hot but not smoking, about 3 minutes. Add the chicken thighs, skin side down, and cook until the skin is golden brown and releases easily from the pan, 7 to 10 minutes. Using tongs, transfer the chicken to a clean plate.

3. Remove all but 2 tablespoons of the rendered chicken fat and reserve for another use. Increase the heat to medium-high and add the onion, garlic, mushrooms, fennel, thyme, chile flakes, bell peppers, the remaining 1 teaspoon salt, and the remaining ½ teaspoon pepper. Sauté until the vegetables soften and release water, 3 to 5 minutes. Deglaze the pot with 1 cup of the stock, and use a spoon to release the browned bits from the bottom. Add the tomatoes and the remaining 2 cups stock and stir to fully incorporate. Nestle the rendered chicken thighs skin side up into the sauce without covering the thighs completely. Offset the lid so that it is slightly vented and cook over medium-low heat for 2 hours. Every 30 minutes, gently stir to avoid the bottom burning. The chicken is done when it is tender and falling off the bone when pierced with a fork.

4. Transfer the chicken and sauce to a deep serving dish and sprinkle with parsley, if desired. Serve immediately. Store in a covered container in the refrigerator for up to 3 days.

HOW TO PURCHASE, STORE, *and* EAT FARM-FRESH PASTURED ORGANIC EGGS

There is no denying that farm-fresh eggs often look and taste very different from eggs you can find at the supermarket. The sheer variety of green and blue pastel, speckled, white, and chocolate-brown eggshells may be the first thing that you notice. Pastured hens are often from more diverse breeds than commercial ones, and they spend their time enjoying outdoor foraging, eating high-quality supplemental feed, and living in clean roosting conditions. This lifestyle changes their egg appearance—but also so much more!

Pastured eggs have stronger eggshells, incredible flavor, taller and brighter golden-orange egg yolks, and firmer egg whites than their commercial counterparts. And their nutrition can't be beat—pastured eggs have significantly higher levels of vitamins A, D, and E, as well as choline, an essential nutrient. They also contain higher amounts of omega-3 fatty acids, which can diminish the risk factors for heart disease, nurture brain development in children, fight inflammation and some autoimmune diseases, elevate mood, and more.

Pastured eggs are handled differently than eggs processed by large-scale poultry operations. Below are some important considerations for purchasing, storing, and cooking with this delicious, nutrient-rich foundational food.

Sourcing Fresh Eggs

Egg labels can be cryptic, especially when you are trying to understand confusing marketing language. We recommend visiting a farmers market or health food store that you can be sure sells local, pastured, organic, and soy-free eggs. Hens that are raised this way aren't given hormones or antibiotics, and they are able to live their best lives frolicking in fields. They forage for bugs and snails, peck at grass, and even coexist with roosters, as nature intended. Maintaining chickens with these methods requires a significant amount of work, and pastured, organic eggs are often more expensive as a result. We use mobile chicken coops to fertilize and aerate the soil, and because our chickens rotate into pasture after the cattle, they are always on the move! We also take measures to ensure chickens aren't crowded. Giving the hens plenty of space with clean litter, fresh water, and a grassy pasture reduces stress, increases egg laying, and enhances cleanliness. But purchasing the eggs produced with these methods not only improves your diet, it also guarantees that the animal has a better quality of life. And it supports the farmer who is making a marginal profit from this labor of love.

Preserving the Quality of Eggs

Another great reason to use locally sourced, pastured, and organic eggs is that they are much fresher than conventional eggs, and they are able to keep their quality longer. Newly laid eggs have an ingenious "bloom," or a layer of protein produced by the hen's body that is deposited over the egg's surface. This cuticle protects the egg from contamination by sealing the porous shell from harmful bacteria while also maintaining the egg's interior moisture. If you are keeping backyard eggs and they don't have soilage, you can simply dry brush them lightly and keep them at a cool room temperature in your kitchen for two to three weeks. They make a beautiful display on the kitchen counter! Wash just before using. Eggs with their protective bloom intact can also be stored in the refrigerator for months! Once an egg is refrigerated, it must stay that way, and unless you have the time to bring them to room temperature for up to several hours before using, we recommend keeping refrigerated eggs in cold temperatures until ready to cook.

When the bloom is washed away, it leaves the egg susceptible to spoilage and must be refrigerated at temperatures no greater than 45°F. Although we take great care to keep our hens' bedding clean and collect eggs daily, we still hand-wash our eggs to remove any soilage before bringing them to market. For this reason, we recommend storing eggs purchased from our farm in the refrigerator once they arrive home. Asking small producers about their practices can help you determine how to handle and store your own eggs.

In contrast to small farms, large-scale processors will often keep their eggs in cold storage for a long period of time (sometimes months) before packaging. Once a large order is received, upward of a quarter- or a half-million units, the labeling begins. When the order is boxed, the label is applied according to USDA laws: "best by" must be thirty days after packaging the eggs, not after they were laid. This loophole means that in many supermarket egg cartons, the eggs may be four to six months old before arriving in the stores and eventually your refrigerator.

One of the big differences with our eggs (and those of many small farms) is that they are always less than one week old when they go to market. We sell out every week and never wait to box them up! We do, however, have to follow the same USDA guidelines for the "best by" date: thirty days from when they were packaged, not laid. Therefore, our eggs should be good for four to six months after purchasing if stored properly. Once our customers taste how amazing free-range fresh eggs are, though, they don't last more than a week or two!

Hard-Boiling Fresh Eggs

The sooner you cook an egg after it has been laid, the better the nutritive quality and also generally its flavor. There are, however, advantages to aging eggs. When the eggs have been aged for several weeks, they lose some moisture and the egg white shrinks, creating more space between the egg's inner membrane and its shell. Once boiled, these eggs are much easier to peel! Try them for recipes such as Blistered Haricots Verts and Fennel Salad with Chopped Egg Vinaigrette (page 196). There are many tips, tricks, and rumored kitchen hacks to avoid the frustration of peeling fresh eggs. And some of them are pretty wacky. Instead, we simply recommend you stock your kitchen with enough eggs to suit your everyday needs in addition to some extras to stow away for later use. Label them with the purchase date, and plan to age them for at least ten days before boiling and peeling.

SPRING FRITTATA
with Fresh Peas, Arugula, Artichokes, Chèvre, and Pesto

Frittatas are a flexible canvas for a variety of savory fillings, including cheese, roasted or sautéed vegetables, and precooked meats. For our farm lunch program, we often serve frittatas, and we have developed four different seasonally inspired versions to choose from! Spring is an excellent time to enjoy fresh greens, artichokes, and sweet shelled peas harvested straight from the garden. This frittata uses Spinach-Pistachio Pesto (page 144) to create a super light and fluffy meal that is rich in flavor.

SERVES 6

1 tablespoon unrefined avocado oil or cold-pressed extra-virgin olive oil

¼ cup drained and finely chopped marinated artichoke hearts

½ cup fresh or frozen and thawed shelled green peas

1¾ cups Spinach-Pistachio Pesto (page 144)

8 large eggs, room temperature

½ teaspoon fine sea salt

¼ teaspoon freshly ground black peppercorns

¼ cup crumbled chèvre (2 ounces)

¾ packed cup arugula

1. Preheat the oven to 350°F and position a rack in the middle.

2. In an 8-inch skillet, heat the oil until it expands, about 1 minute. Add the artichoke hearts and sauté for 2 minutes. Stir in the peas and continue to cook until bright green, about 2 minutes. Add 2 tablespoons of the pesto and stir to combine. Continue cooking until the artichoke hearts are golden brown, about 2 minutes.

3. Line a 10-inch cast-iron skillet with an 11-inch circle of parchment paper. In a small bowl, whisk together the eggs, salt, and pepper. Transfer the filling mixture to the prepared skillet and spread evenly. Pour the whisked eggs over top and gently shake the skillet to settle the mixture.

4. Transfer to the oven and bake for 15 minutes. Remove from the oven and sprinkle the chèvre over the frittata. Return to the oven and bake for an additional 10 minutes, or until the top is a light golden brown and the center is set. Remove from the oven.

5. Using a spatula to assist, tilt the skillet and slide the frittata onto a serving platter. Slice into 6 pieces. Serve hot, topped with the arugula and the remaining pesto on the side. Store any leftovers in a covered container in the refrigerator for up to 2 days.

SUMMER FRITTATA
with Tomato Raisins, Zucchini, Shallots, Rainbow Chard, and Cheddar

This wholesome vegetarian combination uses Tomato Raisins (page 35) for a concentrated sweet pop of flavor to brighten the sautéed vegetables and cheddar.

SERVES 6

1 tablespoon plus 2 teaspoons unrefined avocado oil or cold-pressed extra-virgin olive oil

1 small shallot, thinly sliced into rounds

6 cups loosely packed finely chopped rainbow chard, stems removed and chopped separately (1 large bunch)

1 cup shredded zucchini (½ medium zucchini)

8 large eggs, room temperature

1 teaspoon fine sea salt

½ teaspoon freshly cracked black peppercorns

1 cup Tomato Raisins (page 35)

⅔ cup lightly packed shredded raw mild cheddar (3 ounces)

¼ cup chiffonade-cut fresh basil leaves

1. Preheat the oven to 350°F and position a rack in the middle.

2. In an 8-inch skillet, heat 1 tablespoon of the oil over medium-high heat until shimmering, about 2 minutes. Stir in the shallot and cook until translucent, about 5 minutes. Add the chard and cook until bright green and tender, about 5 minutes. Remove from the heat and set aside to cool, about 5 minutes. Using paper towels, squeeze out the excess moisture from the chard mixture, transfer it to a plate, and set aside.

3. In the same skillet, heat the remaining 2 teaspoons oil over medium-high heat until it expands, about 1 minute. Add the zucchini and cook until bright green and tender, 5 to 7 minutes. Remove from the heat and set aside to cool, about 5 minutes. Using paper towels, squeeze out the excess moisture from the zucchini and add to the plate with the cooked chard.

4. Line a 10-inch cast-iron skillet with an 11-inch circle of parchment paper. In a small bowl, whisk together the eggs, salt, and pepper. Transfer the cooked vegetable mixture to the prepared skillet and spread evenly. Sprinkle in the tomato raisins, cheddar, and basil and pour the whisked eggs over top. Gently shake the skillet to settle the mixture.

5. Transfer to the oven and bake for 25 minutes, or until the top is a light golden brown and the center is set. Remove from the oven.

6. Using a spatula to assist, tilt the skillet and slide the frittata onto a serving platter. Slice into 6 pieces. Serve hot. Store any leftovers in a covered container in the refrigerator for up to 2 days.

AUTUMN FRITTATA
with Kale, Potato, Garlic, and Breakfast Sausage

This filling frittata makes wonderful use of seasonal greens such as kale that become sweeter as the temperatures dip, but you can use Swiss chard as well. Prepare the filling in advance and bring it to room temperature before combining with the eggs to avoid curdling. Serve with Fermented Ketchup (page 87) for a delicious morning or brunch-time meal.

SERVES 6

4 teaspoons ghee or strained pastured bacon fat

1¼ cups small-diced Blue Adirondack potatoes (3 medium potatoes)

2¼ teaspoons fine sea salt

2 cups lightly packed chopped dinosaur kale, stems removed (1 small bunch)

2 thinly sliced garlic cloves

¼ teaspoon freshly ground black peppercorns

8 large eggs, room temperature

1 cup cooked and crumbled Apricot Lane Farms Pork Sausage (page 298)

½ cup Fermented Ketchup (page 87)

1. Preheat the oven to 350°F and position a rack in the middle.

2. In a medium skillet, heat 2 teaspoons of the ghee over high heat until shimmering, about 2 minutes. Add the potatoes and season with 1 teaspoon of the salt. Cook, stirring occasionally, until the potatoes are golden brown and tender, about 12 minutes. Transfer to a bowl and set aside to cool.

3. Place the same skillet over medium-high heat and melt the remaining 2 teaspoons ghee. Add the kale, garlic, ¼ teaspoon of the salt, and the pepper, and cook, stirring occasionally, until the kale is wilted and little to no water remains in the pan, 3 to 4 minutes. Remove from the heat and transfer the kale to the bowl with the potatoes.

4. Line a 10-inch cast-iron skillet with an 11-inch circle of parchment paper. In a small bowl, whisk together the eggs and the remaining 1 teaspoon salt. Transfer the cooked vegetable mixture and cooked sausage to the prepared skillet and spread evenly. Pour the whisked eggs over top and gently shake the skillet to settle the mixture.

5. Transfer the skillet to the oven and bake for 25 to 30 minutes, until the top is a light golden brown and the center is set. Remove from the oven.

6. Using a spatula to assist, tilt the skillet and slide the frittata onto a serving platter. Slice into 6 pieces. Serve hot with the ketchup on the side. Store any leftovers in a covered container in the refrigerator for up to 2 days.

WINTER FRITTATA
with Butternut Squash, Leeks, Collard Greens, and Bacon

This hearty frittata combines sweet winter squash with salty bacon and robust greens but can be further fortified with grated hard cheese sprinkled over the filling before pouring in the eggs if you like. Make sure to wash the collards and leeks thoroughly before chopping, as they can be particularly sandy.

SERVES 6

2 cups peeled small-diced butternut squash

2 tablespoons unrefined avocado oil or cold-pressed extra-virgin olive oil

1 teaspoon fine sea salt

⅛ teaspoon plus ¼ teaspoon freshly ground black peppercorns

6 slices Salt and Pepper Bacon (page 38), roughly chopped

4 cups chopped collard greens, stems removed (1 bunch)

¾ cup thinly sliced leek, white part only (1 medium leek)

8 large eggs, room temperature

1. Preheat the oven to 375°F and position a rack in the middle.

2. Spread the butternut squash over a medium baking sheet and drizzle with the oil. Season with ½ teaspoon of the salt and ⅛ teaspoon of the pepper. Toss to coat and transfer to the oven. Bake for 35 minutes, or until tender and golden. Remove from the oven and set aside to cool. Reduce the oven temperature to 350°F.

3. Line a plate with paper towels. Cook the bacon in a skillet on the stovetop according to the instructions on page 40. Using a slotted spoon, scoop the bacon onto the lined plate to drain. Transfer the bacon fat to a container, leaving about 1 tablespoon in the skillet. Increase the heat to high and stir in the collard greens and leeks. Cook until completely wilted and the moisture has evaporated, 3 to 4 minutes. Remove from the heat, stir in the bacon and roasted squash, and set aside.

4. Line a 10-inch cast-iron skillet with an 11-inch circle of parchment paper. In a small bowl, whisk together the eggs and the remaining ½ teaspoon salt and ¼ teaspoon pepper. Transfer the cooked vegetable mixture to the skillet and spread evenly. Pour the whisked eggs over top and gently shake the skillet to settle the mixture.

5. Transfer to the oven and bake for 25 minutes, or until the top is a light golden brown and the center is set. Remove from the oven.

6. Using a spatula to assist, tilt the skillet and slide the frittata onto a serving platter. Slice into 6 pieces. Serve hot. Store any leftovers in a covered container in the refrigerator for up to 2 days.

ROASTED FENNEL, GREEN OLIVE, AND MANCHEGO OMELETS

Omelets are a simple and light meal, especially when made with quality ingredients such as pastured fresh eggs with bright yolks. This savory vegetable filling combines roasted sweet fennel with buttery green olives, cheesy goodness, and a bright pop of fresh, seasonal herbs. I adore the delicate colors of this dish, and I would be happy putting an olive into just about anything! Serve with sourdough toast (page 54 or 59) and Roasted Garlic Hot Sauce (page 84).

SERVES 2

ROASTED FENNEL

2 cups cored and shaved fennel bulb (1 large bulb)

2 teaspoons cold-pressed extra-virgin olive oil

¼ teaspoon fine sea salt

OMELETS

6 large eggs

¼ teaspoon fine sea salt

¼ teaspoon freshly cracked black peppercorns

4 teaspoons cold-pressed extra-virgin olive oil

¼ cup pitted and sliced green olives (15 to 20 olives)

5 tablespoons finely shredded young Manchego cheese (about 2½ ounces)

1 teaspoon chiffonade-cut fresh tarragon, basil, or parsley leaves

1. Preheat the oven to 375°F and position a rack in the middle.

2. Make the roasted fennel: Line a medium baking sheet with parchment paper. In a medium bowl, toss the fennel with the oil and salt. Spread the fennel over the prepared baking sheet in an even layer. Transfer to the oven and roast for 35 minutes, stirring halfway through, until the tips are brown and the fennel is tender and translucent. Remove from the oven and set aside to cool.

3. In a small bowl, beat the eggs, salt, and pepper together with a fork until frothy. In a heavy-bottomed 8-inch skillet, heat 2 teaspoons of the oil over medium-high heat until shimmering, about 2 minutes. Pour half the beaten eggs (about ⅔ cup) into the pan and let the eggs set until the bottom fluffs and turns opaque, about 30 seconds. Tilt and swirl the skillet in a circular motion to evenly distribute and cook the eggs. Return the skillet to the heat and slide a spatula under the omelet to release it. Using the spatula, flip the omelet, or if you are feeling confident, toss and flip it midair before catching it in the skillet. Reduce the heat to low and evenly spread 2 tablespoons of the olives, 2½ tablespoons of the cheese, and half the roasted fennel over the egg. Fold one side over to sandwich the filling and use the spatula to transfer it to a plate. Sprinkle ½ teaspoon of the tarragon over the omelet and serve hot. Clean the pan with a paper towel and repeat the process for the second omelet.

SUNNY-FRIED EGGS
with Bacon, Kale, and Hominy Grits

In another homage to my Atlanta roots, the savory porridge made from Hominy Grits (page 46) gives this dish an almost floral scent, and it tastes amazing with farm-fresh sunny-side up eggs! If you don't have hominy grits, polenta will still give you a stellar breakfast experience. You can cool and refrigerate parcooked grits ahead of serving. Just cook them with the butter and stock for half the cooking time, and when you are ready to finish, add the water and salt and cook until tender. While the grits do not reheat well on their own, leftovers can still be delicious! Warm ½ cup additional chicken stock with a slab of butter in a small saucepan, and add 2 to 3 cups of cold grits. Gently stir until they reach hot and creamy perfection. This is a light breakfast for four or a hearty meal for two and is delicious with the Roasted Garlic Hot Sauce (page 84).

SERVES
2 TO 4

4 tablespoons unsalted butter

⅔ cup Hominy Grits (page 46) or polenta

1⅔ cups Chicken Stock (page 76), room temperature

1½ to 1¾ teaspoons fine sea salt, to taste

1½ teaspoons cold-pressed extra-virgin olive oil

1 tablespoon minced onion

3 cups loosely packed chopped kale, stems removed (1 large bunch)

4 large eggs

½ cup small-diced pepper jack cheese (4 ounces)

½ cup scallions, green and white parts sliced on the bias (4 scallions)

4 slices Simple Salt and Pepper Bacon (page 38), cooked and chopped

1. In a 3-quart heavy-bottomed pot, heat 2 tablespoons of the butter over medium-high heat and stir in the grits. Continue stirring until you can smell the aroma of toasted corn, about 3 minutes. Pour in 2 cups of water and the stock and bring to a roaring boil. Cook for 5 minutes and then reduce the heat to a simmer. Continue cooking the grits, uncovered, stirring frequently to prevent scorching, until they become thick and creamy, about 20 minutes. Add 1½ teaspoons of the salt and stir well to combine. Reduce the heat to low.

2. In a large skillet, heat the oil over medium-low heat until it expands, about 1 minute. Add the onion and sauté until translucent, 5 to 7 minutes. Add the chopped kale and cook until wilted, about 3 minutes. Remove from the heat and set aside.

3. In a small skillet, melt the remaining 2 tablespoons butter over medium heat. Increase the temperature to medium-high and crack the eggs into the skillet. Fry the eggs for 3 minutes, reduce the heat to medium, and finish cooking the eggs to your preference. Sprinkle the remaining ¼ teaspoon salt over the cooked eggs, or to taste.

4. Add the cheese and scallions to the cooked grits and stir until the cheese is melted. Remove from the heat.

5. Scoop the hot grits into serving bowls and garnish with the cooked kale. Place 1 or 2 hot eggs on top of each bowl and sprinkle with the crispy bacon. Serve immediately.

BAKED EGGS IN TOMATO SAUCE
with Chickpeas and Feta

Baked pastured eggs are a satisfying meal any time of the day, and this dish often falls into rotation because it easily serves a crowd! Even during the height of the pandemic, when our ability to congregate was diminished, the kitchen made this recipe for our WWOOF-ers (World Wide Opportunities on Organic Farms) and apprentice program meals. These dedicated volunteers spend labor-intensive days rotating through each department to gain the knowledge and skills of a regenerative farm. One of the most important aspects of bringing their learning full circle is building relationships with the land that are then experienced at the table, as with irresistible savory dishes like this.

SERVES 4

The sauce can be made ahead of time, and when you are ready to serve it, just add the eggs and bake it off. Serve with toasted and buttered slices of A Crusty Hearth-Style Sourdough Boule (page 59). Firm sheep's milk feta complements the sweet bell pepper and crushed tomatoes, but our milder Farmer's Cheese (page 70) also works well.

1 tablespoon cold-pressed extra-virgin olive oil

1 cup small-diced yellow onion (1 large onion)

1 cup small-diced red bell pepper (about 1 medium pepper)

1 tablespoon seeded and finely minced jalapeño pepper (1 medium pepper)

2 teaspoons minced garlic (2 cloves)

2 teaspoons fine sea salt

½ teaspoon smoked paprika

½ teaspoon ground cumin

1 (18.3-ounce) jar crushed tomatoes

1 cup cooked and drained chickpeas (see page 137)

5 large eggs

Freshly cracked black peppercorns, to taste

A few pinches flaked sea salt, to taste

½ cup crumbled feta cheese (4 ounces)

2 tablespoons finely chopped fresh parsley leaves

1. Preheat the oven to 375°F and position a rack in the middle.

2. In an ovenproof 12-inch skillet, heat the oil over medium-high heat until it expands and shimmers, about 2 minutes. Add the onion, bell pepper, jalapeño, garlic, salt, smoked paprika, and cumin. Sauté the vegetables until the onion is translucent and the moisture has evaporated, 5 to 8 minutes. Pour in the crushed tomatoes and stir in the chickpeas. Reduce the heat to medium and simmer until the sauce is slightly thickened, about 5 minutes.

3. With a spoon, create five equally distanced indentations in the sauce. Carefully crack one egg into each indentation. Season each egg with a crack of black pepper and pinch of salt to taste and sprinkle evenly with the crumbled feta. Transfer the skillet to the oven and bake, uncovered, for 10 minutes, or until the eggs are cooked to your preference.

4. Garnish with parsley and serve hot. This dish is best eaten the day it is made.

PICKLED DEVILED EGGS
with Beets, Horseradish, Honey, and Crispy Chicken Skin

These beautifully pink deviled eggs get their decorative upgrade from beets, which add an earthy flavor. When I was growing up, my mother always made pickled beets and eggs for picnics. This deviled egg recipe developed from my memories of slicing through a pickled egg to reveal the contrast of the yolk—and it is an even more beautiful sight when that yolk is from a pastured egg. A touch of honey mustard sweetness in the filling and a crispy chicken skin to finish create the perfect bite! The filling can be made up to 2 days in advance and assembled up to 24 hours before serving. The longer the eggs sit in the brine, the more color they will acquire; marinate for at least 48 hours for a fully pink egg white while retaining a yellow egg yolk. For another round with a less potent flavor, reserve the pickling brine after the first batch and use it to make more eggs.

MAKES 12 APPETIZERS

PICKLING BRINE

1½ cups peeled and roughly chopped beets (3 small to medium beets)

1½ cups creamed raw honey

1½ cups raw apple cider vinegar

2 teaspoons fine sea salt

6 large hard-boiled eggs, peeled

CRISPY CHICKEN SKIN

1 raw chicken breast and thigh skin

A few pinches fine sea salt

1. Make the pickling brine: In a small saucepan, combine the beets and 5 cups of water. Bring to a low boil over medium-high, reduce the heat to a simmer, and cook, uncovered, until tender, 35 to 40 minutes. Remove the pot from the heat and let cool until the liquid reaches 110°F on an instant-read thermometer, 20 to 25 minutes. Dice the beets and reserve 2 teaspoons for garnishing the eggs.

2. Add 1½ cups of the warm beet water to a 2-quart mason jar with a nonreactive lid. Add the honey, vinegar, and salt and stir to dissolve. Transfer the eggs and diced beets to the brine and fasten the lid. Place in the refrigerator for at least 24 hours or up to 48 hours for optimum color.

3. Preheat the oven to 350°F and position a rack in the middle.

4. Make the crispy chicken skin: Nestle a wire rack into a medium baking sheet. Gently stretch and lay the chicken skin flat on the rack. Sprinkle with a few pinches of salt and place in the oven. Bake for 30 to 40 minutes, until the skin is golden brown. Remove from the oven and let cool for 15 minutes before breaking into 1-inch pieces. The pieces can be stored, covered, in the refrigerator for up to 1 day before serving.

RECIPE AND INGREDIENTS CONTINUE

FILLING

3 tablespoons Avocado Oil Mayonnaise (page 90)

2 teaspoons Fermented Mustard (page 88)

1 tablespoon minced fermented dill pickle

1 teaspoon fermented dill pickle brine

½ teaspoon fresh lemon juice

2 teaspoons freshly grated or prepared horseradish

1 teaspoon mild raw honey

¼ teaspoon fine sea salt

⅛ teaspoon freshly ground black peppercorns

12 small fresh dill leaves (1 frond dill)

5. Make the filling: Slice the eggs in half lengthwise. Carefully remove the yolks and transfer to a small bowl. Add the mayonnaise, mustard, pickle, dill pickle brine, lemon juice, horseradish, honey, salt, and pepper. Mix with a fork until light but creamy, about 3 minutes. Use a small spoon to carefully and cleanly fill the eggs. Garnish with the crispy chicken skin, reserved diced beets, and a sprig of dill.

6. Serve immediately or place in a covered container in the refrigerator for up to 24 hours.

COOKING TIP: *Hard-Boiled Eggs*

When hard-boiling eggs, use older eggs aged for at least 10 days to make them easier to peel. Bring 1 quart of water to a boil in a small, covered pot. Add 6 large room-temperature eggs, lower the heat to a simmer, and cook, uncovered, for 12 minutes. Remove from the heat and ladle the eggs into an ice bath. Let them cool for 5 minutes before peeling.

THE POSTURE *and* PERSONALITY *of* OUR LAYING CHICKENS AND THEIR EGGS

....

Our market eggs come in a jewel box of colors—our customers covet them for their gorgeous, varied appearances as much as for their outstanding flavor and texture! Our hens have a high-quality, diverse diet, which includes foraging, as well as a supplemental organic, soy-free, and non-GMO feed we leave for them to eat whenever they'd like. This creates a fantastic egg—the yolks are rich and silky, and the whites are firm and full of protein. The shells range in color from a rich chocolate or speckled brown to a clean chalky white, buff tan, pastel olive speckled green, and a clear light blue. We raise mostly heritage hens and choose our breeds carefully. Our happy hens live their best lives pecking after grubs, worms, and insects in our fields once the cattle have finished grazing.

Commercial poultry and egg production became industrialized in the 1950s, and many heritage breeds faded in favor of those better suited to confinement. Commercial breed lines are often developed to pump out eggs starting at a young age (around eighteen weeks). These hens tend to have more health problems throughout their lives and burn out after only a few months of laying. We have a more holistic philosophy and choose a variety of slower-growing breeds so that they are healthier as they develop. Most of our hens begin laying at around twenty-two weeks of age and lay slightly fewer eggs each day on average. What we trade in early and high productivity, we gain in the benefit that they lay for a much longer time.

We believe that genetic diversity is key to maintaining healthy ecosystems. By combining many different breeds, our flocks also create a heightened immunity to some diseases and health issues. One breed may be very susceptible to a disease, but by having other breeds that are more resistant, it can slow the spread, giving time for the hens' defenses to build. If the problem does get out of hand, only a small percentage of the flock will be affected. It is the same concept as growing multiple kinds of vegetables instead of just one to protect against a pest outbreak. We select breeds that are best suited to our environment—they are good foragers so they enjoy roaming our fields, and we make sure they can withstand our hot and dry summer months and the harsh autumn winds. We also choose breeds with a pleasant demeanor so they can get along with the whole flock. Each breed has distinct behaviors, and sometimes peculiar personalities, that are a joy to observe. Meet our independent, pastured birds and their beautiful eggs!

Blue Andalusian (hen and rooster)

These robustly healthy heritage chickens have slate-blue to black plumage and white earlobes typical of Mediterranean breeds. They have a graceful upright carriage and are great foragers. The hens are the most consistent white egg-layer that we have, producing medium to large chalky-white eggs. They are small and active, and the roosters are protective and appear almost dragon-like. Walter was our barn mascot for many years, and he took his job of defending the misfit hens in ICU very seriously! Sadly, he passed of old age, but he's buried with the other treasured animals on the farm with a homemade rock epitaph indicating the unknown birthdate of "???"

Sicilian Buttercup

This very old and rare Mediterranean breed gets its name from the cup-shaped comb—particularly dazzling in the rooster—on both sides of its head. It continues over the beak, which has the effect of looking like a crown. These chickens are not well suited to cold environments since their signature showy comb is susceptible to frostbite. Although the plumage of most hens tends to be muted for camouflage, both the male and female Sicilian Buttercups are vibrant looking. The hens do well on pasture in our warm climate and are consistent layers of small to medium white eggs that add variety to our market box. They are very curious and alert—nothing escapes their eye! It is impossible to sneak up behind them, but that is to their advantage. They are typically smaller and lighter than our other hens, adding to the agility necessary to escape predators in the field!

Silver Spangled Hamburg (hen)

Busy and active, Hamburg chickens are attractive birds that consist of six recognized standard varieties. We keep the charming dalmatian-patterned Hamburg hens in our flock as reliable layers of small white eggs. They are popular show birds and excellent foragers. These stylish and graceful hens are small but a bit flighty. When conducting a chicken check in the evenings after the automatic coop doors close, we find them roosted in trees, on top of coops, or generally anywhere we'd prefer them not to be! Thankfully their coloring is easy to spot at dusk, and we can eventually coax them back to safety.

Barred Plymouth Rock (hen and rooster)

Barred Plymouth Rock chickens were the most common barnyard chicken in the United States until the end of World War II due to their hardy but docile and very curious nature; they will often follow you around watching for treats! These iconic American birds made up the bulk of our very first flock and still prove to be some of our most consistent heritage layers. When we release the chickens from their coops in the early morning, they are the most eager to explore the field for food that other chickens wouldn't even consider pecking. They are also friendly and the first to greet you in the evening. Their curiosity and daring will lead them to compromising situations at times, but thankfully they rebound well from most trouble!

These hens' maternal instincts are strong, and they often go broody, stubbornly sitting on or returning to their nest when removed to try and hatch the eggs. Although this may lead to a decrease in egg production, they make good mothers for this reason and are still respectable producers of large brown eggs.

Speckled Sussex

This stunningly beautiful old English breed is very sweet and gentle with an even temper. They are built to be more cold hardy due to their smaller combs and larger body frames; as long as they have access to plenty of shade, they are quite happy in our pasture near a cooling mobile sprinkler or shade cloth when the temperatures are warm. They are good layers of large tan to light brown eggs. Despite their short, white, muscular legs and white four-toed feet, they are typically well camouflaged when free ranging our pastures. A hen named Butterball was the exception, famous on the farm and aptly named due to her rotund appearance—she literally looked like a ball with a head and little feet attached! She was friendly and

CONTINUES

BLUE
ANDALUSIAN

SICILIAN BUTTERCUP

SILVER
SPANGLED
HAMBURG

WELSUMMER

RHODE ISLAND
RED

DELAWARE

BARRED
PLYMOTH
ROCK

FRENCH BLACK
COPPER MARANS

SPECKLED
SUSSEX

OLIVE EGGER

CUCKOO MARANS

EASTER
EGGER

pet-like, and a treasure until we lost her to a hawk. We wish she had known how to curl up and roll away from danger, but she likely tasted delicious!

Rhode Island Red

This distinguished and intelligent American breed is naturally protected from predators due to its non-showy plumage. They are friendly beginner birds (we think of them as the Labradors of birds) well suited for backyard flocks or pasture. The hardy hens are our most prolific layers of large brown eggs, and the happy-go-clucky personalities of these ruby red ladies are a favorite on the farm. One hen named Red is so gregarious that she has become a mascot. She goes out of her way to climb the stairs to visit Maria and communicates digestive distress by pecking at our chicken wrangler Dave's feet. If she hears a meeting is in process, she will show up to be included! Their only downside is that they are the last to leave the pasture party and will often resist going into the coop in the evenings!

Delaware

These beautiful, mostly snow-white chickens are named after the state in which they were developed. They are a cross between the Barred Plymouth Rock roosters and New Hampshire hens and retain some barred feathers on their tails and hackles and occasionally the wings and body. They are intelligent, calm, and playfully curious hens who are very protective of their large brown eggs and will peck your hands to defend them from being gathered! Although they are fast growers and make excellent dual-purpose birds, few small farms kept them, and they steadily declined in popularity. Their status was listed as critical by the American Livestock Breeds Conservancy in 2009, but thankfully a few dedicated people have kept the breed going. Ours are not overly friendly but thankfully don't get spooked too easily when we do handle them.

Welsummer

This sturdy and talkative breed takes its name from the Dutch village of Welsum and is relatively new to North America, having arrived in 1928. We love that they are such good communicators, trilling happy chirps when content with pleasure or clucking brazenly when something is afoul! They are one of only two breeds in the world that lay large and stunning terracotta eggs, at times marked with brown speckles. Unlike the permanent pigment within blue eggshells, the "ink" that overlays brown chicken eggs is unstable. This ink is so richly present in Welsummer eggs that it is easy to wipe away when we clean our eggs by hand before market! Although somewhat underrepresented in most backyard chicken coops, they are a reliable and friendly breed but a little goofy at times: it isn't unusual to find them stuck somewhere that they've perched! They are also one of the best pastured foragers of laying chickens and are known for tolerating the cold with ease. With ample access to heavy shade, they do fine in our Southern California environment.

French Black Copper Marans

These tall and stately birds of French origin lay very large, intensely dark chocolate, almost copper-colored eggs. The birds are difficult to source from hatcheries, and their striking eggs are the most sought after from the farm. Some might even call the plumage a bit gothic, but we think these rare birds are as elegant as they are unusual! The hens that produce the most beautifully colored eggs often lay the fewest—as the season wears on, their ink can run low—and this is true for French Black Copper Marans, which lay only 150 to 200 eggs a year. But the quality and taste of these eggs is unsurpassed, especially when pastured.

Breeders like our team member Dave (see Resources, page 392) work with French Black Copper Marans to try to create eggs with an even darker color. They take extreme pride in this—there is even a grading scale for how dark the eggs are! Our hens are approachable but not overly friendly, are active and hardy, and enjoy free ranging our pastures.

Cuckoo Marans

These friendly and rare hens resemble the Barred Plymouth Rock chickens in plumage, with beautiful, darkly colored feathers marked with irregular, almost black and light slate–colored bars. Subtle differences set them apart, however. They are not a recognized breed but are considered a prized bird for their consistent color that is not quite as dark as the Black Copper Maran. Our Cuckoo Marans have short, tough grayish feathers, a trait known as "hard" feathers that is common among birds of game heritage. The Cuckoo Marans have clean and featherless pinkish-white legs and feet but lay stunning and distinct brown eggs with chocolate spots speckled throughout their shells. These gorgeous eggs have made them an increasingly popular chicken in the United States, and we love them for their personable and hardy disposition. Because of their decent size and weight, they can also make a good dual-purpose bird if necessary.

Easter Eggers and Olive Eggers

Although most chickens are prized purebreds, Easter Eggers are the beloved mutts of the chicken world, displaying a variety of body sizes, feather colors, and plumage patterns. An Easter Egger is not a true breed but a way of characterizing blue-egg-laying chickens. In our flock, they are the ones that get picked on the most because they vary so much in terms of appearances. Because chickens are a flock animal, any bird that stands out is likely to fall to the bottom of the rank.

What they lack in pedigree, however, they make up for in beautiful pastel eggs, amusing and curious personalities, and quiet, low-maintenance behavior. The blue color is the result of a pigment produced by the hen's liver that stays true on both the inside and outside of the shell. Other egg colors are possible within this classification as well. For example, when a brown-egg-laying breed is crossed with the Easter Egger parent breed (Ameraucana), the result is an olive-drab-laying Olive Egger. These pastel-blue eggs with a mottled-brown pigment overlay make a striking addition to our collection!

The hens are heat and cold hardy and get along best with other birds of a similar disposition. Their laser-focused bay-red eyes may appear fierce, but we enjoy these birds for their sweet, sociable character and predator-savvy survival instincts in the field. Nugget, a hen who lives at the barn with Red (and Walter, when he was alive), once famously laid a clutch of eggs in a trash can filled with fifty pounds of pig feed. The chicks couldn't escape the walls of the trash can, but she had cleverly ensured that they had plenty to eat!

Chapter Eight

PASTURED BEEF and LAMB

LAMBING SEASON IS SUCH A GORGEOUS TIME OF YEAR. THE ENERGY THAT OUR Dorper lambs bring with their playfulness and exhaustive curiosity mirrors the feeling of the earth coming alive in spring! We have chosen to focus on this heritage breed, as they are well suited to the hot and arid climate of Southern California but thrive on our lush pasture. The ewes have a long breeding season, and we adore the mild and versatile flavor of the lamb. When we rear these lambs and our heritage-breed cattle, the process is coupled with intentional, sometimes hard choices. Some of the animals, like our Highland cow Firefly, end up being almost like pets because of their long history with us. But, ultimately, as a farmer, you cannot become a hoarder. It adds responsibilities to your team and sometimes compromises the health of the animal. Firefly eventually became so overweight and arthritic that we chose to let her go. We still wrestle with that decision. I have found farming intersects with all the human emotions, including grief.

With the slow passage of time and a focus on best practices, we have been able to create a delicious meat; the health of the pasture is our primary concern because that is the ultimate factor in the health of the animals. What these ruminants eat can significantly affect the nutrient composition of their meat, leading to a real difference in flavor and performance in the kitchen. Grass-fed meats are lean but boast up to five times the amount of beneficial omega-3 fatty acids of conventional meats.

For us, it is important to create recipes that respect the whole animal and also older animals. Mutton is the meat from a mature sheep, and it has different cooking requirements than conventional or even pastured young lamb. When combined with bold spices, however, it is rich and savory—and lets us honor and use the whole cycle of life rather than just the prime cuts of young animals. The following recipes work with the unparalleled flavor of grass-fed beef and lamb and guide you through preparing their cuts for tender, juicy, and succulent results.

Recipes

Roasted Racks of Lamb with Orange-Olive Crust

Shepherd's Pie with Sweet Potato and Chimichurri Sauce

Spiced Lamb Stew with Apricots and Coconut

Spiced Lamb Burgers with Tzatziki

Lamb Kebabs with Meyer Lemon Salsa

Lamb Meatballs with Currants, Yogurt, and Arugula-Mint Pesto

Succulent Beef Short Ribs with Spring Vegetables

Wood-Fired Rib Eye with Fermented Nasturtium Berry Sauce

Crispy Bull Meat Tacos with Romaine Slaw

Grass-Fed Beef Liver Smothered in Spring Onion Medley with Spicy Horseradish Mustard

ROASTED RACKS OF LAMB
with Orange-Olive Crust

Bright and salty Mediterranean-inspired flavors permeate and balance this lamb, which marinates for up to 36 hours before cooking. When sourcing the lamb, look for racks that have been "frenched," or cleaned of fat and sinew that connect the bones, for ease of handling and an impressive presentation. Searing the racks first on a charcoal grill adds a welcome smoky note, but you can skip this step altogether if you don't have access to a grill. Using a low-acid navel orange in the marinade will help the racks brown and create a nuanced flavor. Once the marinade is prepared, taste for assertiveness and adjust the garlic, shallots, and lemon as needed; a strong flavor will tenderize and season the meat. Serve with Roasted Tokyo Turnip and Nantes Carrot Medley with Carrot-Harissa Hummus (page 120) or Kale Salad with Crispy Chickpeas and Parmesan (page 137).

SERVES
4 TO 6

LAMB

Two 5½ × 7½ × 1-inch frenched racks of lamb (about 1 pound each)

CITRUS MARINADE

1 teaspoon orange zest

2 cups fresh orange juice (16 ounces)

3 tablespoons chopped shallot (about 1½ small shallots)

4 teaspoons chopped garlic (about 4 large cloves)

5 teaspoons fine sea salt

½ cup packed chopped fresh parsley leaves (½ bunch)

¼ cup cold-pressed extra-virgin olive oil

1½ tablespoons Preserved Lemon peel (page 34), pith removed (2 to 3 wedges)

1 tablespoon Preserved Lemon liquid (page 34)

1. Make the lamb: Using a thin knife, pierce the racks of lamb all over, about ¼ inch deep and about 1 inch apart, to allow the marinade to penetrate the meat. Set the racks in a deep container or a large plastic bag.

2. Make the citrus marinade: In the pitcher of a blender, place the orange zest and juice, shallot, garlic, salt, parsley, oil, and preserved lemon peel and liquid. Blend on high until the marinade turns a light green, 30 seconds. Pour the marinade over the rib meat, avoiding the bones to prevent burning. Cover with a lid or seal the bag and place in the refrigerator for at least 8 and up to 36 hours.

3. Make the olive paste: In a small bowl, combine the olives, orange zest, oil, salt, and pepper and stir to combine. Set aside until ready to use.

4. Preheat the oven to 425°F and position a rack in the middle. If you have a grill plate, preheat it to high.

5. Remove the racks from the marinade and shake off any excess liquid. Sear the racks on the grill plate, fat side down, for 1 to 2 minutes, rotating as necessary to achieve even grill marks. Transfer the racks to a plate and let them cool, uncovered, until ready to handle, about 5 minutes. If you do not have a grill plate, simply skip this step. Divide the olive paste in half and smear each half evenly over the meaty side of each rack.

OLIVE PASTE

⅔ cup pitted and finely chopped green olives

2 teaspoons orange zest

¼ cup cold-pressed extra-virgin olive oil

¼ teaspoon fine sea salt

⅛ teaspoon freshly ground black peppercorns

6. Nestle a wire rack into a large baking sheet. Place the lamb racks, meaty side up, on the wire rack and transfer to the oven. Roast for 30 to 35 minutes, until the internal temperature reaches 135°F to 140°F on an instant-read thermometer. Remove the pan from the oven and let the racks rest at least 15 minutes before carving into portions. Serve hot.

SHEPHERD'S PIE
with Sweet Potato and Chimichurri Sauce

This savory pie is a comforting and flexible favorite that, when made in advance and frozen, allows us to feed a group in a pinch. The pie and chimichurri sauce can be made separately up to 6 months in advance and thawed in the refrigerator the night before it is baked. Mutton is excellent in this dish, and the chimichurri sauce both brightens and complements the strong flavor of mature meat. If you cannot source it, substitute grass-fed ground lamb or ground beef instead. Orange sweet potatoes provide a gorgeous presentation, but slightly drier white sweet potatoes work as well.

SERVES
8 TO 10

CHIMICHURRI SAUCE

1 cup loosely packed finely minced fresh parsley leaves (1 bunch)

1 tablespoon minced jalapeño pepper (about 1 medium pepper)

1 tablespoon minced garlic (3 cloves)

¼ cup minced red onion (about ¼ large onion)

1 teaspoon fine sea salt

½ teaspoon crushed red chile flakes

¼ teaspoon freshly ground black peppercorns

2 tablespoons plus 2 teaspoons red wine vinegar

¾ cup cold-pressed extra-virgin olive oil

1. Make the chimichurri sauce: In a small food processor, place the parsley, jalapeño, garlic, onion, salt, chile flakes, pepper, vinegar, and oil. Pulse to combine, transfer to a serving dish, and set aside.

2. Preheat the oven to 350°F and position a rack in the middle.

3. Make the pie: Line a large baking sheet with parchment paper and place the sweet potatoes on top. Transfer to the oven and bake for about 45 minutes, or until fork tender. Remove from the oven and set aside until cool enough to handle, 10 to 15 minutes. Remove and discard the skin and place the flesh in the bowl of a food processor. Add the butter, 1½ teaspoons of the salt, and 1 teaspoon of the pepper, and puree until smooth and creamy, scraping down the sides as needed.

4. Increase the oven temperature to 375°F.

5. In a 10-inch cast-iron skillet, heat 1 tablespoon of the lard over medium-high heat. Add half the ground mutton, 1 teaspoon of the salt, and ½ teaspoon of the pepper. Cook, stirring with a spoon, until the meat is dark brown and crumbled, 7 to 10 minutes. Transfer to a large baking sheet and repeat with the remaining mutton.

6. Reduce the heat to medium and add the carrots, onion, celery, garlic, and thyme to the skillet with the residual mutton fat. Sweat the vegetables until the onion becomes translucent, 4 to 5 minutes. Transfer the mutton back to the skillet and add the crushed tomatoes and vinegar.

RECIPE AND INGREDIENTS CONTINUE

PIE

7 small orange sweet potatoes
(about 4 pounds)

4 teaspoons unsalted butter

3½ teaspoons fine sea salt

2 teaspoons freshly ground black
peppercorns

2 tablespoons Lard (page 37)

2 pounds ground mutton

1 cup minced carrots (about 3 medium
carrots)

1 cup minced yellow onion
(1 large onion)

1 cup minced celery (about 3 stalks)

2 tablespoons minced garlic (6 cloves)

1 tablespoon fresh thyme leaves
or 1½ teaspoons dried

1 (18.3-ounce) jar crushed tomatoes

1 tablespoon raw apple cider vinegar

1 cup fresh or frozen shelled peas

Increase the heat to medium-high, stir well, and cook for 10 minutes. Stir in the peas and cook for an additional 5 minutes. Transfer the mixture to a 9 × 11-inch casserole dish and spread evenly.

7. Scoop the pureed sweet potatoes over the top of the filling. Using a spatula, smooth out the top to create an even, attractive layer. Place the casserole in the oven and bake for 30 minutes, or until the filling begins to bubble.

8. Turn the broiler on medium and broil the pie for an additional 4 to 6 minutes on the middle rack to brown the top, keeping in mind that broiling intensity will vary by oven.

9. Remove the pie from the oven and let it cool for 15 minutes to set. Serve warm with the chimichurri sauce on the side. Let cool completely and store, covered, in the refrigerator for up to 5 days or in the freezer for up to 6 months.

COOKING TIP: *Browning Meat*

Taking the time to brown pastured meat only enhances its flavor! Cook in small batches to crispy perfection on the stovetop whenever possible. During cooking, meat undergoes many chemical changes affecting its appearance, taste, and texture. Browning or searing leaner pastured meat produces the rich, deep colors, flavors, and aromas that we love. This browning process is known as the Maillard reaction.

SPICED LAMB STEW
with Apricots and Coconut

Although the meat from our farm is typically mild, the distinctive character of lamb is best when paired with both sweet and spicy ingredients. After you take the time to cook the lamb in small batches, which creates a nice golden crust, this dish comes together with minimal effort beyond the occasional stir. Best made a day ahead, the stew reheats beautifully, and the flavors improve over time. Serve with a rice pilaf or Sourdough Flatbread (page 64).

SERVES 6

LAMB STEW

2 pounds lamb stew meat, cut into 2-inch cubes

2 teaspoons fine sea salt

½ teaspoon freshly ground black peppercorns

4 tablespoons unrefined avocado oil

5 to 6 cups Chicken Stock (page 76)

2 cups small-diced yellow onion (2 large onions)

1 tablespoon minced garlic (3 cloves)

1 tablespoon seeded and finely minced jalapeño pepper (1 medium pepper)

1½ teaspoons garam masala

1 (18.3-ounce) jar crushed tomatoes

2 cups chopped dried Turkish apricots

1 cup full-fat coconut milk

GARNISH

½ cup toasted coconut flakes

½ cup chopped fresh cilantro or mint leaves

⅓ cup sliced jalapeño pepper (3 large peppers)

6 lemon wedges (1½ lemons)

1. Make the stew: In a medium bowl, combine the lamb, salt, and pepper, and mix with your hands to season evenly. In a 4-quart Dutch oven, heat 2 tablespoons of the oil over medium heat until it is shimmering, 2 to 3 minutes. Brown the meat in two batches, searing for a total of 5 minutes per batch, until golden brown. Remove the meat from the pot and transfer to a baking sheet. Remove from the heat and deglaze the pot with ½ cup of the stock, scraping the brown bits from the bottom with a spoon. Pour the deglazing liquid over the lamb and set aside.

2. In the same pot, heat the remaining 2 tablespoons oil over medium heat until it is shimmering, about 2 minutes. Add the onion, garlic, and jalapeño, and sprinkle with the garam masala. Sauté until the onion is translucent, 5 to 8 minutes. Add the seared meat to the pot, along with the tomatoes, apricots, 4½ cups of the stock, and the coconut milk. Cover, reduce the heat to low, and bring to a simmer. Remove the lid and continue to simmer until the meat is fork tender, stirring about every 20 minutes, 2 to 2½ hours. The sauce should be the consistency of a rich, thick gravy and the apricots will have almost dissolved. If the stew becomes too thick for your liking, thin with the remaining cup of stock.

3. Serve sprinkled with the coconut flakes, cilantro, jalapeño, and a squeeze of lemon to finish. Store fully cooled in sealed containers (garnishes kept separate) in the refrigerator for up to 3 days.

SPICED LAMB BURGERS *with Tzatziki*

The first time I cooked for our partners of Apricot Lane Farms, let's just say it was a learning opportunity. As a private chef, my clients rarely requested lamb, and so I was unprepared to cook with meat that can sometimes have a gamey gristle. Our small rental apartment reeked of the pungent aroma of lamb stock, yet our partners were gracious and said nothing as they ate the rack I'd made. I learned that night that Dorper meat is typically mild and delicious no matter what you do, but if you're still not a fan, use grass-fed beef in partial or whole substitution for the ground lamb in these burgers. Serve with your choice of bread bun or flatbread, lettuce, Roasted Garlic Hot Sauce (page 84), Root Vegetable Chips (page 369), or a variety of fresh sides, such as the Roasted Picnic Pepper and Tomato Panzanella Salad (page 170).

SERVES 4

TZATZIKI

⅔ cup thinly shaved English cucumber, cut into half-moons (½ medium cucumber)

1 cup Greek yogurt

1 teaspoon minced garlic (1 clove)

1 tablespoon fresh lime juice (½ medium lime)

¾ teaspoon fine sea salt

1 tablespoon finely chopped fresh mint leaves

BURGERS

1 tablespoon ghee

1 cup minced yellow onion (1 large onion)

1½ tablespoons minced garlic (about 5 cloves)

1 tablespoon minced jalapeño pepper (1 medium pepper)

1 pound ground lamb

1 large egg

1 teaspoon yellow curry powder

½ teaspoon ground cumin

¼ teaspoon ground coriander

1½ teaspoons fine sea salt

½ teaspoon freshly ground black peppercorns

1. Make the tzatziki: In a small bowl, combine the cucumber, yogurt, garlic, lime juice, salt, and mint. Stir well, transfer to a serving dish, and set aside.

2. Make the burgers: In a large cast-iron skillet, melt the ghee over medium heat. Add the onion, garlic, and jalapeño and sauté until the onion is soft and translucent, about 5 minutes. Scoop the vegetables into a small bowl and refrigerate, about 10 minutes. Reserve the skillet for cooking the burgers.

3. Preheat the oven to 375°F and position a rack in the middle.

4. Nestle a wire rack into a medium baking sheet. Place the ground lamb in a medium bowl, add the cooled vegetables, egg, curry powder, cumin, coriander, salt, and pepper and mix to thoroughly combine; the mixture will be moist and soft. Divide into four equal parts and shape into ½-inch-thick patties. Place the skillet over medium-high heat and sear the burgers for 2 minutes on each side. Using a spatula, transfer the burgers to the wire rack and place the baking sheet in the oven. Bake the burgers for 12 to 15 minutes, until the internal temperature reaches 160°F on an instant-read thermometer. Remove from the oven and let them cool for 10 minutes.

5. Serve the lamb burgers hot alongside the tzatziki sauce.

LAMB KEBABS
with Meyer Lemon Salsa

One year Amy Overbeck, the editor of *The Biggest Little Farm*, came over with her family for New Year's Eve, and I served this dish. Her sweet young daughters loved it, as did Beaudie, so I can officially say this is a crowd-pleaser for all ages! Our mild-tasting Dorper sheep spend most of their time rotating through the lemon orchards, browsing the low leaves, whose tannins can serve as a preemptive dewormer. This dish brings the ingredients full circle! Lamb loin is appropriate for grilling, but you can substitute another tender cut or beef steak instead. Remove any sinew or extra fatty bits from the meat before marinating to ensure the texture remains appealing once grilled. A mild or buttery extra-virgin olive oil is best for the salsa; prepare it no longer than a few hours in advance to avoid bitterness from the pith. Serve alongside Sourdough Flatbread (page 64) or pair with the Farro Grain Bowl with Star Ruby Grapefruit, Feta, and Pistachio (page 347).

SERVES 4

MEYER LEMON SALSA

½ cup thinly sliced Meyer lemon (1 medium lemon)

¼ cup thinly shaved shallot (1 small shallot)

½ teaspoon minced garlic (1 small clove)

¼ cup cold-pressed extra-virgin olive oil

¼ cup red wine vinegar

¾ teaspoon fine sea salt

½ teaspoon freshly cracked black peppercorns

MARINADE

¼ cup seeded and roughly chopped jalapeño peppers (2 large jalapeños)

2 teaspoons lightly toasted cumin seeds, crushed in a mortar and pestle

2 teaspoons lightly toasted coriander seeds, crushed in a mortar and pestle

2 cups loosely packed roughly chopped fresh parsley leaves (2 bunches)

1½ tablespoons roughly chopped garlic (4 large cloves)

1. Place eight 10-inch wooden skewers in a container and cover with warm water. Set aside to soak for at least 30 minutes.

2. Make the Meyer lemon salsa: In a small bowl, combine the lemon slices, shallot, garlic, oil, vinegar, salt, and pepper. Stir with a spoon and set aside.

3. Make the marinade: In a food processor, combine the jalapeños, cumin, coriander, parsley, garlic, oil, lemon juice, and salt. Pulse to create a thick green sauce, scraping down the sides as necessary. Set aside.

4. Make the kebabs: Remove any sinew or extra fatty bits from the lamb. Place in a small bowl, sprinkle with the salt, and toss to combine. Divide the lamb into 8 portions and pierce the pieces of each portion onto a skewer. Place the skewers on a large baking sheet and massage the meat with half the marinade and reserve the other half for serving. Cover with plastic wrap and place the lamb in the refrigerator to marinate for 2 to 3 hours. Remove from the refrigerator and let the lamb rest at room temperature for at least 30 minutes before grilling.

5. Preheat a gas grill to medium-high heat for at least 30 minutes. If using charcoal or wood, preheat for about 1 hour according to the instructions on page 186.

RECIPE AND INGREDIENTS CONTINUE

½ cup cold-pressed extra-virgin olive oil

¼ cup fresh lemon juice (1 large lemon)

1 teaspoon fine sea salt

KEBABS

2 pounds lamb loin, cut into 1-inch cubes

1 teaspoon fine sea salt

6. Place the kebabs on the grill and cook over medium-high heat. When the meat easily releases from the grill plate, rotate as necessary to achieve an evenly seared and cooked kebab. Grill for 6 to 8 minutes for rare to medium-rare. Remove the lamb from the grill and let it rest for 5 to 10 minutes before serving. Transfer the kebabs to a large serving platter and spoon some of the lemon salsa over top. Serve with the remaining marinade and salsa on the side.

7. Store the meat separate from the salsa and marinade and keep in sealed containers in the refrigerator for up to 3 days.

LAMB MEATBALLS
with Currants, Yogurt, and Arugula-Mint Pesto

The nuanced flavor of grass-fed lamb shines through in this dish, especially when complemented by warming spices, savory-sweet pesto, and cooling yogurt. Although golden raisins are best to use for a vibrant pesto, you may swap in crimson raisins or a smaller amount of the extremely sweet Uzbek Hunza raisins instead. When shaping the meatballs, do not worry about getting a perfect sphere; you may end up with mini footballs and that is OK. The less you work the mixture, the more tender your meatball will be. Serve this alongside Sourdough Flatbread (page 64).

SERVES
4 TO 6

MEATBALLS

3 tablespoons ghee

¾ cup small-diced yellow onion (about ¾ large onion)

1 tablespoon minced garlic (3 cloves)

2 pounds ground lamb

2½ teaspoons fine sea salt

1 teaspoon smoked paprika

½ teaspoon ground cumin

¼ teaspoon ground green cardamom

¼ cup loosely packed roughly chopped fresh parsley leaves (¼ bunch)

4 large eggs

½ cup dried currants

⅓ cup Sourdough Breadcrumbs (page 61)

1. Make the meatballs: In a small skillet, melt 1 tablespoon of the ghee over medium heat until shimmering, about 2 minutes. Stir in the onion and garlic and gently sweat the mixture until the onion is translucent, 5 to 7 minutes. Remove from the heat and set aside to cool, about 10 minutes.

2. In a medium bowl, break apart the ground lamb. Sprinkle in the salt, paprika, cumin, cardamom, and parsley. Add the cooled onion mixture and the eggs. Gently mix with your hands until just incorporated and few to no lumps remain. It will feel very tacky.

3. Add the currants and breadcrumbs to the bowl and gently mix with your hands to evenly distribute. The mixture will resemble a slightly sticky paste but should come together easily. Do not overwork the meat to avoid any toughness. Allow the mixture to rest, covered, for 5 to 30 minutes in the refrigerator before shaping. The breadcrumbs will soften and absorb moisture, leading to a tender and fluffy meatball.

4. Line a large baking sheet with parchment paper. Form the meat mixture into 2-inch balls and place on the prepared baking sheet. You should have about 2 dozen meatballs.

RECIPE AND INGREDIENTS CONTINUE

ARUGULA-MINT PESTO

1 cup packed arugula

½ cup packed fresh basil leaves

⅔ cup packed fresh mint leaves

¼ cup fresh lemon juice (1 large lemon)

½ cup golden raisins

1 teaspoon fine sea salt, to taste

1 cup cold-pressed extra-virgin olive oil

GARNISH

1 quart Greek yogurt

⅓ cup pine nuts

5. Preheat the oven to 400°F and position a rack in the middle.

6. In a 12-inch cast-iron skillet, melt the remaining 2 tablespoons ghee over medium-high heat. Working in batches, place the meatballs 2 inches apart in the pan and sear. As they begin to brown, use tongs to gently release and rotate them. If they do not lift readily from the pan, cook an additional 30 to 45 seconds. Continue rotating them as necessary to evenly brown on all sides. This should take about 6 minutes total per batch. Transfer the seared meatballs back to the baking sheet and repeat with the remaining meatballs. Transfer the seared meatballs to the oven and bake for 8 to 10 minutes, until the internal temperature registers 150°F on an instant-read thermometer.

7. Make the pesto: In the bowl of a food processor or blender, place the arugula, basil, mint, lemon juice, raisins, salt, and oil. Blend on high until smooth, about 2 minutes, scraping down the sides as necessary. Adjust the seasoning to taste.

8. To serve, spread the Greek yogurt on a large serving platter, making indentations with the back of a spoon to create attractive ripples. Spoon half the pesto in a circular motion on top, allowing it to fill the indentations of the yogurt. Lay the hot meatballs on top and garnish with the pine nuts and remaining pesto, or serve on the side. Serve immediately.

SUCCULENT BEEF SHORT RIBS
with Spring Vegetables

When the days finally lengthen and the sun shines generously over the garden, the first tender spring root vegetables are plucked from the soil. Our carrots and turnips are sweetest at this time and complement the bright, fresh snap peas that we've been waiting to return. This braise is best made with homemade Roasted Beef Bone Stock (page 79), which imparts an unmistakable depth to the dish, but you may substitute a low-sodium store-bought stock instead. Deglazing the skillet with apple cider vinegar adds a bit of brightness, but substitute white wine if you prefer.

SERVES 6

SHORT RIB BRAISE

4¼ pounds pastured boneless beef short ribs (six to eight 1½ × 6-inch pieces)

1 tablespoon fine sea salt

2 tablespoons unrefined avocado oil

¼ cup raw apple cider vinegar

4 sprigs fresh rosemary

10 garlic cloves

1 cup chopped carrot (about 2 medium carrots)

1 cup chopped yellow onion (1 large onion)

2 teaspoons tomato paste

2 teaspoons Fermented Mustard (page 88)

½ teaspoon freshly ground black peppercorns

3½ cups Roasted Beef Bone Stock (page 79)

1. Preheat the oven to 300°F and position a rack in the middle.

2. Make the short rib braise: Evenly sprinkle the short ribs on both sides with the salt and let rest, uncovered, at room temperature for 15 minutes. The salt will draw out some water, creating a brine. In a 10-inch skillet, heat the oil over high heat until it expands and shimmers, about 2 minutes. Sear the short ribs in batches, until nicely browned, about 2 minutes per side. Remove from the heat and transfer the ribs to a plate. Pour off the excess fat from the pan, add the vinegar, and deglaze the pan, stirring to release the caramelized bits of meat and fat. Set aside.

3. Place the seared short ribs in a 9 × 13-inch baking dish and nestle the rosemary, garlic, carrot, and onion in between. Pour the contents of the deglazed skillet over the short ribs. Whisk the tomato paste, mustard, and pepper into the stock to dissolve before pouring over the short ribs. Cover the dish with a sheet of parchment paper before wrapping the top with foil. Place the dish in the oven and braise the short ribs until tender but not falling apart, about 3 hours. Remove the foil and parchment and roast until the meat shreds easily with a fork, about 1 more hour.

4. Make the spring vegetables: In a large skillet, heat 1 tablespoon of the oil over high heat until it expands, about 1 minute. Add the carrots and sear until golden brown, 3 to 4 minutes. Pour in ¼ cup of water, cover, and steam until fork tender, 5 to 7 minutes. Transfer to a large bowl and add 1 tablespoon of the oil to the skillet. Place the turnips in the skillet and sear for 3 minutes, then add ¼ cup of water. Cover and steam until

RECIPE AND INGREDIENTS CONTINUE

SPRING VEGETABLES

3 tablespoons unrefined avocado oil

1½ cups 1-inch-sliced baby carrots (about 12 extra-small carrots)

12 medium turnips, halved

2 cups ½-inch-chopped leeks, white parts only (3 large leeks)

1 cup sugar snap peas, ends trimmed and stems removed (about 12 peas)

¾ teaspoon fine sea salt

the turnips are tender, about 5 minutes. Transfer to the bowl with the carrots and add the remaining 1 tablespoon oil to the skillet. Stir in the leeks and sauté until tender, about 7 minutes. Add the snap peas and cook, uncovered, for an additional 2 minutes. Transfer the leeks and snap peas to the bowl with the carrots and turnips, season with the salt, and toss lightly to coat.

5. Line a fine-mesh sieve with cheesecloth and place over a medium bowl. Spoon the short ribs onto a plate (you can compost the braised vegetables). Strain the stock through the sieve and skim off the fat with a spoon. Transfer the skimmed sauce to a small, wide pot and set over medium heat. Reduce the sauce until it lightly coats the back of a spoon, 5 to 7 minutes.

6. Shred the short ribs with a fork, discarding any excess fat, and transfer to a large serving platter. Ladle the reduced sauce over top, spoon on the vegetables, and serve hot. Store any leftovers in a lidded container in the refrigerator for up to 5 days.

WOOD-FIRED RIB EYE
with Fermented Nasturtium Berry Sauce

Nasturtiums are cool-season annual plants (*Tropaeolum* sp.) that have many edible parts, including beautiful, brightly colored orange, yellow, red, and cream flowers and endearing round leaves with a flavor similar to watercress. The "berries," as they are often called, are actually the young green seedpods that form after the flower is spent. When picked tender, they can be pickled or fermented into something that resembles a caper, although with a much spicier kick. Nasturtiums have naturalized in most of California, where they can be seen blanketing shady hillsides and carpeting the understory of trees. Here in the southern part of the state, their seeds can be harvested in early to mid-winter, while in other four-season climates, late spring or early summer would be more appropriate. Their bold flavor pairs well with steak, and this dish is delicious served alongside French Onion Potato Puree (page 111). Note: You'll want to start fermenting the nasturtium berries at least 3 days in advance (or up to 1 year) before making this dish.

SERVES 4

NASTURTIUM BERRY SAUCE

6 to 8 fresh green nasturtium berries

¾ teaspoon fine sea salt

1 cup Greek yogurt

2 tablespoons Fermented Mustard (page 88)

1 teaspoon minced garlic (1 clove)

2 teaspoons minced fresh parsley leaves

¼ cup thinly sliced scallions or fresh chives (2 scallions)

¼ teaspoon freshly cracked black peppercorns

RIB EYE STEAKS

4 boneless rib eye steaks (13 ounces each)

1 tablespoon fine sea salt

GARNISH

½ teaspoon thinly sliced fermented nasturtium berries (about 3 berries)

6 to 7 fresh nasturtium leaves

9 fresh nasturtium flower petals

1. Place the nasturtium berries in a 4-ounce glass jar. Combine ¼ cup of water with ¼ teaspoon of the salt and pour over the berries. Insert a fermentation weight and position an airlock lid (see page 67). Set aside to ferment at room temperature until bubbly, 3 to 5 days. Remove the weight and replace the airlock with a nonreactive lid. Transfer to the refrigerator to store for up to 1 year.

2. Prepare a wood-fired grill according to the instructions on page 186. When the smoke from the wood fire has subsided, the flames are short, and the embers are glowing, the grill is ready to cook the steaks.

3. Prepare the steaks: While the fire is being prepared, lay the steaks on a large sheet pan and sprinkle the salt evenly over both sides. Let the steaks rest at room temperature for at least 15 minutes, or until ready to grill.

4. Position your grill plate 6 to 8 inches away from the embers. Sprinkle a bit of water onto the hottest part of the grill: it should sizzle and evaporate almost instantly. Transfer the steaks to the grill and cook for 3 to 4 minutes. Rotate the steaks 180 degrees and continue cooking for another 3 to 4 minutes. Using tongs, flip the steaks over and repeat this process until an instant-read thermometer inserted into the meat

RECIPE CONTINUES

registers 135°F for medium-rare, or a higher temperature if desired. Cooking times may vary depending upon the starting temperature of the grill. Place the cooked steaks on a clean plate and let rest for at least 5 minutes before plating.

5. Make the nasturtium sauce: Drain 1 teaspoon of the fermented nasturtium berries and crush in a mortar and pestle to form a chunky paste. Transfer to a small, nonreactive bowl and combine with the yogurt, mustard, garlic, parsley, scallions, remaining ½ teaspoon salt, and the pepper. Stir well and transfer to a serving dish.

6. Serve the steaks on a large platter with the sauce on the side. Garnish with the sliced nasturtium berries, leaves, and petals.

CRISPY BULL MEAT TACOS
with Romaine Slaw

The reality of farming sustainably is occasionally having to harvest a bull. The meat can lack marbling, though, causing it to seize up and toughen when cooking. We have tried all sorts of things to remedy this, like adding pork fat to our burgers or mixing in breadcrumbs and milk to meatballs. The improvements were marginal, but one day our head chef, Kayla, got the idea to pulse cooked meat in the food processor to resemble traditional ground beef. She then tossed in some lard and broiled it, like how we roast carnitas. It was delicious! Lean ground beef works as a substitution for bull meat and benefits from this cooking method as well. It is well worth the extra effort, especially in these savory tacos topped with a refreshing, bright, and creamy sauce and a crunchy slaw!

MAKES
22 SMALL
TACOS

CRISPY BULL MEAT

3 tablespoons Lard (page 37)

1 pound ground bull meat or lean ground beef

1 teaspoon fine sea salt

1 cup minced yellow onion (1 large onion)

1 tablespoon minced garlic (3 cloves)

1 teaspoon chili powder

1 teaspoon ground cumin

1 teaspoon dried oregano

CAPER-LIME AVOCADO SAUCE

2½ cups chopped avocado (about 2 avocados)

2 teaspoons lime zest (1 medium lime)

3 tablespoons fresh lime juice (1½ medium limes)

½ teaspoon fine sea salt

4 teaspoons drained and chopped nonpareil capers

¼ cup minced red onion (about ¼ large onion)

1. Preheat the broiler to high and place a rack 6 inches below the broiler.

2. Make the crispy bull meat: In a 10- to 12-inch cast-iron skillet, melt the lard over medium-high heat. Add the beef and cook, stirring with a spoon, for 5 minutes. Sprinkle with the salt and add the onion, garlic, chili, cumin, and oregano. Continue cooking until crumbly and beginning to caramelize, another 7 to 8 minutes. Remove from the heat and spread the meat over a large baking sheet. Transfer to the oven and broil for 12 to 15 minutes, stirring every 4 minutes, until golden and crispy. Remove from the oven and set aside on top of the warm stove.

3. Make the caper-lime avocado sauce: In the bowl of a food processor or blender, combine the avocado, lime zest and juice, salt, and ½ cup of water. Puree until smooth and creamy. Add the capers and onion, pulse to incorporate, and transfer to a serving bowl.

ROMAINE SLAW

4 cups thinly shredded romaine lettuce, outer leaves removed (about 8 ounces)

⅛ cup thinly sliced red onion

2 tablespoons sliced jalapeño pepper, seeds removed (1 large pepper)

1 tablespoon fresh lemon juice

½ teaspoon fine sea salt

TO SERVE

22 Corn Tortillas (page 44), warmed

1 cup crumbled Farmer's Cheese (page 70)

A few drizzles Roasted Garlic Hot Sauce (page 84), optional

4. Make the romaine slaw: In a medium bowl, toss together the lettuce, onion, jalapeño, lemon juice, and salt and set aside.

5. To serve, spread a dollop of avocado sauce over each warm tortilla. Top with a spoonful of the meat, a pinch of the romaine slaw, and garnish with a light sprinkle of the farmer's cheese. Serve with hot sauce if desired.

GRASS-FED BEEF LIVER
Smothered in Spring Onion Medley with Spicy Horseradish Mustard

When my mom was pregnant with me, she had a wise doctor advise her to eat liver twice a week, as it is a nutritional powerhouse due to its naturally high vitamin B$_{12}$ and iron content. When I became pregnant with Beaudie, I followed suit, and my favorite way to eat it was smothered in spring onions and spicy mustard, much like this recipe! Grass-fed beef liver is ultimately milder than its conventional counterpart, and so we don't soak it in milk, unlike most typical beef liver recipes. Instead, the lemon acts as a marinade that complements the richness and neutralizes more overt iron flavors. It is a great dish for practicing nose-to-tail eating, and if you cannot source spring garlic, substitute tender young leeks instead.

SERVES
3 TO 4

4 fillets ⅜-inch-thick beef liver (about 3 ounces each)

⅓ cup fresh lemon juice (1½ medium lemons)

6 slices Simple Salt and Pepper Bacon (page 38)

3 stalks spring garlic, thinly sliced

1 cup sliced spring onions or sweet yellow onion (1 medium onion)

1½ teaspoons fine sea salt

¾ teaspoon freshly ground black peppercorns

HORSERADISH MUSTARD

¼ cup Fermented Mustard (page 88)

1 teaspoon prepared horseradish

2 tablespoons Greek yogurt

1. Place the liver in a shallow, nonreactive casserole dish. Pour over the lemon juice and cover. Place in the refrigerator for at least 1 hour or up to 3 hours.

2. Line a plate with paper towels. In a 10- to 12-inch cast-iron skillet on the stovetop, cook the bacon according to the directions on page 40. Transfer the cooked bacon to the lined plate. Remove all but 2 tablespoons of the bacon fat from the skillet and reserve. Add the spring garlic, spring onions, ½ teaspoon of the salt, and ¼ teaspoon of the pepper to the skillet and sauté over low heat, stirring frequently, until the onions caramelize to a golden brown, about 30 minutes. Transfer to a plate and set aside.

3. Make the horseradish mustard: In a small serving bowl, stir together the mustard, horseradish, and yogurt and set aside.

4. Remove the liver from the lemon juice, transfer the pieces to a baking sheet, and season all sides with the remaining 1 teaspoon salt and ½ teaspoon pepper. Wipe out the same skillet and place it over medium-high heat. Add 2 tablespoons of the reserved bacon fat and heat until it is shimmering, about 2 minutes. Sear the liver fillets for 2 to 3 minutes per side.

5. Transfer the liver fillets to a serving platter. Smother with the caramelized onions and crumble the bacon over top. Serve warm with the horseradish mustard on the side. Store, covered, in the refrigerator for up to 3 days.

Chapter Nine

PASTURED
PORK

OUR HERITAGE PIGS LIVE AS NATURE INTENDED, ROAMING FREELY THROUGH fields and forest while foraging for roots, grass, nuts, berries, insects, and grubs. For several years, an organic raspberry grower leased the farm next door, and we would feed his #2-grade berries to our loved pigs, in addition to the #3-grade fruits from our orchard. We have even planted mulberry trees in our pig pastures so they can have a late spring indulgence, as well as sorghum-sudangrass (*Sorghum × drummondii*), which they also love to forage. We used to give our pigs the skim that forms from churning Maggie the Cow's cream into butter, but we had to stop as it fattened them up too much! That's saying a lot, as we love using and eating pork fat. In return for these edible gifts, we are rewarded with endearing, healthy little piglets who, despite their cuddly appearance, squeal like the dickens when you attempt to pick them up!

Heritage pigs such as Red Wattle, Large Black, and Berkshire that have been left to roam create deep and complexly flavored meat full of rich, healthy fat. We currently cross our Red Wattle sows with Large Black boars to achieve the ratio of fat to meat that we prefer in the kitchen. This fat is prized for its clean appearance and decadent flavor, and it melts in the mouth. The following recipes celebrate the unique attributes of pastured pork through slow-roasted, stewed, braised, and sautéed dishes.

Recipes

Cinnamon and Orange-Infused Crispy Carnitas

Grilled Pork Sliders in Lettuce Cups with Creamy Apple-Kohlrabi Slaw

Spice-Rubbed Pastured Pork Ribs

Perfectly Brined Pastured Pork Chops with PB&J Sauce

Bacon-Wrapped Pastured Pork Meatloaf with Yellow Pepper Sauce

Chorizo

Apricot Lane Farms Pork Sausage

Something Extra: Recipes for Pastured Animals and Pets
    Horse Cookies
    Canine Feast (Raw Pet Food)

CINNAMON AND ORANGE-INFUSED CRISPY CARNITAS

SERVES 6

Carnitas is a beloved dish of Michoacán origin that has become a staple on our farm. Made from tender pieces of pork that have been slow-braised with cinnamon, bay leaf, and orange, they are shredded and then crisped in the oven before being served as taco filling. It is a simple main dish that has the flavor of home for so many on our team, especially when served with warm Corn Tortillas (page 44) or Cassava and Coconut Flour Tortillas (page 43). Serve with minced onion, fresh cilantro, Lazy Salsa (page 369), Classic Curtido Slaw (page 124), Roasted Garlic Hot Sauce (page 84), and Chipotle Avocado Oil Mayonnaise (page 90). Be sure to also try our Yellow Corn Pancakes with Carnitas and Peach Salsa (page 312). You can use various cuts of pork shoulder, pork butt, or blade end roast that have good marbling for a tender texture. We like to keep some fat on the pork but do recommend removing the sinew.

4 pounds boneless pork shoulder, cut into 2-inch cubes

2 tablespoons fine sea salt

1 teaspoon freshly ground black peppercorns

5 large garlic cloves, crushed

1½ cups chopped sweet onion (1½ large onions)

6 bay leaves

2 medium oranges, sliced into ½-inch-thick rounds

6 cinnamon sticks (about 2½ inches each)

5 cups Lard, melted (page 37)

1. Preheat the oven to 300°F and position a rack in the middle.

2. Place the pork in a large bowl and season with the salt and pepper. Add the garlic, onion, bay leaves, orange slices, and cinnamon sticks. Toss to combine and spread the mixture evenly over a large roasting pan. Pour the melted lard over the meat and cover the dish with parchment paper and then foil. Transfer the pan to the oven and braise until the meat is tender and falls apart when pierced with a fork, about 3 hours.

3. Remove the pan from the oven and let the pork cool for 20 minutes. Discard the bay leaves, cinnamon sticks, and orange slices. Spread the meat on a wire rack set over a large baking sheet to drain completely.

4. Preheat the broiler to low and position a rack 6 inches below the broiler.

5. Shred the carnitas with gloved hands or a fork and spread over a large clean baking sheet in an even layer. Broil the carnitas for 5 to 7 minutes, depending upon the intensity of your oven. The edges will become crispy and dark brown, and the fat will pool and sizzle around the meat. Remove the pan from the oven and set aside. Pat the carnitas with a towel to remove the excess oil.

RECIPE CONTINUES

6. Refrigerate for up to 5 days, crisping again under the broiler when ready to serve.

COOKING TIP:

Recycling Lard

Lard is integral to the process of tenderizing carnitas, but you can recycle it after the meat is cooked: remove the spices, drain the carnitas, and place the roasting pan in the refrigerator for several hours. Once the fat has risen to the surface and hardened, skim it from the cooking liquid and transfer to a medium saucepan. Bring the lard to a simmer and then strain it through a fine-mesh sieve into heatproof containers. Store in the refrigerator for up to 1 month or in the freezer for up to 1 year, using as needed.

GRILLED PORK SLIDERS IN LETTUCE CUPS
with Apple-Kohlrabi Slaw

The shoulder season between summer and autumn is a wonderful time to enjoy the crunchy sweetness of kohlrabi. I am a huge fan of this little-known brassica and am determined to introduce its beauty to those who may think it sounds more like a city in a far-off land! These gorgeous lettuce cups are filled with kohlrabi and fresh herbs that complement the exceptional flavor of pastured pork. If preparing ahead, cover tightly to prevent the meat from oxidizing and remove from the fridge at least 15 minutes before cooking. Serve with Chipotle Adobo Paste (page 82) or Basil Avocado Oil Mayonnaise (page 91), Fermented Ketchup (page 87), and Root Vegetable Chips (page 369).

MAKES
8 SLIDERS

APPLE-KOHLRABI SLAW

2 tablespoons Fermented Mustard (page 88)

1 teaspoon lemon zest

3½ tablespoons fresh lemon juice (about 1 large lemon)

¼ cup fresh orange juice

2 teaspoons champagne vinegar

1¼ teaspoons fine sea salt

¼ teaspoon freshly ground black peppercorns

2 tablespoons cold-pressed extra-virgin olive oil

3 tablespoons finely diced shallot (1½ small shallots)

2½ cups finely shredded red or green cabbage (about ¼ pound)

1⅔ cups julienned kohlrabi (1 large bulb)

1 cup packed julienned kohlrabi leaves

1 cup julienned apple, skin on (1 medium apple)

½ cup pomegranate seeds

1. Make the slaw: In a small bowl, combine the mustard, lemon zest and juice, orange juice, vinegar, salt, and pepper. Whisk the ingredients together while slowly drizzling in the oil to make a creamy and emulsified dressing. Stir in the shallots and set aside until ready to serve.

2. In a medium bowl, combine the cabbage, kohlrabi, kohlrabi leaves, apple, and pomegranate. Toss to incorporate and place, uncovered, in the refrigerator until ready to serve.

3. Preheat your grill to medium-high heat or your oven to 375°F and position a rack in the middle.

4. Make the sliders: Line a large baking sheet with parchment paper. In a medium skillet, heat the oil over medium heat until expanded and shimmering, 2 to 3 minutes. Add the apple, onion, and garlic and sauté until the onion becomes translucent, 5 to 7 minutes. Transfer to a large bowl and let cool for 10 minutes. Add the pork, salt, pepper, sage, and eggs to the bowl and mix with a spoon until thoroughly combined. Divide the meat mixture into 8 equal portions and shape into ½-inch-thick sliders. Lay the sliders on the prepared baking sheet.

RECIPE AND INGREDIENTS CONTINUE

SLIDERS

1 tablespoon unrefined avocado oil

1 cup peeled and finely minced apple (1 medium apple)

1½ cups minced yellow onion (about 1½ large onions)

1 tablespoon minced garlic (3 cloves)

2 pounds ground pork

2½ teaspoons fine sea salt

1 teaspoon freshly ground black peppercorns

2 tablespoons finely chopped fresh sage leaves or 1 tablespoon dried

3 large eggs

8 large lettuce leaves

5. Transfer the sliders to the hot grill and cook until the internal temperature reaches 150°F to 155°F, 7 to 10 minutes per side. Alternatively, heat a heavy-bottomed skillet over high heat and sear the sliders for 1 to 2 minutes per side before transferring to the baking sheet. Bake for 15 to 20 minutes, until the internal temperature reaches 150°F to 155°F on an instant-read thermometer.

6. To serve, arrange the lettuce leaves on a serving platter and place one slider on each leaf. Mix the dressing with the slaw and taste for seasoning. The salad should be sweet and crunchy, and the dressing should be tart and salty and easily coat the salad. Top each slider with a generous helping of slaw or serve on the side.

SPICE-RUBBED PASTURED PORK RIBS

Tender and succulent textures are always the result of slow cooking pastured meats, and these ribs are no exception! Nary a peep is heard at a table full of hungry farmers on a day when ribs are served! The best part is, they are almost always accompanied by our famous Root Vegetable Chips (page 369) and Classic Curtido Slaw (page 124), which simply make you want to weep with culinary joy. Saint Louis–style pork spareribs are cut from the belly of the hog. They are meaty and lie naturally flat, making them perfect for this recipe. You may use baby back ribs instead, but they are shorter cuts and will not require as much BBQ sauce. Other great sides that never disappoint are Summer Corn Salad with Tomato Raisins, Basil, and Chèvre (page 176) or Potato Salad with Preserved Lemon and Mint (page 115).

SERVES
6 TO 8

5 teaspoons fine sea salt

3 teaspoons freshly ground black peppercorns

1½ teaspoons sweet paprika

2 teaspoons onion powder

1½ teaspoons garlic powder

1½ teaspoons ground nutmeg

Two 5½ × 16½-inch slabs Saint Louis–style pork spareribs (about 2 pounds each)

3 cups Family Day Peach BBQ Sauce (page 89)

1. Preheat the oven to 275°F and position a rack in the middle.

2. In a small bowl, whisk together the salt, pepper, paprika, onion powder, garlic powder, and nutmeg until combined. Lay each slab of ribs on a separate piece of 16 × 21-inch parchment paper. Generously season each side of each slab with the dry rub, using the entire mix. Make two enclosed parcels by folding up the sides of the parchment and covering the slabs before laying each parcel on a 16 × 21-inch piece of foil and folding again. Place both parcels on a large baking sheet.

3. Transfer to the oven and roast for 2 hours, or until the meat is tender but not falling off the bone. Remove from the oven and carefully unfold the foil and the parchment away from the ribs using tongs and a gloved hand.

4. Using a pastry or sauce brush, spread ½ cup of the BBQ sauce over both sides of each rack. Return the ribs to the oven and continue roasting for 30 minutes. Remove from the oven and brush an additional ½ cup of the sauce over each rack. Return to the oven and bake for 30 minutes. Repeat once more, using up the rest of the sauce. After 3½ hours total baking time, the sauce should appear lacquered, and the meat should be fall-off-the-bone delicious.

5. Remove the ribs from the oven and let them cool for 15 minutes. Transfer the racks to a cutting board, bone side up. With a sharp knife, portion the ribs and transfer to a platter. Serve warm. Store, covered, in the refrigerator for up to 3 days.

PERFECTLY BRINED PASTURED PORK CHOPS
with PB&J Sauce

We sell pastured pork chops that are thick and have quite a bit of fat that is sweet and nutty, with grassy notes. These juicy chops easily melt in the mouth and pair beautifully with this irresistible combination of sweet stewed blueberries and savory peanut butter. This sauce is similar to a satay sauce and reminds us of a classic peanut butter and jelly sandwich, but with a creative twist!

SERVES 4

BRINE

1 cup apple juice

2 tablespoons mild raw honey

2 teaspoons minced ginger
(¾-inch knob)

2 teaspoons minced garlic (2 cloves)

3 tablespoons fine sea salt

4 boneless 1-inch-thick pork chops
(3¾ pounds)

SAUCE

2 tablespoons unrefined avocado oil

1 tablespoon minced ginger
(1 × 1-inch knob)

1 tablespoon minced garlic (3 cloves)

2 tablespoons minced shallot
(1 small shallot)

1 cup fresh or frozen and thawed
blueberries

¼ cup creamy unsweetened natural
peanut butter

2 tablespoons mild raw honey

2 tablespoons rice vinegar

1½ tablespoons fresh lime juice
(¾ medium lime)

½ teaspoon fine sea salt

1. Make the brine: In a small saucepan, stir together 3 cups of water, the apple juice, honey, ginger, garlic, and salt. Place over medium heat, cover, and bring to a simmer. Remove the lid and reduce for 5 minutes. Transfer to a shallow container and cool, uncovered, in the refrigerator, about 30 minutes.

2. Submerge the pork chops fully in the cooled brine. Return to the refrigerator and marinate for at least 3 or up to 8 hours.

3. Make the sauce: In a medium saucepan, heat 1 tablespoon of the oil over medium heat until shimmering, 2 to 3 minutes. Add the ginger, garlic, shallot, and blueberries. Sauté until the blueberries soften and the garlic and shallot turn translucent, 3 to 4 minutes. Transfer to the pitcher of a blender and add 1 tablespoon of water, the peanut butter, honey, vinegar, lime juice, and salt. Puree until smooth and creamy. Depending upon the quality of peanut butter, add more water, 1 tablespoon at a time, until your desired sauce consistency is achieved.

4. Preheat the oven to 375°F and position a rack in the middle.

5. Remove the pork chops from the brine and pat dry with a paper towel. In a 10-inch cast-iron skillet, heat the remaining 1 tablespoon oil over high heat until shimmering, about 2 minutes. Sear both sides of the pork chops until golden brown, 2 to 4 minutes per side. Transfer the skillet to the oven and roast for 15 to 20 minutes, until cooked through and the internal temperature registers 145°F on an instant-read thermometer. Remove the skillet from the oven and set it aside to rest for 5 minutes.

6. Plate the pork chops and drizzle with the warm sauce. Serve hot.

BACON-WRAPPED PASTURED PORK MEATLOAF
with Yellow Pepper Sauce

We love the deep and rich flavor of our pastured Simple Salt and Pepper Bacon (page 38) and use it whenever we can, including for wrapping this juicy meatloaf! By sealing in the moisture with a crispy outer layer of bacon, the loaves remain incredibly tender. The cheerful yellow sauce lightens this classic comfort food meal, making it lovely to serve for a lunch or brunch. If sourcing all yellow picnic peppers proves challenging, red or orange picnic or bell peppers may be substituted. Use a thin serrated or very sharp knife to carve the meatloaf to avoid crushing the bacon or creating jagged slices. This recipe feeds a crowd, but you can always freeze the cooked and cooled second loaf to reheat for a quick and easy weeknight meal.

SERVES
10 TO 12

PEPPER SAUCE

1½ pounds yellow picnic peppers, stems and seeds removed

4 tablespoons unrefined avocado oil

1 teaspoon fine sea salt

1½ teaspoons minced garlic (about 2 small cloves)

2 tablespoons minced shallot (1 small shallot)

1 tablespoon sherry vinegar

MEATLOAF

1 cup Sourdough Breadcrumbs (page 61)

½ cup Chicken Stock (page 76)

2 tablespoons Lard (page 37) or unrefined avocado oil

2 cups small-diced yellow onion (2 large onions)

2 tablespoons minced garlic (6 cloves)

2 pounds ground pastured pork

1. Preheat the oven to 375°F and position a rack in the middle.

2. Make the pepper sauce: Place the peppers in a large bowl, sprinkle with 2 tablespoons of the oil, and toss to coat. Transfer to a large unlined baking sheet, spread in an even layer, and place in the oven. Roast for 35 minutes, or until the peppers are soft and their skins blistered. Remove from the oven and set aside to cool for 10 minutes. Transfer the peppers to the pitcher of a blender along with the remaining 2 tablespoons oil, the salt, garlic, shallot, vinegar, and 2 tablespoons of water. Blend until the sauce is smooth, 1 to 2 minutes. Pour into a serving bowl and set aside.

3. Make the meatloaf: Line a large baking sheet with parchment paper and place a wire rack on top. In a large bowl, combine the breadcrumbs and the stock and set aside until the breadcrumbs are fully hydrated, about 10 minutes.

4. In a 10-inch skillet, melt the lard over medium heat. Add the onion and garlic and sauté until the onion is soft and light brown, 7 to 9 minutes. Remove from the heat and transfer to the bowl with the breadcrumbs, stirring until fully combined. Add the ground pork, fennel, sage, salt, pepper, and mustard and stir together until

RECIPE AND INGREDIENTS CONTINUE

1½ teaspoons ground fennel seed

1 tablespoon plus 1½ teaspoons chopped fresh sage leaves or 2¼ teaspoons dried

1 tablespoon fine sea salt

1 teaspoon freshly ground black peppercorns

3 tablespoons Fermented Mustard (page 88)

3 large eggs

10 to 12 slices Simple Salt and Pepper Bacon, room temperature (page 38)

combined. Add the eggs and squish the mixture with your hands to fully incorporate. Divide the meat into two equal portions and shape each into a roughly 3½ × 6½-inch loaf. Place the loaves on a piece of parchment paper and cover the surface of each with shingled bacon strips, tucking the ends under the loaves. Transfer the loaves and the parchment paper to the prepared rack and place in the oven. Bake for 1 hour, or until the centers reach 155°F on an instant-read thermometer and the bacon is crispy and brown. Remove the meatloaves from the oven and let them rest for 15 minutes before slicing. Serve warm with the pepper sauce.

CHORIZO

Chorizo is a flavorful sausage that originated in Spain and Portugal but can have several identities, depending upon the origin of influence. This highly seasoned, uncured Mexican recipe is made with a chile and vinegar marinade and will add a savory kick to any dish! We love the heat of dried Japones chiles, but you may substitute the spicy and fruity dried chile de arbol instead. It is a delicious substitute in the Corn Chowder with Jalapeño Pork Crumble (page 173) and is designed for making the Marinated Picnic Peppers Stuffed with Chorizo and Manchego Cheese (page 179). Using a blender is an obvious option to grind the spices into a paste, but if the pitcher of your blender has a wide bottom, an electric spice grinder may be better for the texture of the paste, especially when you are making smaller batches. Leave at least a couple of hours to marinate the pork. Another tip: While not an essential step, refrigerating the chorizo mixture uncovered for 4 hours on a baking sheet before cooking will help with browning.

MAKES
2¼ POUNDS

6 dried guajillo chiles, stem and seeds removed

2 dried ancho chiles, stem and seeds removed

3 dried Japones chiles, stem and seeds removed

4 teaspoons chopped garlic (4 cloves)

⅓ cup raw apple cider vinegar

4 teaspoons fine sea salt

1 teaspoon ground cumin

1 teaspoon ground coriander

1 tablespoon plus 1½ teaspoons chopped fresh oregano leaves or 1½ teaspoons dried

1 teaspoon freshly ground black peppercorns

2 tablespoons fresh thyme leaves or 1 teaspoon dried

½ teaspoon ground cloves

½ teaspoon ground allspice

2 tablespoons Lard (page 37) or unrefined avocado oil

2 pounds ground pastured pork

1. In a small saucepan with a lid, combine the guajillo, ancho, and Japones chiles with 4 cups of water. Bring the pot to a simmer over high heat and cook, uncovered, until the chiles are soft and pliable, 15 to 20 minutes. Remove from the heat and set aside to cool for 5 minutes. Drain the chiles and reserve 3 tablespoons of the cooking liquid. In the pitcher of a blender, place the chiles, reserved liquid, garlic, vinegar, salt, cumin, coriander, oregano, pepper, thyme, cloves, allspice, and lard. Process on high until a smooth paste forms.

2. In a large bowl, combine the marinade and ground pork. Mix with gloved hands until the marinade is well incorporated and the mixture leaves a thin film on the sides of the bowl.

3. Cover the bowl with a lid or plastic wrap and place it in the refrigerator to season for at least 2 hours or up to 5 days before using. If freezing, divide into portions and place in sealed containers or plastic bags and store for up to 6 months.

4. If desired, spread the sausage over a large baking sheet and place it in the refrigerator, uncovered, for 4 hours to help it brown faster when cooking. Cook small batches of the fresh or thawed sausage in a 10-inch cast-iron skillet over medium heat until browned and fully cooked through, 7 to 10 minutes. Serve warm. Store in a sealed container in the refrigerator for up to 3 days.

APRICOT LANE FARMS PORK SAUSAGE

Charles and Maria from our incredible kitchen team frequently make this versatile sausage in bulk before freezing in one-pound portions for regular use in our meal program. It is excellent added to the Autumn Frittata with Kale, Potato, Garlic, and Breakfast Sausage (page 235) or in the Corn Chowder with Jalapeño Pork Crumble (page 173). The simple herbs and spices here elevate the complex flavor profile of pastured pork. If given the option, ground shoulder or pork butt with about 30 percent fat is best for a rich texture in this sausage.

MAKES
1 POUND

1 pound ground pastured pork

1½ teaspoons fine sea salt

1 teaspoon freshly ground black peppercorns

2 tablespoons chopped fresh sage leaves or 1 teaspoon dried

1½ tablespoons minced fresh rosemary or ½ teaspoon dried rosemary powder

½ teaspoon toasted fennel seed, ground into a powder

1. In a medium bowl, combine the pork, salt, pepper, sage, rosemary, and fennel. Mix until the ingredients are well incorporated and the sausage sticks to the bowl, about 5 minutes.

2. Cover the bowl with a lid or plastic wrap and place in the refrigerator to season for at least 2 hours or up to 3 days before using. If freezing, divide into portions and place in sealed containers or plastic bags and store for up to 6 months.

3. Cook the fresh or thawed sausage in a 10-inch cast-iron skillet over medium heat until browned and fully cooked through, 7 to 10 minutes. Serve warm. Store in a sealed container in the refrigerator for up to 3 days.

SOMETHING EXTRA:
Recipes for Pastured Animals and Pets

The following recipes are easy to make to treat your domestic pets and even your farm animals, if you have them! They are also a clever way to reduce food waste by using up less desirable cuts of meat or blemished fruit and vegetables. Of course, it's important to be sure your animals keep a healthy diet and an active lifestyle, so recipes like the Horse Cookies (page 300) are meant to be an occasional indulgence!

The Canine Feast (page 301) is an excellent daily feed alternative to highly processed packaged options and provides a complete nutritional profile for dogs or can easily be tweaked to become suitable for house cats. Unfortunately, commercial pet food formulas often include factory-farmed proteins and high amounts of cheap, low-quality grain fillers. Both ingredients can legally include pesticides, industrial chemicals, drug residues, and microbiological contaminants even though they don't appear on the label. Low-grade food products can degrade an animal's well-being over time, and so making your own can give you peace of mind.

RECIPE CONTINUES

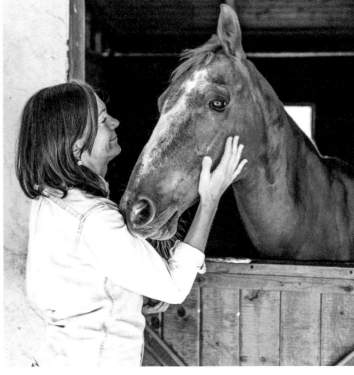

HORSE COOKIES

MAKES 18 COOKIES

Sapphire, a beautiful American Paint, was our first horse on the farm. She had bright blue eyes, just like our late and beloved dog Todd. Later, we added Rico, an American Quarter Horse, who is still with us today. Lavender, our director of business operations, is a horse expert and loves to ride Rico. She also spoils him occasionally with these special cookies but has to make sure that he doesn't sneak them out of her pockets first! Rico is a smart, curious, and handsome guy who has been known to pick the lock of his stall and explore the barn at his leisure!

Offering a horse a treat is one of the easiest ways to bond with your animal. This recipe uses ingredients that are healthy and appropriate for horses who receive plenty of exercise. Our test kitchen chose apple and butternut squash as the base since they are both in season at the same time, although carrot can be used interchangeably with the squash. Natural peanut butter is Rico's favorite, but you can substitute any nut butter your horse finds preferable.

¼ cup virgin coconut oil, melted

1 cup unpeeled shredded apple (1 medium apple)

1 cup unpeeled shredded butternut squash

2 cups sprouted rolled oats

6 tablespoons mild raw honey

6 tablespoons smooth or crunchy natural peanut butter

1. Preheat the oven to 350°F and position two racks evenly apart in the middle third of the oven. Line two large baking sheets with parchment paper or silicone baking mats.

2. In a medium bowl, combine the oil, apple, squash, oats, honey, and peanut butter. Stir with a wooden spoon to combine.

3. Portion the cookies into round, golf ball–size pieces and place 2 inches apart on the prepared baking sheets. Moisten your fingers with water and gently press to flatten each cookie.

4. Transfer to the oven and bake for 30 minutes, rotating halfway through. Remove from the oven when they are golden brown around the edges but still soft. Cool completely on the baking sheets until they are firm and easy to handle, about 1 hour.

5. Place the fully cooled cookies in a sealed container in the refrigerator for up to 1 week.

CANINE FEAST (RAW PET FOOD)

MAKES 10 POUNDS

This simple everyday dog-food recipe will provide your pet with the correct balance of nutrients, protein, fiber, and variety according to Mother Nature. You can also easily adjust it if you have a feline companion. Ground chicken, turkey, beef, pork, or lamb all work well in this versatile recipe, and it is an excellent nose-to-tail use of the animal. The ground meat should include mostly muscle, but it is beneficial to also include some poultry skin, fat, soft bone, and cartilage; use a small meat grinder if possible. Both our golden retriever, Blue, and our partner's border collie, Sparky, tested and gave this recipe four paws up! If you are making this for a feline, simply double the proportion of meat to the other ingredients.

This pet food freezes well in reusable containers and is easy to make in 50- to 100-pound batches, especially for larger dogs. Experiment with what your pet prefers, but root vegetables such as sweet potatoes, squash, carrots, beets, or a mix will provide the proper fiber along with leafy greens such as lettuce, spinach, kale, or carrot tops. The hardest part of making your own pet food is switching your dog or cat over to this wholesome, minimally processed nourishment. It is best to change the diet no more than 10 percent at a time, even though your pet may be ravenous for the tasty new food!

The ideal calorie intake for dogs varies—the average thirty-pound dog will usually require about 2 cups per day. This recipe has no "filler," and so it is shocking to see how much less your pet will need to eat when you make the switch. However, you can add a small amount of cooked whole grain such as rice or oats so the dog can feel fuller and therefore satisfied.

5 pounds ground raw chicken or turkey

8 to 9 cups lightly boiled root vegetables, roughly chopped (about 4½ pounds)

3¾ cups loosely packed chopped leafy greens

2 ounces roughly chopped chicken liver

2 large eggs

1 teaspoon sardine, salmon, or cod liver oil

2 tablespoons raw apple cider vinegar

1. In a large bowl, combine the meat, vegetables, leafy greens, liver, eggs, fish oil, and vinegar. Use two gloved hands to evenly combine.

2. Divide into small storage containers, label clearly with a description of the contents and the date, and cover. Store up to 5 days of portions in the refrigerator and freeze the rest. Remove from the freezer as needed and thaw for 1 day in the refrigerator before serving.

Part IV

THE
ORCHARD

Upon our eager arrival in 2011, the orchards covering the bulk of the growing regions on the farm were full of basic, aging lemon and avocado trees. In spite of their state, they still looked magical through my rose-colored lenses! We chose to keep a few blocks of promising trees and restore their natural root systems for sustenance. Meanwhile, we converted other areas to young, vibrant avocado trees, carefully dipping them in a fertile mixture of compost tea, kelp, and other offerings to the soil microbes before tucking them into their new loving home. One gorgeous section of land remained that spread over twenty-three acres below a towering eucalyptus row on the southwest side. Under the tutelage of Alan York, we imagined planting an oasis along the contours of this land for both erosion control and aesthetic appeal. This shared vision became the Fruit Basket, a swirling, natural habitat for birds, bees, and other wildlife, along with more than seventy-five varieties of citrus and deciduous trees. There is never a day that I am on this farm that I don't make my way through its winding paths, for it is heaven to me.

· · · · · · · · · · · · · · · · ·

It required patience as a land steward while the new trees worked hard to grow and begin bearing fruit. In the first years, sometimes a tree would produce only one or two pieces of fruit per tree. If they produced more, we'd often need to strip the fruit from the trees before it was ripe in order to redirect energy back to the plant. This encourages strong vegetative growth and was what we needed to do to help the trees bear fruit in the coming years. As new-to-me cultivars of summer stone fruits, fall delights, and winter citrus arrived alongside the berries from our gorgeous garden, my heart exploded, and the foundations of my cooking changed. As I became more acquainted with each fruit, the flavor nuances became a part of my culinary perspective and an inspiration for many of the dishes in the following pages. The acid, sweetness, or underlying aromas can be the secret ingredients of a dish. These recipes are held sacred by the fruit, leaving us to only ponder and ultimately hope we are complementing it with our cooking choices.

Chapter Ten

STONE FRUITS
and
BERRIES

AS YOU STROLL BETWEEN THE TREES IN OUR ORCHARD IN JUNE AND July, you smell the perfume of ripening emerging on branches laden with fruit. The sweet nectar that oozes from the first bite of a ripe peach is worth the impatient game of watching and waiting. Crisp salads and savory pancake appetizers celebrate their sweetness and are a welcome marriage to lush garden produce. Cherries dance happily with arugula, and peaches are willing companions to tomatoes and corn. On the hottest days, when the winds blow dusty and dry, fermented coolers or tonics quench our thirst, and strawberry ice cream and plum crisps soothe our appetites with sweet reprieve. These are the days of celebrating abundance, indulging in the spoils of the orchard's generosity.

Unfortunately, nature doesn't provide farmers with a warranty or an instruction manual. Harvests vary by year and are based upon multiple factors, including the long-term health of our trees, the previous winter's chill hours and rains, and when the first blossoms arrive in spring. If we didn't get enough cold or too much at the wrong time, too much rain (never for us!) or not enough (too often for us!), the crop may be light, flavorless, or even nonexistent. We get only one chance at a crop per year, so you can imagine, it is the topic of many conversations on the farm! How many chill hours do we have so far? Do you think we'll get a late spring rain? Is tonight's chill going to affect the early peaches? The answers are usually unknown, but when the stars align, wow, does it feel (and taste) fantastic!

Recipes

LOQUAT GAZPACHO

Loquats are a delicious melon-textured golden-yellow fruit with hints of citrus, depending upon the variety. They are one of the first fruits of the season and a sign that bountiful berries are coming soon. In late spring, grapelike clusters of loquats cover the large trees that line many of our roads on the farm, and it is not uncommon to see an ATV pulled to the side as someone grabs a few to snack on! If picked without the stem attached, this tender and fragile fruit will quickly oxidize into an unattractive brown color, and so they are not often sold at farmers markets and rarely in Chinese or Middle Eastern markets. If you have one growing nearby, however, consider yourself lucky to have a bounty, and this recipe is a perfect use of them! Loquats that are either firm or feel plump and supple can be used for this recipe. If making a few days in advance, omit the fresh herbs until ready to serve.

SERVES
3 TO 4

10 extra-large or 20 small loquats

1½ cups peeled and 1-inch-chopped cucumber (about 1 cucumber)

½ cup small-diced yellow bell pepper (about ½ medium pepper)

1 teaspoon seeded and minced jalapeño pepper (½ small pepper)

¼ cup small-diced yellow onion (about ¼ large onion)

½ teaspoon minced garlic (1 small clove)

2 tablespoons chiffonade-cut fresh mint leaves

2 tablespoons chiffonade-cut fresh basil leaves

2 teaspoons fine sea salt, plus more for garnish

⅛ teaspoon freshly ground black peppercorns

⅓ cup plus 1 tablespoon white wine vinegar

1 tablespoon cold-pressed extra-virgin olive oil, plus more for garnish

1 teaspoon fresh lime juice

1. Lightly rub the loquats under running water before peeling to remove their fine skin fuzz. If the loquats are soft, break the stem starting at the top and peel your way down. Gently press into the flesh with both thumbs and push out the large seeds and inner membrane. If the loquats are firm, however, score a shallow X with the blade of a knife on the blossom end of the fruit. Bring 2 quarts of water to a boil and blanch the loquats for 30 seconds. Remove the fruit with a slotted spoon and transfer to a bowl of ice water. Remove the stems and peel the fruit before popping out the seeds and the inner membrane. Chop the peeled fruit into 1-inch pieces. You should have about 2½ cups of peeled and chopped loquats.

2. In a nonreactive medium bowl, combine the chopped loquats, ½ cup of water, the cucumber, bell pepper, jalapeño, onion, garlic, mint, basil, salt, pepper, vinegar, oil, and lime juice. Toss until evenly seasoned, cover with a towel or plastic wrap, and let macerate for 30 minutes at room temperature.

3. Transfer the macerated mixture to the pitcher of a large blender. Blend on high until the mixture is silky smooth, about 2 minutes. Taste and adjust the seasoning. The gazpacho will be lightly sweet from the loquats and tart from the lime juice and vinegar. Add more vinegar if it lacks brightness and adjust the salt if the gazpacho tastes flat. Pour into a nonreactive container, cover, and place in the refrigerator.

RECIPE AND INGREDIENTS CONTINUE

GARNISH

½ cup small-diced yellow bell pepper (about ½ medium pepper)

½ cup small-diced fresh loquat, pitted and peeled (about 2 loquats)

2 tablespoons torn or chiffonade-cut fresh mint leaves

2 tablespoons torn or chiffonade-cut fresh basil leaves

4. Chill the mixture for at least 2 hours before serving. Garnish with the chopped pepper, loquat, mint, basil, a drizzle of olive oil, and a pinch of salt.

5. Store the gazpacho in an airtight, nonreactive container in the refrigerator for up to 3 days.

COOKING TIP: *Chiffonade*

This slicing technique can be used with any flat leafy green or herb, such as basil, mint, spinach, or Swiss chard. Stack the leaves on top of one another, with the largest leaves on the bottom. Roll the leaves into a cigar-shaped log, and using a sharp knife, make very thin slices perpendicular to the bundle. The result is thin ribbons of greens or herbs, also known as chiffonade.

YELLOW CORN PANCAKES
with Carnitas and Peach Salsa

While we usually soak and then process seeds such as corn to make it more nutritious and digestible as hominy grits or masa harina (page 46), in this recipe, we have chosen to use regular cornmeal because we adore the fluffy, custardy texture and crisp edges that it gives to these pancakes. Although we love it for tortillas, using masa harina here results in a more doughlike batter that tends to fall apart in the pan. Use firm but ripe peaches to make the juicy salsa. It will yield about 1½ cups, more than what is needed, so use the welcome excess for snacking or topping other meals, especially the Spice-Rubbed Pastured Pork Ribs (page 291). Store in a covered container in the refrigerator for up to 2 days.

MAKES
15 MINI-PANCAKES

MINI-PANCAKES

1 cup stone-ground fine yellow cornmeal

2 teaspoons maple syrup

¾ teaspoon fine sea salt

½ cup boiling water

¼ cup raw heavy cream

2 tablespoons strained pastured bacon fat or unrefined avocado oil

1 cup cooked Cinnamon and Orange-Infused Crispy Carnitas (page 285)

PEACH SALSA

1½ cups small-diced peaches (2 medium peaches)

¼ cup minced red onion (¼ large onion)

1 tablespoon minced jalapeño pepper (1 medium pepper)

2 tablespoons fresh lime juice (1 medium lime)

1 tablespoon finely chopped fresh mint leaves

¾ teaspoon fine sea salt

1. Preheat the oven to 400°F for 15 minutes, then turn the broiler to high and position a rack in the middle.

2. Make the mini-pancake batter: In a small bowl, whisk together the cornmeal, maple syrup, salt, boiling water, and cream until evenly incorporated, and set aside.

3. Make the salsa: In a small bowl, combine the peaches, onion, jalapeño, lime juice, mint, and salt. Stir to combine and set aside for about 15 minutes. If the salsa does not become juicy in that time, add up to ¼ cup of water, stir, and set aside.

4. Nestle a wire rack into a baking sheet and place near the stovetop. Set an 8-inch cast-iron skillet over medium heat and melt the bacon fat until it is shimmering, about 2 minutes. Stir the batter to recombine. Using 1 tablespoon of batter per pancake, make four evenly spaced 1½- to 2-inch pancakes. Cook until the edges are set and the center appears bubbly, 2 to 3 minutes. Using an offset spatula, flip and continue to cook the pancakes until golden brown with crispy edges. Place the cooked pancakes on the wire rack and repeat with the remaining batter.

5. Spread the carnitas over a medium baking sheet and place in the oven. Broil for 5 to 7 minutes, until they are golden brown and the edges are crispy. Remove from the oven and set aside.

6. To assemble, top each pancake with 1 tablespoon of the carnitas and 1 tablespoon of the peach salsa. Serve warm with more salsa on the side.

ARUGULA AND PICKLED MORELLO CHERRY SALAD
with Bacon, Chèvre, and Borage Flowers

SERVES 4

California is a top cherry-producing state but only in certain areas that meet the minimum number of chill hours needed to produce flowering buds. Cold weather may not be for everyone, but many fruit trees require temperatures to drop and remain between 32°F and 45°F degrees to initiate and maintain dormancy. During this time, the trees produce the hormones necessary to set flowering buds that will produce fruit. Naturally tart but deliciously sweet Morello cherries fruit well for us, despite our warm winters and low chill hours, and are thankfully self-pollinating! When picked ripe and dark, Morello cherries are delicious cooked into desserts or, when pickled a week in advance, are a bright addition to this refreshing salad. Mix just before serving to avoid wilting and to ensure a beautiful presentation, especially with the bright blue and deliciously edible borage flowers.

PICKLED CHERRIES

½ cup red wine vinegar

3 tablespoons creamed raw honey

1 teaspoon fine sea salt

2 cups pitted fresh Morello cherries or underripe Bing cherries

PRESERVED LEMON VINAIGRETTE

3½ tablespoons unrefined avocado oil

3 tablespoons minced Preserved Lemon peel (page 34), pith removed (5 to 6 wedges)

2½ tablespoons Fermented Mustard (page 88)

1½ teaspoons chopped fresh thyme leaves or ¼ teaspoon dried

2 tablespoons champagne vinegar

¾ teaspoon fine sea salt

¼ teaspoon freshly ground black peppercorns

SALAD

8 cups packed young arugula

6 slices Simple Salt and Pepper Bacon (page 38), cooked and finely chopped

½ cup coarsely chopped hazelnuts

3 tablespoons crumbled chèvre (1½ ounces)

¼ cup fresh borage flowers

1. Make the pickled cherries: In a 1-quart mason jar with a nonreactive lid, mix ½ cup of water with the vinegar, honey, and salt. Seal and shake the jar to dissolve the honey and salt. Add the cherries, seal, and place in the refrigerator for at least 1 week before using.

2. Make the preserved lemon vinaigrette: In a small bowl, whisk together the oil, lemon peel, mustard, thyme, vinegar, salt, and pepper, and set aside.

3. Make the salad: Drain about 1 cup of pickled cherries and chop roughly. In a large bowl, combine the arugula, ½ cup of the chopped cherries, ¼ cup of the bacon, and ¼ cup of the hazelnuts. Drizzle in the dressing and toss until evenly coated. Taste and adjust the seasoning as needed. Transfer to a serving bowl and garnish with the remaining chopped cherries, bacon, hazelnuts, chèvre, and borage flowers. Serve immediately.

YAYA'S HOMEMADE STRAWBERRY ICE CREAM

MAKES
2 QUARTS

My first and lasting inspiration in the kitchen has always been my wonderfully creative mother, whom my son affectionately calls Yaya. We love Yaya so much and had the joy of both her and Buppa (my dad) down the street for many years, where we would happily gather most Sunday nights for a Yaya meal. During that time, she developed this beautiful ice cream using our flavorful Albion strawberries. It never disappoints and has since become a Chester family favorite! The honey may need to be slightly increased if you are working with a less sweet berry. Although this recipe is equally delicious without them, egg yolks are powerhouses of nutrition, and they provide a silky richness that elevates both the texture and flavor. When they are fresh and from reputable sources, they are safe to eat raw.

2 cups fresh or frozen and thawed strawberries, hulled

2 (13.5-ounce) cans full-fat coconut milk

½ cup Toasted Cashew Nut Butter (page 42)

4 medium to large egg yolks

½ cup floral raw honey (orange blossom or clover work well)

2 teaspoons vanilla extract

⅛ teaspoon fine sea salt

GARNISH [OPTIONAL]

½ cup chopped nuts (pecans or pistachios work well)

½ cup toasted coconut flakes

¼ cup carob chips or cacao nibs

2 cups whipped cream

1. If the strawberries are large, slice them in half. Transfer the strawberries to the pitcher of a blender and add the coconut milk, cashew butter, and egg yolks. Process on high until mostly blended. Add the honey, vanilla, and salt, and continue to blend until the nut butter and honey are fully incorporated and the mixture is thick, about 2 minutes. The mixture can be covered and chilled in the refrigerator for up to 2 days before churning.

2. Pour the custard into the frozen container of a 2-quart ice cream maker and process according to the manufacturer's directions, or until the liquid reaches a thick milkshake consistency, 25 to 30 minutes.

3. Transfer the ice cream to a container, cover, and place in the freezer until completely hardened, 2 to 3 hours.

4. Remove the ice cream from the freezer and let it soften at room temperature for 7 to 10 minutes. Scoop into serving dishes and garnish with the nuts, toasted coconut, carob chips, and whipped cream, if desired.

HONEY PANNA COTTA
with Milk Kefir and Fresh Passion Fruit

Passion fruits appear in abundance in Southern California in late summer to early fall, and this panna cotta is the perfect way to enjoy their short window of harvest. Our passion fruit vines are something special to behold, with intricate purple and white flowers that truly outdo themselves. I was floored the first time I saw one, and I must always take a closer look when I pass by them on the fence line of our garden plot, known as Magic Island. If these puckery egg-shaped fruits do not grow in your region, fresh macerated strawberries and mint or simply a generous drizzle of raw honey would be a delightful alternative. This is a perfect dessert for making at least one day in advance of serving so you can allow the vanilla to infuse and enhance the flavor of the tangy milk kefir.

MAKES ONE 8 × 11-INCH MOLD OR TEN ¾-CUP SERVINGS

3 tablespoons plus 1 teaspoon pork or bovine gelatin (see Resources, page 392)

5 tablespoons cold water

2 cups heavy cream, room temperature

3 whole vanilla beans, split (see Resources, page 392)

¾ cup creamed raw honey, to taste

4 cups whole milk kefir, room temperature

1 teaspoon vanilla extract

⅔ cup fresh passion fruit pulp (about 4 large passion fruits)

1. Place the gelatin in a small container and pour in the water. Whisk with a fork to combine and set aside to hydrate for 5 minutes. Once fully hydrated, the gelatin will solidify and take on the shape of the container.

2. Pour the cream into a 3-quart saucepan. Using a small spoon, scrape the seeds of the split vanilla beans into the cream. Add the scraped vanilla pods and place the pan over medium heat. Bring the cream to a simmer, registering between 200°F and 205°F on an instant-read thermometer, and immediately remove from the heat. Use a fork to remove the gelatin from its container and add it to the hot cream. Stir in the gelatin until it is fully dissolved, about 5 minutes. Add the honey to taste and mix to dissolve, then stir in the kefir and vanilla extract. Strain the entire mixture through a fine-mesh sieve into a container with a spout. Compost the vanilla pods.

3. Pour the cream base into an 8 × 11-inch ceramic or glass mold or divide evenly among ten 1-cup ramekins, about ¾ cup per ramekin. Place the filled mold or ramekins on a metal baking sheet and chill in the refrigerator, uncovered, until the panna cotta is completely set, about 2 hours. Cover with plastic wrap and store in the refrigerator for up to 1 week.

4. To serve, remove the panna cotta from the refrigerator and let it rest, covered, at room temperature at least 10 minutes to soften. Cut it into squares or triangles and plate with 1 to 1½ tablespoons of the passion fruit pulp per serving or drizzle the pulp over the individual ramekins and serve.

PLUM CRISP
with Grain-Free Nut Topping

I see food as only one of the pieces of wellness, albeit an important one. I also prioritize mental health, community, creativity, restoration, and, of course, playfulness! Just like biodynamic farming, it takes a little bit of everything to find that ever-elusive, perfectly imperfect spot to operate from, and food has been the gateway to my more balanced well-being. When I want a sweet bite to finish a meal, this grain-free crisp is my absolute favorite example of what I crave! It is only lightly sweetened beyond the farm-fresh fruit, and it is easy to assemble, leaving time for community and restoration. If using store-bought red and black plums, add 2 to 3 teaspoons of fresh lemon juice to balance their sweetness. Avoid older plums—they can become mealy, and their dry flesh will likely scorch your pot.

SERVES 4

5 cups ½-inch-diced Satsuma plums (about 2 pounds plums)

¼ cup plus 2 tablespoons mild raw honey

1 cup coarsely chopped macadamia nuts

1 tablespoon white chia seeds

1 tablespoon black sesame seeds

1 tablespoon virgin coconut oil

1 cup large unsweetened coconut flakes

1. Preheat the oven to 325°F and position a rack in the middle.

2. In a 3-quart nonreactive pot, combine the plums and ¼ cup of the honey. Cook over low heat, stirring frequently, until the plums soften to a chunky jam consistency, 20 to 25 minutes. Transfer to an 8 × 8-inch casserole dish and set aside to cool.

3. Line a medium baking sheet with parchment paper. In a small bowl, combine the macadamia nuts, chia seeds, sesame seeds, oil, and the remaining 2 tablespoons honey. Rub the ingredients with the tips of your fingers to combine. Gently fold in the coconut flakes with a spoon or combine with your fingertips, being careful not to break the flakes. Spread the topping over the prepared baking sheet in an even layer and transfer to the oven. Bake for 10 to 15 minutes, stirring halfway through. The topping is ready when it is lightly toasted, golden brown, and fragrant. Remove from the oven and let cool for 15 minutes.

4. Spread the topping over the warm plums in a thick layer, covering the entire surface. Serve immediately or at room temperature.

5. To store, let the crisp cool completely, then cover and store in the refrigerator for up to 1 week. Warm, uncovered, in a preheated 350°F oven for 15 minutes before serving.

FERMENTED PLUM AND PINK PEPPERCORN CORDIAL

SERVES
4 TO 6

The attractive Peruvian pepper tree (*Schinus molle*) has naturalized in Southern California, and we inherited quite a few on the farm. They have weeping branches with feathery leaflets that droop over fence rows and provide welcome shade along a lovely farm road we call Lemon Pepper Lane. It isn't uncommon to see someone enjoying a late-afternoon hammock nap under their canopy on the hottest days of summer, while clusters of berries sway overhead. These peppercorns are ready to pick when their papery outer husk is a rosy- to bright-red pink, and they can be used fresh or dried. Their resinous flavor is balanced with a fruity and floral aroma that is excellent when used in sweet or savory recipes or a refreshing cordial. The Satsuma plum's predominantly tart, slightly sweet, floral profile is perfectly suited as a companion to the spicy peppercorns. We prefer the cordial only lightly fermented before it becomes more alcoholic and slightly funky. Taste as you go and bottle when it is to your liking!

5 pounds pitted and juiced Satsuma plums, unstrained (about 1 quart juice)

2 tablespoons mild raw honey

1 tablespoon plus ½ teaspoon pink peppercorns, crushed in a mortar and pestle

1 to 2 quarts chilled sparkling water, to taste

3 to 6 tablespoons fresh lime juice, to taste

GARNISH

Six to eight ⅛-inch-thick slices lime (1 lime)

4 to 6 sprigs mint or edible flowers

1. In a 1-quart mason jar, combine the plum juice, raw honey, and peppercorns. Mix with a spoon until the honey is fully dissolved. Clean the rim of the jar with a cloth and position an airlock lid (page 67). Ferment the mixture at room temperature until effervescent, 3 to 5 days.

2. Transfer the cordial to a 1-quart swing-top bottle and secure the lid. Store in the refrigerator for up to 2 weeks.

3. When ready to serve, strain the cordial through a fine-mesh sieve into a 2-quart glass jar or serving pitcher. For an intensely flavored sweet beverage, mix equal parts sparkling water and cordial (1:1), and add 3 to 6 tablespoons of lime juice, to taste. Or for a lighter, lower-sugar flavor, opt for a 2:1 ratio with 6 tablespoons lime juice.

COCKTAIL TIP: *A Sophisticated Twist*

This gently spiced nonalcoholic cordial also translates well into a cocktail! Our partner and drink mixer extraordinaire Jessica Gurinas suggests placing 2 or 3 ice cubes in a cocktail shaker before adding ¾ cup plum cordial and ¼ to ⅓ cup gin for a sophisticated cocktail twist.

Secure the top, shake to mix until the shaker sweats with condensation, and then pour into a chilled lowball glass. Top with ¼ cup sparkling lime water and garnish with the lime slices and mint.

Chapter Eleven

HARVEST FRUITS

AUTUMN IN SOUTHERN CALIFORNIA CONTINUES TO BE AN ABUNDANT TIME AS our orchard shifts from stone fruits and berries to the sun-ripened flavors of juicy figs, my favorite glowing persimmons, and bursting pomegranates. We welcome the first harvest of apples in tandem with the warming aromas of cinnamon and vanilla that waft through our kitchen. Although harvest-season fruits are remarkably sweet from a long period of ripening, their deep flavors complement savory salads, comforting soups, and appetizers as much as desserts and jammy spreads, maximizing the use of produce that shares the season between summer and fall.

Recipes

STRAWBERRY-APPLE BUTTER
with Vanilla

MAKES
1 PINT

Strawberries and apples may seem like an odd pairing, as they don't typically fruit in the same season. We have found, however, that the smoothest fruit butter is made from frozen and thawed strawberries that are pureed in a blender and cooked down slowly with apples. Sweet Albion strawberries have low acidity, and when harvested juicy and perfectly ripe, they freeze very well. You can use store-bought pure apple juice without preservatives or added sugar instead of fresh pressed, and 2 teaspoons of vanilla paste for the vanilla beans if need be. Allow at least 1½ to 2 hours for cooking, and watch carefully toward the end to avoid scorching. To encourage evaporation, it is best to use a wide and shallow pot about 12 inches in diameter. Maria, from our kitchen team, earned the name "Maria Machine" a few years ago when we brought her on to make apple butters, a job that requires her to stir a large pot for hours before processing multiple batches. She recommends wearing long sleeves to protect from dangerously hot splatters as the butter reduces and thickens.

1 quart fresh apple juice

8½ cups peeled, cored, and diced Pink Lady apples (about 10 medium apples)

2 cups strawberry puree (about 2½ cups halved strawberries)

2 whole vanilla beans

1. In a large pot, heat the apple juice over medium heat until reduced by half, about 15 minutes. In the pitcher of a blender, place the apples and the strawberry puree. Blend until smooth and transfer to the cooking pot. Split the vanilla beans down the middle and scrape the seeds into the pot. Stir to combine, cover, and reduce the heat to medium.

2. When the mixture comes to a simmer, remove the lid. Lower the heat to low and continue to cook, stirring often to prevent scorching and sticking, until it has reduced by at least half. When approaching the proper consistency, a spoon will form distinct ribbons in the butter when stirred and the color will be a matte brownish-red that holds its shape well on a spoon. Although the final consistency can be adjusted by adding a bit of water to loosen, avoid overcooking, which will result in a darkened color and scorched flavor.

3. Remove from the heat and scoop the apple butter into two sterilized 8-ounce mason jars. Wipe the rims of the jars with a clean cloth or paper towel and release trapped air bubbles by carefully sliding a knife between the apple butter and the sides of the jar. Fasten the lids, let cool at room temperature until warm, and place in the refrigerator to store for up to 2 months.

CLASSIC CHICKEN LIVER PÂTÉ
with Gordon Apples

Gordon apples give this deeply savory liver pâté some welcomed fragrance, accentuated by the caramel notes of bourbon. Journeyman Featherbone Bourbon Whiskey (see Resources, page 392) is our choice, as it is distilled from organic corn, wheat, and rye with a warm and earthy but sweet character. If Gordon apples aren't available, Fuji, Pink Lady, or another low-acid variety is best for this recipe. Purchase bright red organic chicken livers from a reputable source no earlier than one day before making this recipe, or freeze the fresh livers and thaw the day of use. This pâté is very thick but will spread nicely if left to rest at room temperature for at least 15 minutes before using. Serve with A Crusty Hearth-Style Sourdough Boule (page 59) or with the Multi-Seed Herb Crackers with Thyme and Rosemary (page 153).

MAKES
1 PINT

4 tablespoons unsalted butter

1 cup peeled and minced Gordon apple (1 large apple)

½ cup minced red onion (about ½ large onion)

1½ teaspoons minced garlic (1½ large cloves)

4 teaspoons chopped fresh sage leaves or 2 teaspoons dried

1½ teaspoons fresh thyme leaves or ¾ teaspoon dried

1 teaspoon fine sea salt

4 slices Simple Salt and Pepper Bacon (page 38), chopped

1 pound chicken livers, excess fat and sinew removed (about 12½ ounces cleaned liver)

¼ teaspoon freshly ground black peppercorns

¼ cup bourbon

3 tablespoons heavy cream

¼ cup ghee, melted

1. In a medium skillet, melt the butter over medium heat. Cook the apple, onion, garlic, sage, thyme, and ½ teaspoon of the salt, stirring until the apple softens and the onion turns translucent, about 7 minutes. Transfer the mixture to the bowl of a food processor and set aside.

2. Line a plate with paper towels. In a skillet, cook the bacon over medium heat until golden and crispy, about 7 minutes. Transfer to the lined plate to drain and add the chicken liver to the skillet. Season with the remaining ½ teaspoon salt and the pepper and cook over high heat for 3 to 4 minutes per side, being careful not to burn the livers or the bacon fat. Transfer the livers, bacon fat, and bacon to the food processor. Deglaze the pan with the bourbon, and use a spoon to scrape the pan drippings into the food processor. With the blades running, stream in the cream and process until a smooth and creamy paste forms, 3 to 4 minutes.

3. Divide the pâté into two 8-ounce jars and smooth the tops with the back of a spoon. Divide the ghee in half and pour over the top of each jar. The butter should cover the pâté entirely and be ¼ inch thick. Store in the refrigerator for up to 1 week.

KALE TABBOULEH
with Apples, Almonds, and Pomegranate

Kale salads are some of our staple dishes. This tabbouleh-inspired combination uses almonds as its base instead of the *burghul* (bulgur) that is traditionally used. The subtle sweet taste the almonds have after soaking and dehydrating (page 41) is delightful here, and they pair deliciously with a combination of seasonal farm flavors and textures that are both bright and filling. For best results, pulse the almonds in a food processor to the size of a medium-textured couscous. To balance the acidity of lemon and sumac, which are both essential to this dish, choose crisp and firm sweet apples such as Gordon or Pink Lady and a sweet pomegranate variety such as Parfianka, or decrease the amount of lemon juice to taste. The red, green, and white colors of this salad are festive for holiday meals, and the salad can be made several hours in advance, covered, and placed in the refrigerator. Although we use dinosaur or curly-leafed kale, any tender-grown variety will perform well.

SERVES
4 TO 6

6 cups loosely packed finely chopped kale, stems removed (2 large bunches)

2 cups medium-coarse-ground almonds

2 cups unpeeled small-diced apple (2 large apples)

½ cup finely minced red onion (about ½ large onion)

1 cup fresh pomegranate seeds (about 1 pomegranate)

½ cup finely chopped fresh mint leaves

6 to 8 tablespoons fresh lemon juice (1½ to 2 large lemons)

¼ cup cold-pressed extra-virgin olive oil

1 teaspoon minced garlic (1 clove)

2 teaspoons fine sea salt

1 teaspoon ground sumac

1. In a large nonreactive bowl, combine the kale, almonds, apple, onion, pomegranate, mint, lemon juice, oil, garlic, salt, and sumac. Toss to mix and serve immediately.

2. Store in a covered nonreactive container for up to 2 days. Alternatively, combine the lemon juice, oil, garlic, salt, and sumac and store separately from the salad for up to 1 week before mixing and serving.

ROASTED FIG AND FENNEL SALAD
with Walnuts and Chèvre

This simple, warm, and satisfying salad is a wonderful balance of sweet and savory. The Fruit Basket section of our orchard is home to four varieties of figs, yet each year I most look forward to the ripening of Violette de Bordeaux, which tastes just like my memories of a childhood fig cookie. I don't think nature could have crammed any more figgy flavor into such a small package! That said, Black Mission figs, which are popular for a good reason, lend a similar robust color and fragrance to this salad and hold up well when roasted. If you are making the salad in the autumn months, try using earthy hazelnuts instead of walnuts or rich and buttery macadamia nuts for a milder experience.

SERVES 4

SALAD

4 cups cored and ¼-inch-sliced fennel bulbs (about 6 small bulbs)

3 tablespoons unrefined avocado oil

1 teaspoon fine sea salt

¼ teaspoon freshly ground black peppercorns

8 ripe but firm fresh brown figs, stems removed and halved

¼ cup chopped toasted walnuts

3 tablespoons crumbled chèvre (1½ ounces)

¼ cup fennel fronds

1 tablespoon chiffonade-cut fresh mint leaves

DRESSING

1 teaspoon minced garlic (1 clove)

1 tablespoon fresh thyme leaves or 1½ teaspoons dried

2 tablespoons cold-pressed extra-virgin olive oil

2 tablespoons fresh lemon juice (½ large lemon)

½ teaspoon fine sea salt

1. Preheat the oven to 375°F and position a rack in the middle.

2. Make the salad: In a medium bowl, toss the fennel with the oil, salt, and pepper. Spread over a large unlined baking sheet and roast for 45 minutes, or until golden. The fennel will shrink to half its size and develop dark, caramelized tips. Remove from the oven and transfer to a bowl.

3. Preheat the broiler to high and position the oven rack 6 inches below the broiler.

4. On the same baking sheet, place the figs cut side up. Place the pan under the broiler and broil for 5 to 7 minutes, until the edges of the figs darken. Remove from the oven and let the figs cool for at least 10 minutes.

5. Make the dressing: In a small bowl, whisk together the garlic, thyme, oil, lemon juice, and salt and set aside.

6. To serve, pour the dressing over the roasted fennel and toss to combine. Add the figs and walnuts and fold gently. Transfer the salad to a serving platter and garnish with the chèvre, fennel fronds, and mint. Serve immediately, at room temperature.

WHITE BEAN TARTINE
with Bacon, Arugula, and Pickled Persimmons

This is a beautifully presented autumn appetizer that can be easily assembled and served at room temperature for a small party or in larger portions as open-faced sandwiches. While small and tender navy beans provide a nice color contrast with the warmly spiced Pickled Persimmons (page 33), pinto or cranberry beans also have complementary flavors and textures. Cook the bacon until it is nice and crispy for a delightful textural contrast with the puree and the toasted sourdough.

MAKES
16
APPETIZERS

2 cups cooked navy beans

¼ cup reserved bean cooking liquid

2 teaspoons minced garlic (2 cloves)

½ teaspoon lemon zest

2 teaspoons fresh lemon juice

½ teaspoon fine sea salt

2 tablespoons cold-pressed extra-virgin olive oil

8 large slices A Crusty Hearth-Style Sourdough Boule (page 59), toasted

1 quart Pickled Persimmons (page 33), drained

16 slices Simple Salt and Pepper Bacon (page 38), cooked

½ cup micro-arugula

1. In a food processor, combine the beans, cooking liquid, garlic, lemon zest and juice, salt, and oil and process to a smooth paste. Scrape down the sides and the bottom of the processor bowl to incorporate any large pieces of bean. Process for an additional minute, until the puree is smooth and creamy. Transfer to a bowl and set aside.

2. To assemble, lay the slices of toast on a cutting board and spread about 3 tablespoons of the bean puree on each slice. Arrange about 6 pickled persimmons on top of each slice of bread. Lay 2 slices of the crispy bacon diagonally on top of each slice and then sprinkle some of the micro-arugula on top. Cut each slice diagonally into a triangle, making 16 appetizer-size servings. Serve immediately, at room temperature.

CHOCOLATE PERSIMMON PUDDING

SERVES 6

As a friendly reminder, astringent persimmons are the type that must ripen to a pudding-like texture before being consumed; otherwise, they suck every bit of moisture from your mouth and give my favorite fruit a bad rap! On the farm, we grow only one astringent type, called Chocolate, and we love to use it in this dreamy pudding. Its name can mislead some, but it refers to the flesh, which has a freckled brown appearance, and doesn't taste a bit like chocolate. The most complicated part of this recipe is simply waiting for the persimmons to ripen! If you cannot source Chocolate, substitute another fully ripe astringent type of Hachiya persimmon. It makes a unique autumn pudding when combined with orange, maple, and warming cinnamon, and it uses both heavy cream and coconut cream for a rich complexity that can't otherwise be achieved by using just one. Serve chilled for a light but satisfying midafternoon or after-dinner treat!

3 Chocolate persimmons

1 cup raw heavy cream

½ cup full-fat coconut cream

¼ cup maple syrup

A pinch of fine sea salt

½ teaspoon ground cinnamon

½ teaspoon vanilla extract

½ cup fresh orange juice (4 ounces)

2 tablespoons arrowroot powder

4 large egg yolks, room temperature

6 tablespoons chopped walnuts

1. Remove the stems of the persimmons and transfer the flesh to a blender. Puree until smooth. You should have about 1¾ cups.

2. In a medium saucepan, combine 1 cup of the persimmon puree, the heavy cream, coconut cream, maple syrup, salt, cinnamon, and vanilla. Bring to a simmer over medium heat and cook, stirring frequently with a whisk, for 15 minutes. In a small bowl, whisk together the orange juice, arrowroot, and egg yolks until well combined and no lumps remain.

3. To temper the egg yolks, reduce the heat to low and in a slow and steady stream, pour ¼ cup of the hot cream over the egg mixture, whisking vigorously to prevent the eggs from scrambling. Transfer the tempered eggs to the saucepan, whisk to combine, and increase the heat to medium. Cook, whisking often, until the mixture thickens and coats the back of a spoon, 8 to 10 minutes.

4. Remove the pot from the heat, transfer the pudding to the blender, and puree on high speed for 1 minute. Divide the pudding equally among six 6-ounce ramekins, about 4 ounces per ramekin. Transfer to the refrigerator and chill, uncovered, until the pudding has fully set, at least 3 hours.

5. To serve, garnish with the remaining persimmon puree and the walnuts. To store, cover each ramekin with reusable waxed linen or plastic wrap and refrigerate for up to 4 days.

CHERIMOYA BREAD PUDDING
with Lemon and Macadamia Nuts

SERVES 6

Cherimoyas (*Annona cherimola*) are subtropical fruits from dry, cool highland areas in the Andes that have found a home in coastal Southern California. Although they resemble a peculiar-looking dinosaur egg, they are beloved by many, including the late Alan York, our original mentor. Cherimoyas are naturally pollinated by a beetle that we don't have in California, and so we pollinate their flowers by hand, often with a paintbrush. We continue to try to find ways around this, however, by suspending banana peels nearby and sowing rows of corn in between to attract similar pollinators. Often called an "ice cream" or "bubble-gum" fruit, cherimoya has a uniquely sweet and delicate tropical flavor and a soft, pear-like, but smooth texture. It is worth the extra effort to grow the fruit, which are picked firm, like an avocado, and then slowly ripen to a rich and custardy texture. They are very aromatic when ripe and can fill the kitchen with an overwhelming fragrance. You can eat them fresh or pair them with brighter flavors such as lemon when cooked. Our crop is still small and somewhat precious, but we love the challenge they bring and like to use them in this decadent bread pudding. Search for firm but ripe cherimoyas at farmers markets in Southern California or Latin or Middle Eastern markets elsewhere, and avoid overripe fruits that may develop an oxidized, brown color that turns bitter once cooked.

1 cup cherimoya segments, skin and seeds removed

4 large eggs, room temperature

½ cup maple sugar

2½ cups raw heavy cream, room temperature

¼ teaspoon fine sea salt

2 teaspoons vanilla extract

2 tablespoons lemon zest (2 large lemons)

4½ cups ½-inch cubed A Crusty Hearth-Style Sourdough Boule (page 59)

⅓ cup chopped macadamia nuts

1 cup raw heavy cream

7 tablespoons maple syrup

½ vanilla bean

1. In a small saucepan, bring 2 quarts of water to a simmer. In the pitcher of a blender, place the cherimoya, eggs, maple sugar, cream, salt, vanilla, and lemon zest. Puree until combined, about 20 seconds.

2. In a medium bowl, combine the bread cubes and cream mixture. Mix with a spatula until soggy and then transfer to a 7½ × 12-inch baking dish or a 12-inch-round braising pan. Evenly sprinkle with the macadamia nuts and cover with parchment paper before securing with a layer of foil. Let soak for 15 minutes at room temperature.

3. Preheat the oven to 350°F and position a rack in the middle.

4. Nestle the pudding dish into a larger baking dish with at least 2 inches of extra space on all sides. Into the larger dish, pour in enough of the hot water to reach halfway up the sides and carefully transfer to the oven. Bake for 40 minutes, uncover, and continue baking for another 20 minutes, or until the pudding is set and the top is golden brown. Remove from the oven and set aside to cool for 20 minutes prior to serving.

RECIPE AND INGREDIENTS CONTINUE

5. In a medium chilled bowl, pour in the cream and 1 tablespoon of the maple syrup and scrape in the seeds from the vanilla bean. Using a handheld mixer, whip on medium-high speed until stiff peaks form, 5 to 7 minutes.

6. To serve, divide the pudding into portions and spoon a dollop of whipped cream on top. Serve warm, drizzled with 1 tablespoon of the maple syrup over each serving. Once fully cooled, store tightly covered in the refrigerator for up to 4 days.

BLACKBERRY-FIG JAM
with Caramelized Onion

MAKES
1 PINT

The Blackberry Path lines a walk from our home to the barn and is a popular spot for a summer snack. These plump and juicy berries were growing on the farm when we arrived, and they were one of the very first fruits that I got to harvest. Our first few summers, my mom and I used to collect and freeze them on trays before bagging them to store and enjoy all year, or we would use them in recipes like this unique jam. Black Mission figs or similar cultivars with dark, burgundy skins are a fitting choice for this recipe—they impart a deep color and flavor and are best used when gooey, overripe, and almost syrup-like. The rich sweet and savory notes of this creative combination can enhance so many meals, especially when paired with anything pork. It's especially tasty slathered on a ham sandwich! Or try it spread over prepared Sourdough Pizza Dough (page 62): crumble with blue cheese and cooked Simple Salt and Pepper Bacon (page 38), then bake until crispy, and finish with fresh, lightly dressed arugula. For breakfast, smother a layer of this jam on a hearty piece of sourdough toast (pages 54 or 59) and then pile on a heaping portion of fresh, creamy ricotta or Farmer's Cheese (page 70). It is also at home simply served alongside artisan cheeses and cured meats.

1 tablespoon cold-pressed extra-virgin olive oil

1 cup minced red onion (1 large onion)

1½ cups fresh blackberries (12 ounces)

3 cups fresh or frozen and thawed Black Mission figs, stems removed and halved (1 pound)

½ teaspoon chopped fresh thyme leaves or ¼ teaspoon dried

1 tablespoon mild raw honey

2 tablespoons fresh lemon juice (½ large lemon)

½ teaspoon fine sea salt

½ teaspoon freshly cracked black peppercorns

3 tablespoons aged balsamic vinegar

I. In a medium heavy-bottomed pot, heat the oil over medium heat until it expands, about 1 minute. Add the onion and sauté until translucent and beginning to caramelize, 8 to 10 minutes. Add the blackberries, figs, thyme, honey, lemon juice, salt, and pepper. Cook, stirring occasionally, until the mixture thickens and the fruit softens and breaks into small chunks, 15 to 20 minutes. Remove from the heat, stir in the vinegar, and set aside to cool for 15 minutes. If desired, use an immersion blender or food processor to create a smooth jam before scooping into a sterilized 1-pint mason jar.

2. To store, fasten the lid and place in the refrigerator to cool and seal. Store for up to 2 weeks in the refrigerator or in the freezer (after it has cooled) for up to 6 months.

Chapter Twelve

WINTER
CITRUS

DURING THE DARKNESS OF WINTER, OUR CITRUS TREES GROW HEAVIER BY THE day with glittering jewels of oranges, grapefruits, lemons, limes, and kumquats. For many years, Nathan, who is our director of sales, and I had our meetings in the citrus orchards during this time, and still do sometimes! We call Nathan our chef in the field due to his culinary background working in fine-dining restaurants for ten years before joining our team. We tasted for ripeness as we went and compared notes, always cleansing our pocketknife at the end with a lemon, ready for next time. Whereas many citrus skins will remain green when ripe in warmer climates, our cooler winter weather induces color change but not ripeness; we must first taste the fruit to test its balance between sweet and sour before picking. Unlike the avocado, citrus stop ripening after they are picked because they do not possess starches that can convert to sugars. While some, like the Mexican lime, are everbearing, the window of availability of others makes them a little more precious.

Nathan and I have built a professional relationship through our palates; sharing experiences through flavor has built a trust that carries into our sales program and keeps our team connected. With our combined experience as chefs, we enthusiastically share recipes with each other and brainstorm ideas to help our team feel equipped to share tips on these foods at the market. In truth, we sell food to share our love of a good meal.

These heavenly, much-anticipated fruits are full of vitamins, and they arrive just in time to fortify us with the equivalent of edible sunshine for the long months ahead. Sweet treats, bright salads, fresh juices, and grain bowls bring vibrant life to our meals when most else remains otherwise dormant.

Recipes

Farro Grain Bowl with Star Ruby Grapefruit, Feta, and Pistachio

Cara Cara Orange and Avocado Salad with Sesame and Jalapeño-Miso Dressing

Fennel and Melogold Salad with Blue Cheese and Pickled Shallot

Almond Avocado Oil Cake with Meyer Lemon Curd

Honey-Sweetened White Limeade with Lemongrass, Coconut, and Ginger

Kumquat Cocoa Bites

FARRO GRAIN BOWL
with Star Ruby Grapefruit, Feta, and Pistachio

Grapefruit is at its glorious, juicy peak during the height of California winter when Star Ruby really tastes like candy. Pink grapefruits don't always grow well for us because they require extreme, consistent heat, which our coastal winds keep at bay. The Fruit Basket section of our orchard originally had another pink-fleshed variety that struggled before we finally grafted it over to Melogold. But for some unknown reason, Star Ruby thrives, and we are happy to have her! If you cannot source them or they are unavailable at our markets (possibly because our farmers market manager, Kevin, ate them all), you can easily substitute sweeter types such as Oro Blanco, Melogold, or even Cara Cara oranges, especially if you find grapefruit too bitter. If the citrus is excessively juicy, chop and lay it on a clean towel to absorb excess liquid before tossing with the salad. The components of the salad can be prepared and stored separately in advance for up to 3 days and brought to room temperature before tossing and serving.

SERVES
4 TO 6

1 cup whole farro wheat berries

1¼ teaspoons fine sea salt

2 tablespoons rice vinegar

2 tablespoons cold-pressed extra-virgin olive oil

¼ teaspoon crushed red chile flakes

¼ cup finely minced red onion (about ¼ large onion)

¼ cup chopped pistachios

¼ cup dried cherries

1 tablespoon roughly chopped fresh dill fronds

¼ cup crumbled feta (2 ounces)

1 cup supremed and ½-inch-chopped Star Ruby grapefruit (2 medium grapefruits) (see Cooking Tip, page 350)

1. In a medium bowl, combine the farro, ¼ teaspoon of the salt, and 3 cups of water. Soak for 8 to 10 hours, drain, and rinse well. Transfer to a small saucepan and add 2½ cups of water. Cover and bring to a boil over medium-high heat. Reduce the heat to medium-low and cook at a gentle simmer until the farro is al dente and the water has been absorbed (adding ½ cup more water if necessary), 20 to 25 minutes. Drain and pat dry. This will yield about 2½ cups of cooked farro.

2. In a large bowl, combine the farro, rice vinegar, oil, the remaining 1 teaspoon salt, and the chile flakes and set aside at room temperature until ready to serve. Just before serving, add the red onion, pistachios, cherries, dill, and feta to the bowl, tossing to combine. Add the chopped grapefruit and toss lightly to incorporate.

3. Transfer to a serving platter or bowl and serve at room temperature. Although the liquid from the citrus will pool and soften the farro, you may store in a sealed container in the refrigerator for up to 3 days.

CARA CARA ORANGE AND AVOCADO SALAD
with Sesame and Jalapeño-Miso Dressing

Winter may be a sparse time for fresh green vegetables in some parts of the country, but this bright and tangy salad uses the best of the season's juicy citrus to summon some cheer. And oh how my family loves this dressing! John has been known to swing by the barn kitchen to request an extra jar of it for himself! White miso can easily be found at most grocery stores, but I prefer to use chickpea miso to avoid soy (see page 29). It has a delicious earthy flavor and can be ordered online (see Resources, page 392) or found at health food stores. This recipe yields ⅔ cup dressing, possibly more than you need, depending upon your preference. Store, covered, in the refrigerator for up to 1 week, or use the extra on a simple green salad with shredded chicken.

SERVES
4 TO 6

JALAPEÑO-MISO DRESSING

1 tablespoon peeled and finely minced fresh ginger (1 × 1-inch knob)

2 teaspoons minced fresh garlic (about 2 large cloves)

2 teaspoons seeded and minced jalapeño pepper (1 small pepper)

2 tablespoons chickpea or white miso (see page 29)

3 tablespoons rice vinegar

½ teaspoon mild raw honey (optional)

SALAD

3 Cara Cara oranges, peeled and sliced into ¼-inch-thick rounds

2 ripe avocados, cut into ⅛-inch slices (about 1 pound)

½ jalapeño pepper, seeds removed, thinly sliced into rounds

Flaked sea salt

½ teaspoon toasted white sesame seeds

½ teaspoon toasted black sesame seeds

1½ cups microgreens or sprouts of choice

1. Make the dressing: In the bowl of a food processor or blender, combine ¼ cup of water, the ginger, garlic, jalapeño, miso, vinegar, and honey (if desired) and puree until creamy with some texture. Set aside until ready to use or cover and store in the refrigerator for up to 1 week.

2. Make the salad: Arrange the orange segments, avocado slices, and jalapeño rings onto individual plates. Lightly sprinkle salt over the avocado and garnish with the sesame seeds. Drizzle the dressing over the salad. Sprinkle with the the microgreens and serve immediately.

FENNEL AND MELOGOLD SALAD
with Blue Cheese and Pickled Shallot

Melogold citrus is a sweet and juicy cross between a grapefruit and a pomelo. Its golden flesh easily separates from the interior membrane, making it one of the easiest to portion into supremes (see below). Melogold is such a special citrus: its light and bright flavor devoid of bitterness is almost spa-like! Once the ingredients of this salad are combined with the vinegar and salt, it produces a dressing that is thin but full of flavor. It is best to toss the salad right before serving to avoid the dressing settling to the bottom of the bowl. If you cannot source Melogold, try substituting other sweet cultivars such as Oro Blanco. Use a mild, nutty, and buttery blue cheese for this dish rather than one that is overpowering.

SERVES 6

PICKLED SHALLOT

¼ cup raw apple cider vinegar

½ teaspoon fine sea salt

1 tablespoon mild raw honey

¼ cup shaved shallot (1 large shallot)

SALAD

7 cups cored and thinly shaved fennel bulbs (3 to 4 medium fennel bulbs)

3 cups Melogold grapefruit supremes (2 medium grapefruits)

1 tablespoon Melogold juice, reserved from the grapefruit supremes

2 tablespoons cold-pressed extra-virgin olive oil

¾ teaspoon fine sea salt

¼ teaspoon freshly cracked black peppercorns

2 tablespoons roughly chopped fennel fronds

1 tablespoon ½-inch-sliced fresh chives or scallion greens

¼ cup crumbled raw blue cheese (1 ounce)

1. Make the pickled shallot: In a small nonreactive saucepan, combine the vinegar, ¼ cup of water, and the salt and bring to a simmer over medium-high heat. Stir to dissolve the salt and remove from the heat. Let the mixture cool to 110°F before adding the raw honey. Stir to incorporate the honey, add the shallot to the brine, and then transfer the mixture to the refrigerator for at least 30 minutes or up to 3 days.

2. Make the salad: In a large bowl, combine the fennel, grapefruit supremes, reserved juice, oil, salt, and pepper. Toss gently before folding in the cooled shallot and brine, fennel fronds, and chives.

3. Transfer the salad to a serving plate and garnish with the blue cheese. Serve immediately.

COOKING TIP: *Citrus Supremes*

Citrus supremes are the segments of the fruit that have had the peel, pith, and connecting membranes sliced away and removed, leaving the brightly colored sections to be admired and enjoyed! It takes a little time, but the presentation is worth it. With a sharp knife, slice about ¼ inch off the top and bottom of the fruit. Standing the fruit on a flat surface, steady it with your nondominant hand. With the tip of your sharp knife, cut into the citrus about ¼ inch deep, following the curve, until the peel and pith are removed. Repeat until the entire citrus is peeled and no pith remains. Slice into segments with the knife blade cutting as closely as possible to the membrane. Repeat on the other side of the segment to release the citrus section. Repeat with the remaining segments.

THE CITRUS
of Apricot Lane Farms

· · · · · · · · · ·

Citrus trees and shrubs are one of our most productive and deliciously juicy crops on the farm. They grow naturally in tropical and subtropical climates and are commercially viable only in areas with some seasonal change but no sustained frost, making Southern California and our farm prime areas for growing! Because of our unique microclimate, we grow citrus that will perform well accordingly and have a wide range of use besides just snacking out of hand, including refreshing beverages, bright dressings, curries, curds, and baked goods. We have included our favorite recipes in this book using the best of what we have to offer, hoping to inspire you to explore with culinary curiosity!

A unique feature of citrus plants is that they readily interbreed, producing hybrids as sour and complex as the rare Yuzu or as sweet and ambrosial as the Cara Cara, a pink-to-ruby-fleshed orange that we adore and anxiously await to ripen. The variety of colors, flavors, and textures of citrus means that each has a distinctive flavor and culinary characteristics dependent upon genetics, growing conditions, and harvest. Most citrus hybrids owe their genetic lineage to four original species: the pomelo (*Citrus maxima*), the mandarin (*Citrus reticulata*), the citron (*Citrus medica*), and the commercially rare Ichang papeda (*Citrus ichangensis*).

All citrus plants, regardless of size, are evergreen. Some are short and squat while others are large and dangerously thorny! Apart from only a few, most of our citrus trees bear fruit in the coldest months of the year and are an excellent source of vitamin C, an antioxidant that can strengthen the immune system with anti-inflammatory properties.

The following is a description of our most beloved citrus and their attributes to help you seek what is in season. Look for fruits that are heavy in the hand, and avoid any soft or tender skins with a wrinkled appearance. Citrus with a sweet, strong fragrance is most promising for the best experience in the kitchen!

Melogold grapefruit (*Citrus maxima* × *Citrus paradisi*, January to February)

This large and squat hybrid is a cross between an acidless pomelo (*Citrus maxima*) and a white Marsh grapefruit, and most resembles the sweet pomelo parent in flavor. It is our sweetest grapefruit, and in our microclimate, it outperforms other red-fleshed grapefruits that need more extreme heat. Many kids, who can be finicky about grapefruit, have been known to love our Melogold! We much prefer it as a breakfast or salad fruit because of how utterly surprising its honeyed flavor can be.

Oro Blanco grapefruit (*Citrus maxima* × *Citrus paradisi*, December to January)

These large and heavy squat-oval fruits have a smooth, aromatic green-to-yellow skin when ripe and are coveted by chefs for their juicy sweetness. In Spanish, *oro blanco* means "white gold," which accurately

CONTINUES

LISBON

MEYER

AUTUMN GOLD

WASHINGTON

CARA CARA

FUKUSHU

HEIRLOOM VALENCIA

TAROCCO

MORO

ORO BLANCO

MELOGOLD

TANGO

MAKRUT

PAGE

CLEMENULE

MEXICAN

BEARSS

SATSUMA

YUZU

describes their delectable, floral flesh. Oro Blanco have a thick and bitter rind but are wonderful to eat fresh when peeled or cut into supremes. Like Melogold, Oro Blanco were developed from the same cross and released to commercial trade only in the early 1980s. They are still considered a specialty citrus and are popular among our market customers. Slice them into winter salads or juice them for a morning beverage.

Fukushu kumquat (*Fortunella obovata* 'Fukushu', January to February)

This small, thornless citrus tree produces 1½-inch-long oval fruit with a noticeably thin, sweet, edible rind and tart, acidic flesh with few seeds. The leaves are longer and broader than other kumquat species, and the fruit is also larger, slightly different in shape, and much sweeter than the more common Nagami kumquat. For years, we would find mysterious little piles of kumquat innards under our trees and couldn't determine the source until one day a similar pile showed up on our kitchen counter. Turns out, Beaudie had been enjoying the sweet skins for a snack, but he won't eat the more puckery flesh! Enjoy these addictive little sweet-tart fruits sliced into salads or salsas, stewed with fish, made into marmalades, or added as a flavor to honey syrups. We especially love their bright flavor in the Kumquat Cocoa Bites (page 363).

Indio mandarinquat (*Citrus × citrofortunella* 'Indio', everbearing)

This deliciously fragrant, adorable fruit is a cross between a Nagami kumquat and a Dancy mandarin. Like a kumquat but larger and with a novel bell-shaped appearance, the mandarinquat has a sweet peel that is completely edible and full of essential oils and nutrients. When the fruit is eaten whole or sliced, the tender peel perfectly balances the acidic flesh. Enjoy these playful fruits preserved in marmalades or honey syrups, sliced into winter salads, diced into fruit salsas, or added to beverages.

Lisbon lemon (*Citrus × limon* 'Lisbon', January to December)

This classic heirloom citrus is one of the most widely planted lemons in the world. They are so enticing that our wholesale customers place their orders early to be sure they get some each week! In our first few years, our lemons were filled with seeds, a sign that the fruit was under stress. Now, I marvel each time I slice into a lemon, both at the pleasantly tart flavor and at the nominal seeds they contain. It's like the trees are telling me they are happy! Lisbon is a vigorous and cold-hardy commercial variety that originated in Portugal but has since made a home in nearly every citrus-growing region. It produces a heavy crop of large, oblong fruit similar in appearance to the Eureka lemon.

Meyer lemon (*Citrus × meyeri* 'Meyer', January to March, May to June)

These thin-skinned, remarkably fragrant, and floral sweet lemons are native to China, where they originated as a cross between a citron and a hybrid of mandarin and pomelo. Meyer lemons did not rise to culinary fame in the Western world for many decades due to their thin, fragile skin that pierces easily during shipping. When we first planted them, I was amazed at how many fruits they began producing almost immediately! Yet we often thin the harvest, as the trees will stay very stunted otherwise. They are smaller than the more common Lisbon or Eureka lemons, with a smoother, deep golden-yellow to orange-hued skin that resembles our egg yolks. They are excellent in desserts such as Meyer Lemon Curd (page 359) but can be used in savory sauces and vinaigrettes, preserved with salt (page 34), or used whenever you want a floral lemon flavor without the sharpness of a more common lemon.

Pink Eureka lemon (*Citrus × limon* 'Eureka Pink Variegated', January to February)

This unique lemon tree has an arresting variegated cream-and-green pattern on its leaves and a beautifully yellow-and-green-striped fruit with pink flesh! It is a natural mutation of the Eureka lemon commonly found in grocery stores but has a rougher skin and very tart juice. This treasured ornamental "sport" (spontaneous mutation) has become a popular tree in home landscapes and is a darling of specialty farmers markets. Its juice has a delightful salinity and a bright acidic flavor that is delicious in cocktails or as a natural accompaniment to shellfish. A thin slice of this lemon is a captivating addition to a glass of ice water!

Mandarins (*Citrus reticulata* 'Satsuma', December to January; 'Page', November to January; 'Clemenule', January; 'Tango', February; and 'Gold Nugget', March)

These small, drought-tolerant, but frost-sensitive trees are valued for their sometimes diminutive fruits with loose, easily peeled skins and remarkably sweet flesh. They are so popular that more than two hundred cultivars have been developed! We have chosen a variety of cultivars that are productive over a long period of harvest. Our son (like most kids) loves mandarins, especially the zipper-peel varieties, because he can actually pick and peel them by himself. At the farm, our visiting children learn to twist mandarins off the tree without leaving behind a piece of the skin that would otherwise harbor pests. It is a ready-made snack that brings profound joy to their sticky faces!

Cara Cara navel orange (*Citrus sinensis* 'Cara Cara', January to February)

The Cara Cara orange is a beautiful pink-to-ruby-fleshed citrus that graces our orchards in mid- to late winter. Its shape and skin resemble one of its parents, the heirloom navel orange, but the flesh is sweeter and only slightly acidic. It also contains an impressive 20 percent more vitamin C than the navel! Exotic hints of cranberry or blackberry further distinguish it from any other orange that we grow. Use it as an alternative to Star Ruby grapefruit for less bitterness in the Farro Grain Bowl with Star Ruby Grapefruit, Feta, and Pistachio (page 347) and to brighten winter salads such as the Cara Cara Orange and Avocado Salad with Sesame and Jalapeño-Miso Dressing (page 348).

Washington and Autumn Gold navel oranges (*Citrus sinensis* 'Washington', December to May; 'Autumn Gold', February to March)

The navel orange was discovered in Brazil in the early 1800s and then cloned and heavily planted in Southern California in the 1870s, helping to establish the state as a leader in citrus production. Both our early-to-midseason Washington and the late-season Autumn Gold are fruits with robust, juicy flesh. Their sweetness is balanced with a notable acidity, making them excellent for juicing or adorning salads as well as for snacking. Their most distinguishing physical characteristic, however, is their endearing belly button. This "navel" is an undeveloped twin fruit formed inside the blossom end and results from the same gene mutation that also led to the fruit being seedless.

CONTINUES

Makrut lime (*Citrus hystrix*, November to February)

The knobby appearance of this animated lime is special, and the slightest hint of zest can lift a dish to aromatic heights. The juice is sharply sour and slightly bitter and should be used carefully. The zest and the leaves of this distinctive citrus are, however, highly valued, especially in the curry dishes of Thailand and Southeast Asia. The winged leaves have a unique shape and can be dried and used similarly to bay leaves or sliced thinly and used fresh as a garnish for Curried Coconut Soup with Chicken and Yellow Squash Noodles (page 209).

Yuzu (*Citrus junos*, January to March)

Describing this rare citrus is difficult using common culinary language. It would be easy to pass over these fruit, with their pockmarked and rough skin and rather small and squat stature, for something much less than extraordinary. But if you were to walk into a room of ripe yellow yuzu, you might think you were stepping into a lush jungle thick with exotic flowers! Although yuzu originated in China over one thousand years ago, Japan is the most notable location of cultivation. The USDA has made it illegal to import the fruit or propagation stock, and they are difficult to find in markets outside of citrus-growing regions in the United States. Yuzu are not a snacking citrus, but every bit of this coveted fruit and its puckery-tart juice can be used to flavor creative condiments, sauces, cocktails, and vinaigrettes or to garnish savory fish or chicken dishes. From ponzu (soy sauce combined with yuzu juice) to yuzu kosho (a paste of the rind fermented with salt and fiery hot chiles), a little goes a long way!

Mexican lime (*Citrus aurantifolia*, everbearing)

These aromatic small limes are known in the United States by many common names, including Key lime, bartender's lime, or West Indian lime, but they are grown in many other parts of the world such as Mexico, Egypt, Morocco, and India and have more localized names there as well. The rind and blossoms are remarkably floral and fragrant, and the trees are generous, bearing fruit year-round that drops to the ground when ripe. The juice is extremely acidic, and of course, most of us know its signature flavor from Key lime pie! Mexican limes are also excellent in savory marinades, dressings, or guacamole. Use them to brighten Flavio's Guacamole (page 371); to squeeze over Smoky Potato and Greens Tacos (page 150) or Crispy Bull Meat Tacos with Romaine Slaw (page 276); or to make Honey-Sweetened White Limeade with Lemongrass, Coconut, and Ginger (page 360).

Palestine sweet lime (*Citrus limettioides*, December to April)

This low-acid lime can be traced to the Middle East, where it is enjoyed in the cuisine of that region. The bright yellow fruit are beautiful and large with an oblong to round shape and a subtle flavor profile that is unique but similar to the Bearss lime, although less sweet or tart. Our trees took quite a few years to mature, and we were unsure if they would ever produce a flavor better than floor cleaner! After the third year, however, the limes went from being harshly astringent to having a mild and pleasant quality that we adore. Use the juice or zest where a more common acidic lime would overpower a dish: grated into baked goods or curries, squeezed into teas or fresh fruit beverages, or to flavor kombucha.

Bearss lime (*Citrus latifolia*, September to November)

This nearly thornless tree is a cross between a Mexican lime (*Citrus aurantifolia*) and a lemon (*Citrus limon*). These prolific trees bear juicy, delightfully seedless, lemon-size yellow fruit. They have the most robust, rounded flavors once fully ripe and yellow, without the traces of bitterness when picked green, as is typical of supermarket limes. Bearss is more cold hardy than the Mexican lime and is one of our favorite and most versatile citrus for cooking or preparing beverages such as the Honey-Sweetened White Lime-ade with Lemongrass, Coconut, and Ginger (page 360). Use it to make the Simple Jicama Salad with Sumac, Bearss Lime, and Ancho Chile (page 125) and the Citrus and Garlic Sea Salt (page 93), or use to brighten Marinated Picnic Peppers Stuffed with Chorizo and Manchego Cheese (page 179).

Moro blood orange (*Citrus sinensis* 'Moro', December to February)

The dramatic, deep-red flesh and blushing-sepia to deep-purple skin of this blood orange owes its color to the presence of anthocyanins, a type of flavonoid or class of compounds with antioxidant effects. Anthocyanins are commonly found in red grapes, purple cabbage, and blueberries and only sometimes in citrus. The pigments of blood oranges are not produced in significant amounts unless the fruit is exposed to cold conditions during its development or post-harvest in storage. Moro are one of the most commonly cultivated commercial blood oranges, and we love them tossed in salads, made into beverages, baked into beautiful cakes, or juiced and reduced into a glaze for meat.

Tarocco blood orange (*Citrus sinensis* 'Tarocco', December to February)

Blood oranges are considered to have a general Mediterranean origin, and this landrace Sicilian variety has a remarkably sweet and flavorful flesh that varies in color from deep raspberry pink to a streaked red. Unlike the Moro, the Tarocco's thin skin rarely shows any signs of blushing until the late season. It is considered to be one of the best-tasting blood oranges, though it rarely has the same intensity of dark-red flesh as the others. When displayed next to citrus of contrasting color or added to Cara Cara Orange and Avocado Salad with Sesame and Jalapeño-Miso Dressing (page 348), they seem jewellike and almost extravagant!

Valencia orange (*Citrus sinensis* 'Valencia', April to May, August to September)

In addition to our bountiful selection of winter-bearing citrus, we grow summer-bearing sweet Valencia oranges. We push off harvesting this variety to maximize sugar content, even at the sacrifice of texture, as this is the ultimate juicing orange! Our favorite fruits come from three heirloom trees that were already mature on the property when we moved to the farm. We estimate the trees are over fifty years old, and their fruit belongs in the "ugly but delicious" category—not much to look at, but such an intensely sweet flavor! Our director of sales, Nathan, calls these special citrus the "Capri Sun" of oranges, and our visitors would agree. In the early years of the farm, when there weren't many fruits ready to harvest, we would swing by these trees so our touring guests could have a taste. Once they picked an orange, we would show them how to roll it between their hands to soften and encourage maximum juiciness. Then, we'd instruct them to take a mouth-size bite of the skin from the stem end and squeeze the sweet, sun-warmed orange directly into their mouths. It gave them a memorable experience, and a delicious thirst quencher!

ALMOND AVOCADO OIL CAKE
with Meyer Lemon Curd

This gluten-free cake is only slightly sweetened, making it an excellent snacking cake. Unrefined avocado oil gives the lavender-scented crumb a beautiful hue and buttery flavor that is complemented by the bright curd, which has a gentle tartness. With pastured chicken eggs, the curd appears impressively bright! If using soaked nuts (page 41), the skins can be removed before dehydrating to make your own blanched almond flour, or source it from sustainable farms (see Resources, page 392).

MAKES
1 LOAF

CAKE

2 cups blanched almond flour

½ cup coconut flour

1 teaspoon baking soda

1 teaspoon baking powder

½ cup unsweetened almond milk

½ cup Lavender-Infused Honey (page 158)

½ cup unrefined avocado oil

3 large eggs, room temperature

1 teaspoon Meyer lemon zest (½ medium Meyer lemon)

1 tablespoon fresh Meyer lemon juice (1 medium Meyer lemon)

2 teaspoons vanilla extract

CURD

4 tablespoons unsalted butter, softened

⅓ cup creamed raw honey

6 large egg yolks, room temperature

1 tablespoon Meyer lemon zest (1½ medium Meyer lemons)

⅔ cup Meyer lemon juice (about 5 medium Meyer lemons)

1. Preheat the oven to 325°F and position a rack in the middle.

2. Make the cake: Line a 4 × 9 × 4-inch loaf pan with parchment paper and lightly grease the paper with butter. In a medium bowl, whisk together the almond flour, coconut flour, baking soda, and baking powder. In a separate large bowl, whisk together the almond milk, honey, oil, eggs, lemon zest and juice, and vanilla extract. Using a spatula, fold the dry ingredients into the wet ingredients to create a thick batter. Scoop the batter into the prepared loaf pan and evenly smooth the top.

3. Bake for 50 to 60 minutes, rotating halfway through, until a toothpick or knife inserted into the center comes out clean. Let cool for 5 minutes. Tip the cake from the pan, carefully remove the parchment, and transfer to a wire rack. Let cool completely before slicing, about 2 hours.

4. Make the curd: Using a handheld mixer and medium bowl or a stand mixer fitted with the whisk attachment, beat the butter with the honey on medium speed until soft and fluffy, about 2 minutes. Add the egg yolks one at a time, incorporating each fully, and continue beating until the volume has doubled, about 2 minutes. Add the lemon zest and juice and mix just to combine—it will curdle, but this is normal. Pour the mixture into a small saucepan and cook over low heat, stirring occasionally, until warmed through, 4 to 5 minutes. Increase the heat to medium and cook, stirring often to prevent scorching, until thickened or the curd registers 170°F on an instant-read thermometer—do not boil. Remove from the heat and strain through a fine-mesh sieve into a small bowl. Cover with a vented lid to prevent a skin from forming and place in the refrigerator to cool.

5. Serve the sliced cake with the curd on the side.

HONEY-SWEETENED WHITE LIMEADE
with Lemongrass, Coconut, and Ginger

This refreshing blended beverage has the underpinnings of a tropical escape with hints of floral lemongrass and ginger balanced by a frothy, spoonable coconut foam. Although using more coconut cream will make it extra decadent, too much will mute the subtle balance of citrus and herbs. Bearss limes are abundant in winter, but Mexican limes are available for year-round harvest to make this drink. Serve with spicy meals, at a BBQ, or for a summer gathering, where its impressive presentation can be admired! For a more adult cocktail version, try adding ¾ to 1 cup of white rum or good-quality silver tequila before blending.

SERVES
4 TO 6

2 tablespoons peeled and finely minced fresh ginger (1 × 2-inch knob)

3 tablespoons minced lemongrass (1 hefty stalk)

½ cup mild raw honey

4 teaspoons lime zest (2 medium limes)

1 cup fresh lime juice (8 medium limes)

½ cup full-fat coconut cream

1 cup ice, plus more to serve

GARNISH

4 to 6 lime wedges

4 to 6 sprigs fresh mint (optional)

1. In a 1-quart saucepan, combine the ginger, lemongrass, and 1 cup of water. Bring to a boil over medium heat and simmer for 5 minutes. Remove the pan from the heat and let it cool for 5 minutes. Transfer the contents to the pitcher of a blender and blend until smooth, then strain through a fine-mesh sieve into a heatproof bowl. Let the mixture cool to 85°F or lower, and whisk in the honey until fully dissolved. Cool the mixture in the refrigerator for 30 minutes or over a bowl of ice water until chilled.

2. Pour the chilled syrup into the blender. Add 3 cups of water, the lime zest and juice, coconut cream, and ice. Blend on high until light yellow and decadently frothy, about 2 minutes. Pour over ice, spooning the foam evenly into each glass. Garnish with a wedge of lime and fresh mint (if desired).

KUMQUAT COCOA BITES

My fabulous childhood friend Kevin is such a fan of our kumquats that for his birthday each year, which falls during kumquat season, I ship him a box of fresh fruit. And he's not the only lover of these special treats! The kumquat trees are a frequent pitstop on winter farm tours, and the comments always revolve around the surprisingly sweet flavor of the kumquat rind. Small but satisfying, these tasty cocoa bites pair the sweet but bright peel of kumquats with the robust flavor of chocolate. The coconut sugar and cacao nibs stay crunchy once rolled, and give these morsels a playful texture that melts nicely in the mouth. Remove the peel from the kumquat using a small paring knife, and scrape away the bitter white pith prior to finely chopping.

MAKES
15 BITES

¼ cup unrefined coconut sugar

¼ cup Dutch-process cocoa powder

2 tablespoons virgin coconut oil

⅛ teaspoon fine sea salt

½ teaspoon ground green cardamom

1 tablespoon finely minced kumquat peel (about 3 Fukushu kumquats)

2 tablespoons raw tahini, room temperature

2 tablespoons cacao nibs

¼ cup finely chopped pistachios

1. In a medium bowl, combine the coconut sugar, cocoa powder, oil, salt, cardamom, kumquat peel, tahini, and cacao nibs and mix to incorporate. The sugar will become soft but retain some of its crunchiness. Cover with plastic wrap and refrigerate for 20 minutes so the mixture stiffens slightly.

2. Line a medium baking sheet with parchment paper. Place the pistachios in a small bowl. Using the small end of a melon baller (about 1 teaspoon), scoop a portion of the chocolate mixture and roll between your palms to form a small ball. Roll the ball in the crushed pistachios to evenly coat and transfer to the prepared baking sheet. Repeat this process with the remaining mixture. Transfer the baking sheet to the refrigerator and chill until firm, at least 1 hour.

3. Once the bites are firm, serve cold or transfer to a covered container and store in the refrigerator for up to 1 week.

Chapter Thirteen

THE
AVOCADO

THE AVOCADO IS NATURE'S PLANT-BASED BUTTER, RICH WITH HEALTHY FATS AND a creamy, decadent texture. We boast an impressive collection of fifteen different kinds of avocados, many of which are often overlooked by other growers but worth seeking out whenever possible. The ingredient combinations in this chapter highlight the versatility of our cultivars, which come in many shapes, sizes, and nuanced textures (see page 374 for detailed descriptions). That said, Hass is the most ubiquitous and easy-to-source avocado and will work beautifully in the following recipes.

Recipes

LAZY SALSA
with Root Vegetable Chips

Tomatillos are a generous crop, and I created this recipe back when we had a surplus of these small green fruits. Initially, I felt my new dish was quite clever until one of my teammates informed me: *"That's lazy salsa!"* I now understand it is a common, quick technique used frequently in Mexico with a truly perfect name! Choose tomatillos that are bright, have a thick outer husk, and are not overly ripe to avoid any cloying sweetness. I love making this beautiful green and tangy salsa in large batches and pairing with other dishes such as baked fish and tacos or mixing into grain bowls.

Making your own chips at home is a fun and delicious project. The results are fresh and slightly thicker than store-bought. You get to control the ingredients, including the amount of salt, the quality of oil, and the growing practices that go into the vegetables. We use virgin coconut oil to fry our chips—it provides a delicate flavor and crispiness that you won't get with cheaper, more refined expeller-pressed oils. Keeping the temperature low maintains the oil's integrity and prevents the root vegetables—which are high in natural sugars—from burning. If you keep it under 350°F, you can filter it and use it again at low temperatures. It is worth slicing the chips on a mandoline to ensure an even thickness; thus the cooking time is consistent and you avoid the risk of unevenly cooked batches. If you are making the chips in advance, store them in a sealed container for up to 3 days. These colorful, crunchy chips are wonderful accompaniments to Spiced Lamb Burgers with Tzatziki (page 262), Grilled Pork Sliders in Lettuce Cups with Apple-Kohlrabi Slaw (page 287), or Spice-Rubbed Pastured Pork Ribs (page 291).

SERVES
10 TO 12

SALSA

½ cup small-diced yellow onion
(about ½ large onion)

1 teaspoon chopped garlic
(1 large clove)

4 cups quartered tomatillos
(about 15 medium tomatillos)

2 tablespoons fresh lemon juice
(½ large lemon)

2 teaspoons fine sea salt

¼ teaspoon freshly ground black peppercorns

1¼ cups chopped avocado
(about 1 extra-large avocado)

2 tablespoons minced jalapeño pepper
(1 large pepper)

1. Make the salsa: In a food processor, pulse the onion and garlic into small pieces, scraping down the sides as necessary. Add the tomatillos, lemon juice, salt, and pepper and pulse until combined. Add the avocado and the jalapeño and pulse again. The salsa should be chunky, with the tomatillos and avocado as distinct, recognizable pieces. Pour the salsa into an airtight container to keep the avocado from oxidizing and chill until ready to serve.

2. Make the chips: Peel the white sweet potato, orange sweet potato, and beets, and place in separate bowls. Prepare a fourth bowl for the unpeeled fingerlings. In a 2-quart pot, heat the oil to between 325°F and 335°F on an instant-read thermometer. Nestle a wire rack into a large baking sheet and place next to the frying oil. As the oil is heating, slice the root vegetables into ¹⁄₁₆-inch-thick pieces in order from lightest to

RECIPE AND INGREDIENTS CONTINUE

VEGETABLE CHIPS

1 large white sweet potato

1 large orange sweet potato

4 small red beets

3 large Red Adirondack or French Fingerling potatoes (½ pound)

3 cups virgin coconut oil

½ to 1 teaspoon Flavored Sea Salts of choice (page 93) or fine sea salt, to taste

darkest pigmentation to prevent the darker vegetables from staining the lighter vegetables or the oil. Keep the slices in their respective bowls until ready to fry.

3. With a slotted spoon, lower up to 10 slices of the white sweet potato into the hot oil. As the oil bubbles vigorously, stir the chips to prevent them from sticking together. After 3 to 5 minutes, the chips will be golden brown and the oil will slow to a gentle bubble. Use a slotted spoon to transfer the chips to the wire rack and spread in a single layer. Let cool for 5 minutes and then check for crispness. If the chips still bend when folded, they require more frying time; return them to the hot oil and continue frying for another minute or two. Transfer the cooled crispy chips to a large bowl and repeat with the remaining sliced vegetables, working in order of color and ending with the beets. When the chips are finished frying, the orange sweet potatoes will brighten in color and the edges will curl like chanterelles. The Adirondack Red potatoes will turn a pink-periwinkle color, with a brown halo around the edges. Fry the beet chips at 325°F for best results; these are the trickiest to judge and will be done when the middle has traces of mustard yellow and the edges turn a deep red-wine color.

4. Season the cooled chips with salt to taste. Plate and serve with the chilled salsa on the side.

INGREDIENT TIP: *Ripening Avocados*

All avocados are seasonal and ripen only once picked from the tree; shop for fruit according to either firmness or skin color, depending upon the variety. Place rock-hard avocados in a paper bag with a ripe banana to build and circulate ethylene, a naturally produced gas that hastens ripeness. Store avocados at room temperature until fully ripe, or to slow ripening, place them in the refrigerator. Whole, ripe avocados will keep for 2 to 3 days in the refrigerator, while cut avocados will keep for a day, maybe two. Although refrigerating avocados is a great way to avoid food waste, it is worth noting that it does increase bitterness. Most avocado flesh darkens when exposed to air (with a few noted exceptions); to prevent discoloration, sprinkle cut avocados with lemon juice or vinegar and wrap before refrigerating.

FLAVIO'S GUACAMOLE

MAKES
3½ CUPS

In the early days, our farm team consisted of me, John, and Raul Rios, our infrastructure and irrigation technician, who has lived on the property through three prior owners. Flavio Vidales was the first new member of our now expanded team, and as our holistic livestock specialist, he has continuously supported the evolution of the farm's animals through so many ups and downs. Regardless of the long days, he would often hurry home and whip up this dish for our potluck social gatherings, and he has finally shared his coveted recipe for this book! His precision with each ingredient, and the timing he uses to add them, creates a unique guacamole flavor and texture. I love Flavio's guacamole, and there is truly nothing like it! Try serving it as a side to Cinnamon and Orange-Infused Crispy Carnitas (page 285), as a topping for Smoky Potato and Greens Tacos (page 150), or mounded on top of sourdough toast (pages 54 or 59)! Although traditional Mexican cooking uses pungent, raw white onions to cut through assertive flavors, we replace them with red onion because it is most often what we grow. Choose firm but ripe avocados that can both hold their shape and also add a silky creaminess. Hass works best for this guacamole, but creamier Gwen or Lamb Hass can hold up to the lime and raw onion as well. Wait until just before serving to stir in the tomatoes, and if you cannot source the meatier, acidic Roma, substitute an heirloom tomato and additional lime juice.

1½ tablespoons fresh lime juice
(¾ medium lime)

3 tablespoons minced jalapeño peppers (about 1½ large peppers)

½ teaspoon minced garlic
(1 small clove)

¼ cup minced red onion
(about ¼ large onion)

1½ teaspoons fine sea salt

¼ teaspoon freshly ground black peppercorns

3 large Hass avocado, halved
(about 1½ pounds)

½ cup seeded small-diced Roma tomato (about 2 tomatoes)

¼ cup chopped fresh cilantro

1. Pour the lime juice into a medium bowl and add the jalapeños, garlic, onion, salt, and pepper. Stir to combine and set aside to macerate for at least 5 minutes.

2. On a cutting board, place the avocados cut side down and dice into ¼-inch cubes—you should have about 3 cups. Add the diced avocado to the macerated mixture and stir gently to combine. Add the diced tomato and cilantro right before serving to prevent the salad from oxidizing too quickly. With a spoon, gently fold the ingredients until evenly distributed, leaving the avocados chunky. Taste for seasoning and adjust as needed. Serve immediately.

3. To store, place a piece of parchment paper directly on top of the guacamole to discourage oxidation and discoloration. Store in the refrigerator for up to 3 days.

WHOLE AVOCADO SALAD
with Aged Balsamic and Extra-Virgin Olive Oil

This quick and easy recipe accentuates the pairing of creamy, sweet avocado with rich balsamic vinegars. If you do not have aged balsamic vinegar, substitute additional unaged balsamic and a little honey for sweetness. Use the fruits when they are firm but ripe to make them easier to peel and slice. When Beaudie was only five years old, I served this dish for dinner, and before I scooped one for myself, he had eaten the entire plate of four halves! I have learned that a small drizzle of aged balsamic on just about any food will encourage kids to eat with enthusiasm. This salad is best prepared right before serving so the natural oils in the avocado remain creamy at room temperature.

SERVES 4

2 tablespoons diced shallot
(about 1 small shallot)

1 teaspoon fine sea salt, to taste

¼ cup aged balsamic vinegar

2 tablespoons balsamic vinegar

2 tablespoons cold-pressed
extra-virgin olive oil

2 large firm but ripe avocados, halved,
peeled, and room temperature
(about 1 pound)

1 teaspoon chopped fresh chives

1. In a small glass or nonreactive metal bowl, stir together the shallot and ½ teaspoon of the salt. Set aside for 5 minutes. The salt will soften the shallot and mellow its sharp flavor. Add the vinegars and oil and mix thoroughly.

2. On a serving platter, arrange the avocado halves facing upward so the interiors act as little cups for holding the dressing. Stir the dressing well and spoon over the avocado wedges. Generously sprinkle the remaining ½ teaspoon salt, to taste, and the chives over the dressed avocado wedges and serve at room temperature.

THE AVOCADOS

of Apricot Lane Farms

· · · · · · · · ·

Avocados are one of the main crops of Apricot Lane Farms—we have 5,425 trees spread throughout our orchards. When we first took over the farm, there were only Hass cultivars, commonly known as "green gold," and a few trees of Zutano and Bacon that were used to pollinate the Hass. Faced with replanting, we considered growing more Hass, a variety that has swept the market—and for good reason: it has an incredibly creamy texture, tasty flavor, and thick skin, which makes it easy to ship and store. But instead, we were drawn to rediscovering new and exciting varieties that have become harder to find because they are rarely grown commercially. This desire to support diversity led us to create what we now call the Avocado Conservation Project. We planted hundreds of trees on the south part of the mainland property near what is now the Farm School. We were not able to source to test many of the varieties we planted, and so we have waited years until the trees finally produced fruit. But our patience has brought rewards! For example, though we only recently tasted our first Sharwil avocado, it has quickly become a favorite on the farm because of its creamy flesh that lacks any overbearing flavors. We still have many Hass trees in our orchards and enjoy their high-quality fruit, particularly for pressing into our glowing-green avocado oil, but we proudly grow fourteen additional cultivars. Each has a unique skin appearance, texture, pit-to-flesh ratio, and flavor. Some weigh a hefty two pounds or more and have pebbly green alligator skin and watery flesh, while others have shiny black and tender edible skin and can be eaten like a peach! The range of fruit is incredible to see. But Miguel can identify each tree simply by looking at its trunk or leaves.

Embarking on the Avocado Conservation Project was a calculated risk—we knew that the pack-houses in our region, which operate as distributors for growers, wouldn't take all our unique varieties. But we trusted that our customers would prize diversity as much as we do, and so we planned to bring our fruit to farmers markets. So far, it has worked! It has been thrilling to share these new and exciting ingredients, and they have also brought fresh life to our kitchen at the farm.

The avocado originated in south-central Mexico and was domesticated between nine and ten thousand years ago. The domesticated culinary avocado is so different from its ancestors that it is now considered its own distinct species (*Persea americana*) in the laurel family. Avocado cultivars are now divided into three landraces: the Mexican highlands (*aoacatl*), Guatemalan highlands (*quilaoacatl*), and the West Indian lowlands (*tlacacolaoacatl*). Each has unique qualities formed by the ecological conditions of these different growing regions.

Though demand for avocados has exploded in the United States in the last thirty years, cultivar diversity of the avocado has shrunk dramatically as the Hass cultivar has become increasingly common. Heritage fruits with specific growing conditions and even wild species in their ancestral habitats are in danger of being lost as more land is cleared. Growing older cultivars on our farm not only preserves their identity but improves cross-pollination carried out by bees and thus fruiting among our trees. Avocados have a complicated system of reproduction and are classified as either Type A or Type B cultivars. Both cultivars have unique flowers that essentially change sexes depending upon the day and time: Type-A avocados bloom first in the morning with their female reproductive parts available to pollinate. Type-B avocado flowers also open in the morning, but as male flowers. The following day, the flowers switch it up, opening as the opposite sex in the afternoon! Because avocado flowers take turns exposing their male and female parts, it is more difficult for a single tree to pollinate itself and thus bear fruit. That is why nearly all avocado farms such as ours will have a few different varieties to facilitate cross-pollination, which is merely a happy by-product of our commitment to diversity. Below are our personal favorites, many of which are unique to Southern California.

Hellen (June to September)

This very large, pear-shaped, and extremely rich avocado contains over 20 percent oil and has a thick and beautiful green skin. It is sometimes difficult to determine when this delicious fruit is ripe, but it will peel easily when it is ready to eat. We believe it is an overlooked but versatile avocado and enjoy using it in salads and as a toast topper.

GEM (April to October)

The teardrop-shaped GEM features complex flavor characteristics that are poised to compete with its relative, the Hass. It has a creamy, tasty flesh with a subtle nutty aroma. Once sliced, it oxidizes much more slowly than other cultivars. The trees are prolific, and the fruit can hang on to its branches for long periods before harvest without compromising fruit quality. When ripe, the pebbly green skin of the GEM turns a deep, almost purple-black color and is soft to the touch when squeezed. Our director of sales, Nathan, loves to add GEM avocados to his hummus, blended with avocado oil for a smooth and creamy finish.

CONTINUES

PINKERTON

BACON

HASS

SIR PRIZE

FUERTE

GEM

NABAL

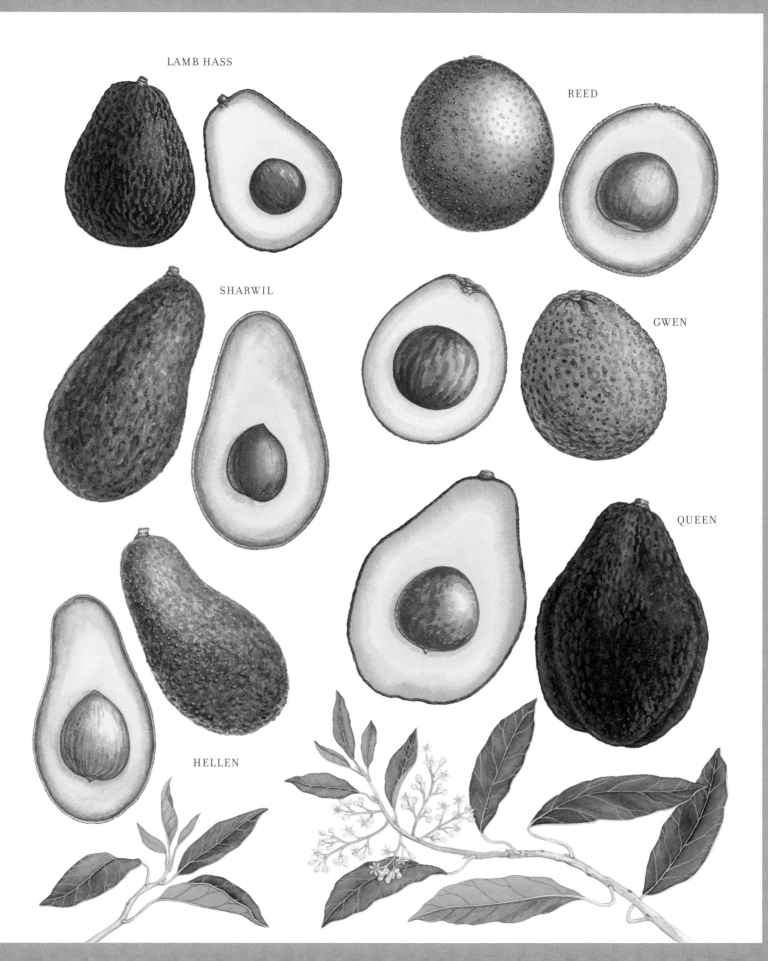

LAMB HASS

REED

SHARWIL

GWEN

QUEEN

HELLEN

Nabal (June to September)

Our sales and transportation manager, Chris, swears that the best guacamole he's ever had was made with a combination of Nabal and Hass avocados, and it is no surprise. This very rare Guatemalan cultivar is coveted as the avocado grower's avocado. They rarely leave the ranch where they are grown! Nabal is curiously round in shape, larger than a softball, with a smooth green skin that easily peels when ripe. We enjoy its clean and unique taste adorned very simply with a sprinkle of good-quality sea salt and maybe a squeeze of lime. Its unparalleled creamy flesh is also excellent in desserts and, combined with the large size, it is our test kitchen chef Stephanie's favorite for making Creamy Avocado Honey Ice Cream (page 387).

Sharwil (April to July)

The rough skin of this pear-shaped avocado remains green when ripe and is a nod to its Guatemalan ancestry. Its smooth, buttery flesh surrounds one of the smallest seeds of any avocado and has a high oil content, making this one of our creamiest cultivars when harvested after a long period of maturation. The flesh hints at a slight salinity, contains no trace of bitterness, and lacks the overbearing nuttiness of more commonly available cultivars such as Hass. For this reason, it is an avocado connoisseur's favorite and is considered to be one of the best-tasting cultivars on the market. Combine the rich flavor of Sharwil avocados with seasonal companions such as citrus; pair with acidic dressings or vinaigrettes; or use to make milkshakes, desserts, or savory dishes such as guacamole.

Sir Prize (November to March)

This highly sought-after avocado has a high flesh-to-seed ratio and is of excellent eating quality. The skin yields to touch and darkens when ready to eat, and it does not oxidize or brown once sliced! Sir Prize is one of the few avocados that is in season for us during the winter. It is an excellent garnish for warming soups and pairs great with pomegranates, which are in season at the same time. The sweet and tart burst from the pomegranate combined with the rich, smooth avocado and a squeeze of lime is something we look forward to every year! Eat the creamy, nutty flesh of Sir Prize on Avocado Toast with Tokyo Turnips, Spinach, Pastured Egg, and Bagna Cauda (page 381).

Queen (August to November)

Under the rough purple-to-black exterior of this enormous pear-shaped avocado rests the rich and regal flesh of an impressive fruit with a small seed and high oil content. It is excellent in salads, blended into sweets, or will make a large party's worth of guacamole! It was discovered in Antigua, Guatemala, and brought in 1914 to Southern California, where it has earned a reputation as a supersize fruit. Unlike the other Guatemalan varieties that are typically sensitive to cold temperatures, our Queen trees can withstand a frosty nip without suffering much damage.

Reed (May to November)

These large round fruits with a thick, leathery green, pebbly skin are believed to be a seedling of the Guatemalan Nabal. They have a delicious nutty, smooth, and creamy flesh and a large pit.

It takes a little skill to learn when a Reed is ready to eat, as it will give less when squeezed than other thinner-skinned avocados. Chop them into fruit salads or mash into guacamole and use their large, sturdy skins as a serving bowl! You can harvest them early in the season when their flesh is firm but ripe. Try splitting one in half, removing the pit, and brushing with oil before searing face side down on a hot grill. Finish with a squeeze of lime and a sprinkle of salt for a special treat! The season often extends well into summer, and when they are softer, they are delicious mixed with chile, fresh mint, lime juice, and sea salt. Serve either as is or on sourdough toast (page 54 or 59).

Fuerte (December to March)

Our winter-bearing Fuerte avocado has developed a cult following for its hazelnut flavor and other subtle but complex nuances. Its name translates from Spanish as "strong," a moniker it earned as virtually the lone survivor of the famous 1913 freeze in Southern California. It ascended as the most popular commercial variety until it was usurped by the Hass in the late 1990s, when the eighty-three-year-old ban on the importation of Mexican avocados into the United States was lifted. Fuerte remains a strong contender, and it is an excellent pollinating companion—we plant it adjacent to our Hass for this reason. A hybrid of the Mexican and Guatemalan types, it has a thin skin that retains a strong green color like the latter when ripe, and if it gives with a gentle squeeze, it is worthy of devouring. Once ripened, Fuerte avocados remain at their zenith much longer than other cultivars. Nathan's favorite way to enjoy these is in a citrus and avocado salad using a juicy sweet-and-tart mixture of oranges, mandarins, and grapefruits that are at peak season in February. Mixed with fresh arugula and a liberal drizzle of our avocado oil, the rich Fuerte is a perfect companion to the spicy contrast of the greens.

Lamb Hass (June to December)

This prolific tree is a cross between Gwen and Hass but produces bigger fruit than the Hass and matures later, making it a nice companion to round out our market offerings. Dark green, pebbly skin turns purplish black as the fruit ripens. It is easily peeled, revealing an exceptionally rich and creamy flesh that can be used similarly to Hass. Its large size lends well to big batches of Flavio's Guacamole (page 371), when the chile, cilantro, lime, and tomatoes are also in season. Head Chef Kayla likes splitting them in half and stuffing them with all manner of savory fillings. For a hearty snack, try blending creamy chèvre with some Tomato Raisins (page 35), fresh basil, and garlic before drizzling with a balsamic glaze and sprinkle of sea salt!

Pinkerton (February to March)

This large, pear-shaped avocado with a long, graceful neck has a small seed and a deliciously oily and slightly sweet flesh. Its green skin is thin and pliable, and easy to peel when ripe. This versatile avocado is excellent in desserts such as Mexican Chocolate Avocado Pudding (page 389) but is equally at home in savory dishes as well. It is in season right at the beginning of spring, when our pastured chickens are beginning to increase egg production. Try Pinkerton paired with a creamy scrambled egg, or use it as a binder instead of mayo in egg salad. Garnish with tender pea shoots and shaved spring garlic for a special seasonal brunch!

CONTINUES

Bacon (December to February)

This oval, dark green, and smooth-skinned winter avocado with a large pit is unique in both flavor and texture. It was named after the farmer who first developed it (not after cured pork!) and has a higher water content and less oil than other avocados. Because it doesn't overpower more delicate flavors, it is excellent chopped into fruit salads or blended into smoothies. To make a bright and versatile salsa, combine it with segmented sweet citrus, diced red onion, minced jalapeño, lime juice, cilantro, and salt and use as a refreshing topping for fish or grilled shrimp. You can also use this salsa as an alternative in Yellow Corn Pancakes with Carnitas and Peach Salsa (page 312).

Gwen (June to October)

This cultivar of avocado is my absolute favorite—it is so buttery and smooth, we joke that it is nature's fudge! It has a nutty flavor and particularly dense texture that is excellent blended into Mexican Chocolate Avocado Pudding (page 389) or served in a wide array of savory dishes. These avocados reach their full potential when lamb comes into season on the farm, and our Spiced Lamb Burgers with Tzatziki (page 262) pair wonderfully with these! Gwen avocados are modest in size, and the skin remains green once ripe.

Hass (March to August)

This popular avocado is our orchard foreman Miguel's favorite selection. It has become so ubiquitous that it now is the standard by which all other avocados are judged. It is the most cultivated variety in the world and comprises around 95 percent of the avocados exported from Mexico. Its nutty flavor is balanced by a high fat content, making it a good choice for most culinary applications, and its modest size means it can be consumed within a meal. It turns an almost purple color when ripe, which takes the guesswork out of knowing when it is best to eat. Many customers ask us why our Hass are so flavorful. In addition to a focus on soil health, we begin picking Hass much later—many farmers in our region begin harvesting them as early as late January, whereas we never begin picking before the third week of March. This allows the avocados more time on the tree to increase their fat content and flavor. Come peak Hass season (end of May or beginning of June), they can be larger than usual, and it is hard to choose a better avocado! Hass are the easiest to source most times of the year and excellent for use in any of the recipes of this book.

AVOCADO TOAST
with Tokyo Turnips, Spinach, Pastured Egg, and Bagna Cauda

Although *bagna cauda* has medieval Provençal origins, this version translates from the Italian regional Piedmontese dialect as a "hot dip" or "hot gravy." It includes local olive oil, anchovies, and garlic and has the magic ability to make just about anything dunkable and delicious! This super-savory, lush avocado toast is a well-balanced meal for breakfast, lunch, or a light dinner. Choose avocados with a milder flavor and soft flesh for mashing such as Sir Prize. We prefer our mild Tokyo turnips for this dish and harvest them while they are still very small, but if yours are larger, simply slice them into 1-inch-thick pieces before julienning. For an alternative leafy green, try using baby kale leaves, or lightly chop more mature leaves.

SERVES 2

BAGNA CAUDA

¼ cup cold-pressed extra-virgin olive oil

¼ cup minced garlic (12 cloves)

2 tablespoons chopped salted anchovies (1 ounce)

1½ teaspoons sherry vinegar

⅛ teaspoon fine sea salt

TOAST AND TOPPINGS

¾ cup ½-inch-diced hard-boiled egg (2 large eggs)

½ plus ⅛ teaspoon fine sea salt

⅛ teaspoon freshly ground black peppercorns

1 large avocado, roughly chopped (about ½ pound)

½ teaspoon minced garlic (1 small clove)

1 teaspoon fresh lime juice

⅔ cup lightly packed julienned Tokyo turnip (4 small turnips)

2 teaspoons minced scallions (green parts only) or fresh chives

2 teaspoons fresh lemon juice

2 teaspoons cold-pressed extra-virgin olive oil

2 thick slices A Crusty Hearth-Style Sourdough Boule (page 59)

1 cup packed small baby spinach leaves (1 ounce)

RECIPE CONTINUES

1. Make the bagna cauda: In a small skillet, warm the oil over high heat until shimmering, about 2 minutes. Add the garlic and anchovies and stir to infuse the oil, about 30 seconds. Remove from the heat and stir in the vinegar and salt. Set aside.

2. Make the toppings: In a small bowl, sprinkle the egg with ⅛ teaspoon of the salt and the pepper. Gently mix and set aside. In a small bowl, mash together the avocado, garlic, lime juice, and ¼ teaspoon of the salt with a fork until smooth and creamy. Set aside. In a small bowl, stir together the turnips, scallions, lemon juice, the remaining ¼ teaspoon salt, and the oil and set aside.

3. Preheat the oven to 350°F and position a rack in the middle.

4. Using a pastry brush, spread some of the bagna cauda on one side of both slices of bread. Nestle a wire rack into a baking sheet and place the bread on top, oiled side up. Transfer to the oven and toast for 5 to 7 minutes, until lightly browned. Flip the bread and toast for an additional 3 to 5 minutes. Remove from the oven and set aside to cool.

5. Spread half the avocado mixture over each slice of toast. Divide and spread the spinach over each slice. Divide and top with the seasoned egg and turnip. Serve immediately with the remaining bagna cauda and a small spoon on the side for drizzling.

BLT SANDWICH
with Egg, Avocado, and Basil Mayonnaise

Oh how I love a fried pastured egg on a sandwich! This everyday classic, made with A Simple Sourdough Sandwich Loaf (page 54) and perfectly seasoned components, is a sublime experience. Pastured egg and bacon, juicy-ripe but firm heirloom tomato, garden greens, and California avocado make it a true tribute to the land, especially when it's made with our unrefined avocado and olive oils. Though we grow tomatoes for market only in the peak of summer, I keep a few tomato plants going near the house until almost November, as Beaudie isn't into any sandwich without the moisture of a good tomato! That said, it is best to make this sandwich at the height of summer, when tomatoes are the most flavorful.

MAKES
1 SANDWICH

Two ¼-inch-thick slices A Simple Sourdough Sandwich Loaf (page 54)

One ¼-inch-thick slice heirloom tomato

A few generous pinches Flavored Sea Salts (page 93) of choice or fine sea salt, to taste

Freshly ground black peppercorns, to taste

¼ cup lightly packed arugula

¼ teaspoon fresh lemon juice

1 tablespoon plus 2 teaspoons cold-pressed extra-virgin olive oil

1 large egg

4 teaspoons Basil Avocado Oil Mayonnaise (page 91)

3 slices Simple Salt and Pepper Bacon (page 38), cooked

Three to four ⅛-inch-thick-slices avocado

1. Preheat the oven to 350°F and position a rack in the middle.

2. Nestle a wire rack into a baking sheet and place the bread on top. Transfer to the oven and toast until lightly browned, 5 to 7 minutes. Remove from the oven and set aside to cool.

3. Place the tomato slice on a paper or cloth towel to absorb excess moisture. Sprinkle the top with a generous pinch of flavored sea salt, followed with a sprinkle of ground pepper, and set aside.

4. In a small bowl, mix the arugula, lemon juice, 1 tablespoon of the oil, and a pinch of salt. Mix until well combined and set aside.

5. In a small cast-iron skillet, heat the remaining 2 teaspoons oil over medium heat until it expands, about 1 minute. Crack the egg into the hot pan and cook until the bottom of the egg is opaque, 3 to 4 minutes. With a fork, pierce the yolk and let it run. Season the top with a generous pinch of salt and pepper. Flip the egg over and cook for 2 additional minutes. Remove the egg from the pan and set aside.

6. Spread the mayonnaise over the bread slices and lay the warm egg on the face of one slice. Stack the bacon, arugula, avocado, and the tomato on top, keeping each component as neat as possible. Top the sandwich with the last slice of bread and two sandwich picks. Slice in half on the diagonal and serve.

CREAMY AVOCADO HONEY ICE CREAM

This unique, dairy-free ice cream is one of our test kitchen chef Stephanie's favorites for its rich mouthfeel, light sweetness, and gorgeous brilliant color, especially when it's made with Nabal avocados. If you cannot source Nabal, the more common Hass avocado will work well, although it will lend a more distinctive vegetal flavor. Whichever you choose, do make sure the avocados are fully ripe to create the most delicious, creamy base. To avoid crunchy ice crystals, chill the cans of coconut milk in advance to separate the fat from the water. Alternatively, you can use full-fat coconut cream and skip this step. The custard base is lightly sweetened so that the avocado flavor remains prominent. If you fancy a sweeter dessert, use an additional tablespoon of honey.

MAKES
1 QUART

3 (13.5-ounce) cans full-fat coconut milk

4 large egg yolks

½ cup plus 1 tablespoon mild raw honey

1 teaspoon vanilla extract

1½ cups 1-inch-diced ripe avocado

1 tablespoon fresh lemon juice

1. At least 4 hours or up to several days before making the custard base, chill the cans of coconut milk in the refrigerator. Open the cans and use a spoon to remove the separated layer of coconut cream that has risen to the top, leaving behind the coconut water. Transfer 2¼ cups of coconut cream to a 2-quart, heavy-bottomed saucepan, preferably enamel coated.

2. In a small bowl, whisk the egg yolks to an even consistency and set aside. Add the honey to the coconut cream and place over low heat, stirring until the honey dissolves completely. Raise the heat to medium and stir until the mixture registers 130°F on an instant-read thermometer. Remove from the heat and slowly drizzle ¼ cup of the hot cream mixture into the egg yolks while whisking vigorously. Continue drizzling an additional ¼ cup cream before stirring the tempered eggs into the saucepan. Adjust the heat to low and stir continuously until the mixture thickens and easily coats the back of a spoon. When finished, it will register between 190°F and 200°F on an instant-read thermometer, 5 to 7 minutes. Remove the saucepan from the heat.

3. Immediately strain the ice cream base through a fine-mesh sieve into a nonreactive bowl. Add the vanilla extract and whisk to combine. Cover and chill in the refrigerator for at least 2 or up to 8 hours.

RECIPE CONTINUES

4. Transfer the base to the pitcher of a blender. Add the diced avocado and lemon juice and blend on low until the mixture is thick and creamy, about 3 minutes. Pour the ice cream base into the frozen bowl of an ice cream maker, and churn for up to 30 minutes according to manufacturer's instructions, or until it reaches the texture of soft-serve ice cream. Transfer the ice cream to a container, cover with a lid or plastic wrap, and freeze until hardened, at least 2 hours.

5. Remove the ice cream from the freezer and let it sit at room temperature for a few minutes to soften slightly. To serve, dip an ice cream scoop into a glass of hot water before scooping the ice cream into bowls, repeating, if necessary, to ease the process. Cover and store the ice cream in the freezer for up to 2 months.

MEXICAN CHOCOLATE AVOCADO PUDDING

SERVES 4

For years, avocado pudding has been a dessert we've served up for special occasions on the farm, from celebrating a birthday to honoring the passing of a cherished farm animal. Originally, I created a velvety and delightful version without cinnamon and spices. One Valentine's Day, our kitchen team experimented with it to create a treat for our team and landed on this silky pudding full of chocolate flavor, natural sweetness, and the spicy warmth of traditional Mexican hot chocolate. Hass avocados whip up well here, but if you have the option, try Gwen or Nabal for a creamier result or the Fuerte for a rich and distinctively nutty flavor. Use avocados at their peak of ripeness for the smoothest consistency. This pudding is best served the day it is made but stores well in the refrigerator for 2 to 3 days.

2 large avocados (about 1 pound)

1 cup almond milk

¾ cup full-fat coconut milk, shaken well and at room temperature

9 pitted Medjool dates, roughly chopped

½ teaspoon fine sea salt

3½ tablespoons raw cacao powder

½ teaspoon ground cinnamon

⅛ teaspoon ground cayenne pepper

GARNISH

A few flakes Maldon sea salt

A sprinkling of raw cacao powder

A few generous pinches shaved chocolate

1. Scoop out the avocado flesh and chop into 1-inch pieces. Measure 3 cups of chopped avocado into a bowl and set aside.

2. In the pitcher of a blender, combine the almond and coconut milks, avocado, dates, salt, cacao powder, cinnamon, and cayenne. Blend on low for 1 minute, then increase the speed to high and blend until smooth, about 3 minutes. Scrape down the sides as necessary.

3. Pour the pudding into individual serving dishes or store in a sealed container in the refrigerator for up to 3 days. When ready to serve, stir gently if separation has occurred. Garnish with a few flakes of Maldon salt, a dusting of cacao, and shaved chocolate.

Acknowledgments

Anyone who has sat at the helm of a large passion project knows that it takes a village to accomplish anything! Considering the complex backdrop of Apricot Lane Farms, there is certainly a village to thank!

This book would not be the same without my culinary teams of both past and present. Ofelia, Chris, and Alex—thank you. Stephanie Bolanos, your commitment and hard work are seen on every page. Maria and Charles, you served as the vital backbone of our team's creative efforts. And last but certainly not least, Kayla Roche, the shared language we speak is a true blessing in my life. It has been a joy to witness your creativity flow with wild abandon. You are a skilled leader, a generous collaborator, and a true artistic force who has further shown me what a relationship that has grace and ease feels like.

To my farm team: Big, big love to you. Our collective effort is in these pages, and this book is a lovely fruit sprung from our thriving ecosystem. To my farm directors, Nathan, Shawn, and Lavender, thank you for taking the time from your busy schedules to answer questions and read book passages. Thank you, Sandra, for your producing and editing support. Connor, Dave, Chris, Kevin, Miguel, Ruby, Lucas, Sophie, Shal, and more, thank you for sharing your expertise to ensure we captured our depth effectively. To our partners, Paul and Jessica, thank you for helping our wildest dreams come true. We will always strive to honor that unquantifiable gift. Rachel, your intuitive support is a true blessing. And to our customers and our fans, thank you for trusting us to feed your families and allowing us to be a representation of your love of Mother Earth.

I am deeply grateful for the extended team of this book, which includes my talented agent, Rica Allannic; amazing photographer, Ed Anderson; and refined stylist, Val Aikman-Smith. To my powerful writer, Sarah Owens, who pored through hours of interviews and research to distill this expansive project into the beautiful prose found in these pages—thank you. To my outstanding illustrator, Andy Raville, who began this journey as a gardener at Apricot Lane Farms, your work captivates me. To my talented editor at Avery, Lucia Watson, thank you for seeing me and supporting this vision without waver. It was a joy to work with you. And, the rest of the Avery team, Ashley, Suzy, and more, thank you for elevating this work with a detailed artistic eye and careful attention to our tone. To Will Winters, who not only consulted the beginnings of our animal program but developed the amazing dog food recipe that Blue and our guardian dogs adore, thank you. And Min Kim, thank you for your guidance in developing our bread recipes. Alice Waters, thank you for making a dream come true by not only visiting the farm, but believing in us enough to support with your time and beautiful words.

Mirna, there's never a day that I am not deeply grateful for you. And Natalie, your conscious attention and playful presence is a gift to our family. To my wellness team, Arash Jacob, Bob Cooley and team, David Simons, David Ross, Dennon Rawles, Jennifer Freed, Jia Yu, Tanja Seagraves, Stefan Hagopian, and Sherry Sami—thank you.

To my brother, Matt, thank you for your kindness and for supporting me before the dream of Apricot Lane Farms ever manifested. Mom, thank you for plopping me on the kitchen counter, sharing your innovative creativity, and always believing my dreams were possible, even if you didn't want to clean up after them!

And finally to my partner in all things, John Chester, thank you for believing in me and always prioritizing our creative expression. It is through the powerful combination of our strengths that we are getting to experience our wildest dreams in this life. And speaking of dreams manifested, thank you to our son, Beaudie. Your love of the farm is a beautiful thing to see.

Resources

SUSTAINABLE HERBS, HONEY, SPICES, SALTS, AND TEAS

Burlap & Barrel
www.burlapandbarrel.com
Equitably sourced unique spices.

Frontier Co-op
www.frontiercoop.com
Organic bulk herbs and spices.

Healthy Traditions
www.healthytraditions.com
Coconut oil, raw honey, and grass-fed meats and meat products.

Honey Pacifica
www.honeypacifica.com
Southern California–sourced raw honey since 1978.

Jacobsen Salt Co.
www.jacobsensalt.com
Hand-harvested sea salt and raw honey.

Mountain Rose Herbs
www.mountainroseherbs.com
High-quality organic, sustainably sourced, and wildcrafted bulk herbs and spices.

Stavoren Trading Co.
www.stavorentrading.com
Sustainable, ethically sourced vanilla beans, paste, and extract.

SPECIALTY INGREDIENTS

Alma Semillera
www.almasemillera.com
Ingredients dedicated to the preservation and revitalization of Mesoamerican foodways with a focus on precolonial and heirloom wheat, beans, maize, and masa harina.

Apricot Lane Farms
www.apricotlanefarms.com
Our very own avocado oil, extra-virgin olive oil, and cool swag such as T-shirts and sweatshirts!

Atlantic Holdfast Seaweed Company
www.atlanticholdfast.com
Sustainable sea vegetables hand-harvested by the lunar cycle from the Gulf of Maine.

Brightland
www.brightland.co
Raw champagne and balsamic vinegars and extra-virgin olive oils that are consciously made in California.

Great Lakes Wellness
www.greatlakeswellness.com
Grass-fed, pasture-raised beef and pork gelatin products.

Journeyman Featherbone Bourbon Whiskey
www.journeymandistillery.com
Certified organic using locally sourced Midwest grains and unfiltered, untreated water from an underground aquifer in Three Oaks, Michigan.

Keepwell Vinegar
www.keepwellvinegar.com
Founded to embrace local, sustainably farmed flavors through fermentation and time. Unique raw vinegars, miso, and sauces produced with attention to detail and craftsmanship.

Maine Coast Sea Vegetables
www.seaveg.com
Sustainably harvested and frequently tested seaweeds and sea vegetable products.

Masienda
www.masienda.com
An excellent source for purchasing a quality tortilla press, molino, and comal of heirloom quality as well as ingredients for nixtamal and heirloom maize.

Pure Indian Foods
www.pureindianfoods.com
Grass-fed, organic ghee made by fifth-generation artisans.

South River Miso
www.southrivermiso.com
Small-batch misos and kōji made with craft and respect for ingredients and tradition.

Ziba Foods
www.zibafoods.com
Heirloom and wild-grown nuts and dried fruits.

STONE-GROUND ARTISAN FLOURS

Camas Country Mill
www.camascountrymill.com
Whole grains and whole flours from the heart of the Willamette Valley.

Roan Mills
www.roanmills.com
Whole-grain flours and breads available in the greater Los Angeles area.

EQUIPMENT

Breadtopia
www.breadtopia.com
Bread-baking equipment, supplies, and sourdough starter.

Cookshack Smoker
www.cookshack.com
Residential and commercial equipment for smoking and grilling.

Etsy
www.etsy.com
A good source for vintage cast-iron skillets and other refurbished cookware. Look for "Made in America" to avoid iron contaminants.

Excalibur Dehydrators
www.excaliburdehydrator.com
Professional-quality dehydrators with convenient options including sizes to fit every need, adjustable thermostat, and a timer.

Mockmill Tabletop Home Mill
www.mockmill.us
Electric tabletop grain and seed mills at an affordable price point with self-sharpening ceramic milling stones.

Onggi Ferments & Foods
www.onggi.com
Fermentation equipment, books, and small-batch unpasteurized ingredients.

Preserved
www.preservedgoods.com
Fermentation equipment, books, and instructional classes.

FARMS

David Uribe, Ventura, California
Uriberuribe77@icloud.com
Live heritage-breed baby chicks such as Black Copper Marans.

Grass Roots Farmers' Cooperative
www.grassrootscoop.com
Grass-fed and finished beef, pastured chicken, and forested pork sourced from family farms across the Midwest and Southeast. Shipped anywhere in the United States.

Marian Farms, Fresno, California
www.marianfarmsbiodynamic.com
Biodynamic almonds, grapes, raisins, oranges, lemons, and high-quality copper-pot distilled spirits.

Novy Ranches Grass-Fed Angus Beef, Simi Valley, California
www.novyranches.com
A good source of grass-fed meats and bones shipped direct and frozen.

SonRise Ranch, Oceanside, California
www.son-riseranch.com,
Excellent source of pastured pork, chicken (and their feet!), and grass-fed and finished beef sold as whole, half, or quarter cows. Shipped anywhere in the United States or available for pickup in Southern California.

Index